WIN A FEW, LOSE A FEW

Cover photo of the team

Back Row (from left): Nigel Rees, Susan Solomon, the author, Adele Weston, Dick Durden-Smith, Jane Somerville, John Gould

Front Row (from left): Michael Palin, Michael Sadler, David Wood

"Not expected to win, but keen not to lose."

WIN A FEW, LOSE A FEW

Bob Scott

The Book Guild Ltd

First published in Great Britain in 2022 by
The Book Guild Ltd
Unit E2 Airfield Business Park,
Harrison Road, Market Harborough,
Leicestershire. LE16 7UL
Tel: 0116 2792299
www.bookguild.co.uk
Email: info@bookguild.co.uk
Twitter: @bookguild

Copyright © 2022 Bob Scott

The right of Bob Scott to be identified as the author of this
work has been asserted by him in accordance with the
Copyright, Design and Patents Act 1988.

All rights reserved. No part of this publication may be
reproduced, transmitted, or stored in a retrieval system, in any form or by any means,
without permission in writing from the publisher, nor be otherwise circulated in
any form of binding or cover other than that in which it is published and without
a similar condition being imposed on the subsequent purchaser.

Typeset in 11pt Minion Pro

Printed and bound in the UK by TJ Books LTD, Padstow, Cornwall

ISBN 978 1914471 735

British Library Cataloguing in Publication Data.
A catalogue record for this book is available from the British Library.

In memory of my beloved grandmother Barbara Easton Scott
1886 – 1991

CONTENTS

Preface   xi

1   **Childhood**   1
From Somerset to Surrey by way of Cairo and Cape Town
My family – birth in Somerset – the end of War – Egypt – back to England – austerity – father goes to Whitehall – posted to South Africa – a large boy – tough schools – sunshine and holidays – back to England again

2   **More Schools**   8
A Pupil in England, a Teacher in Africa
English Prep School – still larger – holiday in Singapore – English Public School – briefly keen Christian – acting and singing – Head Boy – Queen's Visit – Gap Year in Southern Rhodesia – end of colonialism

3   **Arrival at University**   21
An Unusual First Year at Oxford and in the West End
Oxford – Dick Durden-Smith – Hang Down Your Head And Die – theatres not libraries – vacation in the West End – important new friends David, Adele, Michael, John, Braham – reunions

4   **University Continues**   32
More Oxford Follies and Burton and Taylor
Oxford continues – holiday in Delhi – funeral of Winston Churchill – Dr. Faustus with Richard Burton and Elizabeth Taylor for 3 weeks – exam fiasco – Four Degrees Over in Edinburgh and London – now what?

5	**A Grandmother**	44

An Amazing Friend and Lady

Amazing lady – in loco parentis – loved and not – a big influence – extraordinary talks – sport and theatre – generous and mean, serious and funny – letter-writer – dies at 95

6	**Arrival in Manchester**	56

The Road to the Royal Exchange Theatre

Arts Council bursary – Manchester – Administrator, 69 Theatre Company – big stars, big success – London transfers – leads to building Royal Exchange Theatre – LS Lowry and JB Priestley – Princess Alexandra – Michael Elliott

7	**Manchester Theatres Part Two**	75

The Palace Theatre Revived

Raymond Slater – Palace Theatre – Royal Opera House connections – hair-raising Royal Gala Opening – debt to Andrew Lloyd Webber – full houses – excitements with Nureyev, Olivier, Rex Harrison, Cosi Fan Tutti, Pavarotti and a horse

8	**Manchester Theatres Part Three**	89

Bingo Hall back to Opera House

Take over Manchester Opera House – Michael Crawford in Barnum – Topol in Fiddler on the Roof – Evita and Lloyd Webber again – more stars – first trip to USA – Cornerhouse – Raymond Slater in trouble – theatres sold

9	**Manchester and Abroad Part One**	100

Olympic Flights of Fancy Landing in Tokyo

Olympic dreams – Olympic journey begins 21/2/85 – committee formed – Graham Stringer – slow start – great team of volunteers – visit Los Angeles –attend Calgary (Eddie the Eagle) and Seoul (Ben Johnson) in 1988 – Duke of Westminster – Mrs. Thatcher – team and Princess Anne in Puerto Rico – IOC Members – lose in Tokyo

Contents

10   **Mostly on Aeroplanes**   **114**
Two Letters to David at School
Letter one – with Princess Anne in Manchester and Budapest – letter two on the vote trail in Bali, Cairo and Rabat – help from Bobby Charlton and Clive Lloyd

11   **Manchester and Abroad Part Two**   **122**
Olympic Flights of Fancy Concluded in Monte Carlo
Second Bid for 2000 – John Major – £55 million for Manchester – Meet Alicia in Greece – Barcelona Games – 'gross hospitality' for IOC Members – team on the road – Queen meets IOC Member in Paris – corruption and British unpopularity – 2nd failure in Monte Carlo – BOA abandons Manchester – still a great legacy

12   **Russian Adventures**   **134**
Wonderful, Woeful St. Petersburg
Love affair with Russia started in teens – Chaliapin and Tolstoy – visits to Moscow and Leningrad – Gorbachev at Bolshoi – Russian IOC Members – Anatoly Sobchak, Mayor of Leningrad and adviser, Vladimir Putin, in Manchester and Leningrad – with Prince Charles in newly renamed St. Petersburg – final work visit to Russia

13   **Roundabout Route to Greenwich**   **149**
Apollo, the Commonwealth Games, Bermuda and a New Life
Marriage over, no job, a knighthood, awards – strange time – portfolio life – Alicia moves to England – Apollo Leisure – London Lyceum fiasco – Commonwealth Games and wedding in Bermuda – leave Manchester for Greenwich for Millennium planning

14   **Greenwich**   **161**
The Dome and Way Beyond
The Dome – cock-ups – Jennie Page – new life in Greenwich – consultant and chairman – Picturehouse Cinemas, Greenwich Theatre, Greenwich Waterfront Partnership, South London Business, the Oval, Bexley Heritage, Trinity Laban Conservatoire

15   Liverpool   173
European Capital of Culture 2008
Liverpool – Chief Executive of Liverpool Bid to be European Capital of Culture in 2008 – weekly visits – compare Liverpool in crisis and Manchester booming – heart attack – Liverpool wins – bumpy build-up to great year – International Ambassador – Cities on the Edge – Granada Foundation

16   Europe   188
Almost a Eurocrat
President of European Commission Jury for European Capitals of Culture – much travel for no pay – highlight when Marseille wins for France – UK involvement now finished – a Remainer – resists concept of one European Culture

17   Somerset to Greenwich   199
Reflections on a Life Mostly Lived
Reflections – world in crisis – is our blessed generation to blame? – Uncle Tim – bidding – marriage – travel – Alicia – win a few, lose a few!

PREFACE

Memoirs, as someone else said, are unreliable. What to include, what to remove, what to hide? And did it really happen like that? I think so, but I am not sure. Some places choose themselves: Southern Africa, Oxford, Manchester, Russia, Greenwich, Liverpool. So do some people, for their fame: Burton and Taylor, Bobby Charlton, Princess Anne, Nureyev, Mrs Thatcher, LS Lowry, Andrew Lloyd Webber, John Major, the Queen, Pavarotti, Vladimir Putin. Indeed, it has occasionally felt like a long voyage through a celeb-infested sea. More important, I believe, are the key figures in my life like Dick Durden-Smith, David Wood, Michael Elliott, Raymond Slater and Graham Stringer. Finally, of course, my family and children are here, but especially the ones who have gone, like my parents, Uncle Tim and Gran.

For the mistakes I can blame no-one but myself, but I do thank friends for their support: my sister Diana, John Causer, Helen Hindle, Nick Raynsford, Rosie Oliver, Chantal Lapergue and Kathy Arundale. Almost nothing in my life was planned. I have known success and failure. I just enthusiastically followed paths. The best was the one that led to Alicia.

1

CHILDHOOD

From Somerset to Surrey by way of Cairo and Cape Town

My family – birth in Somerset – the end of War – Egypt – back to England – austerity – father goes to Whitehall – posted to South Africa – a large boy – tough schools – sunshine and holidays – back to England again

My parents met at Birmingham University in 1938 when they were both nineteen. When war was declared the following September, my father, who was reading Mining Engineering, joined up almost immediately. With something of a scientific bent he joined a Searchlight Battalion of the Royal Artillery. He was commissioned and moved into Radar. His asthma stopped him from active service and he spent most of his years as a Radar Instructor at various spots along the west coast, mostly in Somerset and North Wales. I teased him that if he was intent on defending our shores he seemed to have been consistently looking the wrong way. My parents, David and Vera, were married in deep snow in January 1941. My sister, Diana, was born in June 1942 and I was born in January 1944. I nursed the secret for years that I was conceived in a Bristol Air Raid Shelter only to be disabused of such frivolity by my mother when I had grown up. I am not sure where that came from, but by then I had impressed lots of friends. The equally lustful truth was the spare room of her in-laws.

Meanwhile, my father had been rapidly promoted to the rank of Major and was posted to teach Radar in the aptly named Somerset village of Watchet. The nearest town is Minehead and at that General Hospital I was born. My mother's rude health at the time is best described by the fact that she bicycled three miles to the shops on the morning of my birth that night, when I weighed in at ten pounds. At the end of the war my father had a scruffy piece of paper from his Birmingham University tutor (by then deceased) saying that if he had completed his studies he would probably have got a second-class degree. My mother stayed on at Birmingham to complete an Economics degree but by April 1945 she had two children under three to look after.

My father chose not to be demobbed at the end of the war. He had spotted and successfully responded to an advertisement for the Chief Radar Instructor in the British Military Mission to Egypt. He went out ahead and in early 1946 my mother, sister and I joined him in Cairo for over a year. His main role was to teach Radar to the Egyptian Army. Again, I teased him that his teaching skills had clearly been no preparation for the Israeli attack a few years later. I remember little of Egypt. My sister reminded me that my father greeted us off the ship with the first bananas we had ever tasted – ecstasy. Later, on a beach in Alexandria I tasted my first Coca-Cola – more ecstasy. The same afternoon, aged two, presumably in celebration, I upped from the family group and walked straight into the sea and almost drowned. I remember our Nanny and our steward, Hassan; I remember being plagued by boils and I remember watching, fascinated, as a poor bullock walked round and round in a small circle to pump up water. I also remember the delivery of huge ice blocks in sacking from a bicycle rickshaw every morning to feed a crude refrigerator. I confess, however, that some of these so-called memories may only be the results of old photographs being brought to life.

As an extended family we survived the war well. All four of my grandparents, both uncles and my parents were still alive. We came home in 1947 in the famous troopship of later fame, the Empire Windrush. It was memorable because as a troopship it had three military bands on board. Diana and I would sit on the companionway steps, mesmerised and in heaven, listening to an almost endless concert of marches and stirring music. My father flirted with a few short-term jobs when we got back and became increasingly worried. Finally, he became a civil servant and joined the Dominions Office, later renamed

Childhood

the Commonwealth Relations Office. He reckoned his interview had been a disaster. He missed his train and arrived very late at the distant rural training college where a group of mostly Oxbridge graduates had gathered for a two-day selection session. So, he decided to enjoy himself at a free bar and told us later he showed off for thirty-six hours. To his astonishment it seemed to work. My parents had liked Egypt and were optimistic that the new job would bring exciting foreign postings. Happily, that is exactly what it did.

With a wife and two children to support, his annual salary of £500 meant that times were not easy in post-war austerity Britain. A childhood without money has rather pompously convinced me that today's multiple treats and presents lose their specialness. Pleasure is diluted. Going to the local 'snack bar', called the British Restaurant, believe it or not, for egg and chips very, very occasionally in 1949 was much more exciting than today's endless trips to McDonalds. One teddy bear meant more than today's cupboards full of toys.

All in all, therefore, I came from a straightforward post-war, middle-class, mid-twentieth-century family, but a family which has always been lucky. My grandfathers survived the First World War as officers. They were both schoolteachers but at rather different kinds of schools. My paternal grandfather (Grandpa Scott) was a Housemaster at Wellington College and my maternal grandfather (Grandpa George) who had been injured in the First War and suffered with his hearing was a supply teacher at a school in Eltham. Neither grandmother worked for a living, but one (Granny Scott) was tremendously involved in public and charitable work, while the other (Granny Ibbitson) was an efficient, but rather moaning, housewife. My mother and father were striking people, talented, confident and good-looking. My father became a senior diplomat, was knighted (ending up as British Ambassador in South Africa) and then moved effortlessly into the world of non-executive directorships. As a diplomatic wife it was impossible for my mother to work full-time, but she would certainly have been successful if she had married differently. In Egypt she briefly became a spy. She was a good mother but she certainly would have liked to be 'something' more as well.

My sister Diana, who is eighteen months older than me, was also cleverer and a good deal better-looking, slim and with wonderful auburn hair. She has a PhD and made a very good marriage with Brian Unwin, who became a Permanent Secretary at the Treasury before finishing as President of the European Investment Bank in Luxembourg. They have three sons. My brother Andrew, who is about eight years younger than me, is a gifted music teacher and choral conductor who also made an excellent marriage in Newcastle with Elspeth, a GP, and they have a son and a daughter. The three of us were well-behaved children and never seemed to give our parents any real problems. We gave them an easy time. In 1972 I married an Australian TV producer, Su Dalgleish. We had three children, David who was home-grown and Tom and Anna who were adopted. We divorced twenty-three years later.

My chief youthful characteristic was that, before the rest of the world caught up, I was large. All my childhood I had the vague feeling that I was unusual. I wish I could use the word 'special', but I can't. I was just very big. My talents were moderate. I did not work particularly hard or well at school. I was enthusiastic and noisy. I was a curious combination of naturally lazy but, when enthused, energetic. I always seem to have had an unhealthy desire to show off. I sat the eleven-plus exam and, apparently, I answered the question 'Do you have any hobbies?' with 'Being in charge.' How appalling! Years later when I was able to look back on a rather complicated 'career', my father remarked that over the years I had proved conclusively that 'bullshit baffles brains'. Anyway, I do not really believe in planned careers. Careers are things to look back over.

No, special I was not; as I was growing up I just had the feeling that I was different. My mother used to tell me that I was the third longest baby ever born in Somerset, and that when I made my first appearance into the world, the doctor said, 'Good god, he looks six months old'. Also, our childhood was unusual. We changed countries and schools regularly. My sister, with whom I have always been very friendly without being particularly close, was my only constant friend until I was nine. With one or two exceptions we made and lost friends on a regular basis. When I finally went to boarding school I saw little of my parents, as they were always abroad, and much more of my grandparents. I suppose this was 'different' too. It did not make me at all unhappy. Indeed, I mostly enjoyed this sense of being on the outside, looking in. At least I could claim that I was never just average, and I never got lost in a crowd.

For a few years we lived in North Kent in awful, rented accommodation and then in a pretty dismal little house in Chislehurst, so that my father could be close to London for the new job and we could be near my mother's parents. I now live in Greenwich, which is not far from Chislehurst, and I can never quite get used to the notion that Chislehurst is considered posh. To me it was grim. My first school was a girls' school in Eltham called Babington House. I was the only boy there, which was unusual, but I was sent there to be with my sister. I still have my first report – 'Robert talks too much and needs to sit still.' The

Childhood

appalling winters of the late 1940s remain a powerful memory. I remember feet of snow. We used to be able to make one room downstairs warm, but going upstairs to our freezing bedroom at night was something my sister and I dreaded. Meanwhile, my father was settling into Whitehall in the private office of the Secretary of State for Commonwealth Relations, Philip Noel-Baker. The Secretary of State's office overlooked Horse Guards Parade, and one exciting day in June 1950 we were allowed to watch Trooping the Colour from his balcony. I also remember the thrilling day when the rationing of sweets was removed. A few months later we got the news that my father's first foreign posting was to be South Africa. I remember the four of us dancing round the little front room in Chislehurst chanting 'We're going to South Africa! We're going to South Africa!' What excitement.

We left Southampton on a poisonous January day in 1951 on the Pretoria Castle, escaping from the grey world of a British winter to the sun and the colours of South Africa in summer. Two weeks on board going from austerity to luxury, from war-torn wintry London to the beauty and blue skies of a Cape Town summer was mind-blowing. The two of us were befriended by an elderly peer, the Earl of Munster, who was travelling alone and seemed to find the two of us engaging. On our last day he took us to the ship's shop and said, 'Choose anything you want!' What a world! The transformation of our lives was amazing. With a big house, a smart new car (a Morris Oxford, forsooth), several servants and two brand new bikes for my sister and me, we felt we had arrived in heaven. We made friends easily. All of them have left South Africa.

I went to several schools during our two and a half years there. We had to keep changing schools because every six months the whole government circus of Parliament, Ministries, Embassies, etc. moved up and down from Cape Town to Pretoria – an incredibly expensive way of trying to keep the peace between the Cape and the Transvaal. Perhaps the toughest school I went to (my third of four in South Africa) was the Maritz Brothers in Cape Town where I had the most bizarre first day. I arrived there with my still strange English accent as a large eight-year-old in February 1952. This was the first day of the official autumn term, so we wore heavy corduroy shorts, a grey flannel shirt, a long-sleeved sweater, a blazer and full-length woollen socks. The trouble was that the temperature was touching 100°F. Summer was still in full swing. But rules were rules and they required us to wear the full winter rig.

The school was divided into houses and the first thing we did on that first morning was to meet as a house with Brother Peter, both a priest and our housemaster. I sat sweating like a pig on the floor at his feet with my legs crossed, along with the other new boys. He told us what was expected of us particularly on the sports field and how we were to behave. At the back of the room two boys were mucking about. They were warned to stop. They continued to muck about, and they were warned for a second time. No change. After three warnings, Brother Peter dispatched the head of the house to get his cane. He returned with a four-foot-long whippy stick of bamboo. The two miscreants were called to the front and commanded to kneel with their hands over their heads side by side on the floor about twelve inches away from my nose. Brother Peter proceeded to thrash them together across their backs and bums. Maybe ten or twelve strokes jointly. They got up, shook themselves down and returned to the back. Five minutes later they were mucking about again. Good training to be a Springbok, I suppose. I was transfixed.

The school I remember best was in Pretoria – Waterkloof House Preparatory School – or WHIPS when we were screaming on our first teams. One of South Africa's leading cricketers, Eddie Barlow, was a senior boy when I was very junior. I remember watching him score a century in the fathers' match, which was an opportunity to experience passionately competitive South African sport. The fathers did not enjoy one little bit being put to the sword by a twelve-year-old. They would clearly have killed him if they could. It was a very tough school. There was a ritualistic punishment for a boy caught swearing. The whole school was assembled to watch the boy wash his mouth out with soap and water. In front of all of us he had to gargle and then swallow the contents of a pint milk bottle filled with grey soapy water. At the end he was violently sick. Of course, all the schools I attended were white.

Schools apart, South Africa was heaven for young white children. The Cape, with Table Mountain and its beaches, was sensational. In Pretoria we were only a few hours from the Kruger National Park and lions and elephants and the rest. We discovered grown-up barbecues called *braaivleis*. Visits to places like Ystherfontein, the Drakensburgs, the Karoo, Hartebeestport Dam, the Victoria Falls are all golden memories. In February 1952 I remember rushing home from my new school shouting and singing, to be met by my mother at the gate telling me to keep my voice down because King George VI had died. I wondered if, somehow, I was responsible. A magical event was the Van Riebeeck Festival to celebrate the 300th Anniversary of the arrival of Captain Jan Van Riebeeck and his small Dutch fleet in Table Bay in 1652. It was, I suppose, a major Afrikaner thrash but it had the most thrilling funfair I had ever seen. We spent the day at the festival with my parents' friend and my father's colleague Nicholas Monsarrat who was running the British pavilion. His famous novel *The Cruel Sea* had just been published. My brother Andrew was born in Pretoria in September 1952 but it was a bad time for our mother who suffered for weeks from a difficult pregnancy and birth.

I can only excuse myself for having no sense of the injustices of the country by my age. All I knew was that the relatively few black people we got to know as children were lovely to us. We got on especially well with our servants, particularly Lydia, who was really in charge of us children and the house. I suppose whatever happens to a seven-year-old is roughly what he expects. I was not surprised at going to different schools every six months, I was not surprised that life in South Africa felt so much better than life in England. It was just where we were and it was wonderful. Nor was I surprised that my friends were white, not black. There was complete separation. It felt normal. My eyes were opened ten years later, when I spent eight months as a teacher in Southern Rhodesia (now Zimbabwe) between school and university.

By September 1953 the dream was over. We returned to England on the Winchester Castle arriving back on the same kind of dank, grey day as the one when we had departed. Those two long Union Castle voyages to and from South Africa, travelling First Class, I might add, were highlights of our childhood. The food, the swimming, Crossing the Line, the deck games, watching films on deck (I remember *Limelight* with Charlie Chaplin) lying on our stomachs on the deck with our heads in our hands – it was all bliss. As the ship berthed in Southampton I looked down from the side of the ship to watch the dockers playing out the ropes and pushing the ramps up to the ship from the quay. I was now nine and was astonished to see white men doing the work. I thought all manual labourers were black.

Life would now continue in two to three year sections with my father alternately serving time abroad and time at home. But the fun of living with our parents abroad was over. We were off to boarding schools in Surrey: Diana to Bramley, me to Camberley.

2

MORE SCHOOLS

A Pupil in England, a Teacher in Africa

English Prep School – still larger – holiday in Singapore – English Public School – briefly keen Christian – acting and singing – Head Boy – Queen's Visit – Gap Year in Southern Rhodesia – end of colonialism

Now the roles were reversed and I was to go to an English prep school with my strange South African accent rather than the other way around. I would also be joining my form two years late, which meant that the gangs and teams had already been formed and I would have to try to break in. I did not lose my sense of being unusual. It was decided that I would go to Eagle House, a rather good boys boarding prep school outside Camberley, which had the advantage of being around the corner from my paternal grandparents' house next to Wellington College in Crowthorne. My parents would probably have a year or two in Britain, but then they would be off again to foreign parts. From now, Granny Scott would become the major parental force in my life, from schools through university; but more of her later.

Eagle House had several wonderful teachers. In fact, I think they were the best teachers I ever had. I enjoyed lessons. The headmaster was a rather fierce but fair man called Paul Wootton. The best teacher was the French master, John Watson, who believed that young people should learn to speak a foreign language before they started trying to write it down. We all left Eagle House with good French conversation. He was famous too; he wrote the pop song 'Looking High, High, High', which came second as the British entry in an early Eurovision Song Contest. But for me, his real significance was that he used to produce the annual school play. I remember performing a crazed Russian spy with false moustache and sideburns in the farce *The Crimson Coconut*. I can still remember the heat and glare of the footlights and the smell of the moustache glue. There is no doubt that my love of dressing up and showing off had begun to flower.

For Christmas 1956, Diana and I had an exciting holiday in Singapore, my father's second posting. We flew from the Nissen Huts, which formed the main terminal at Heathrow, in a BOAC Argonaut. The journey took three days, which included a night at a hotel in Rangoon. There were fifteen stops. The plane was not pressurised and never flew higher than 8,000 feet. It was extremely bumpy and the sick bags were in constant use. My poor sister had to sit with a brother who insisted on eating every offered meal, which he then proceeded to lose! When you consider international flights today it is amazing to remember that every time you climbed back into the plane after each stop you were met by a stinking wall of the smell of vomit. Nevertheless, I remember it as very glamorous. Singapore was foreign and exciting. The markets and streets were full of Asian people (mostly Chinese and Malay), brilliant colours and strange smells, but, again, the separation of the Brits from the locals was complete. We spent most of our time either at the swimming club or the yacht club. Our journey home was much quicker and posher on a BOAC Super Constellation.

Back to Eagle House where sport played a big part in my life. I was in all the teams – rugby, cricket and hockey – and played them enthusiastically rather than well. I drew the line at running. I liked chasing balls (relatively slowly) but I loathed cross-country runs. I also developed my love of watching sport, both live and on television. I went to see England play South Africa on the grass at the Oval and MJK Smith and DO Brace playing rugby for Oxford at Twickenham against Major Stanley's XV. On special occasions we had the thrill of watching sport live on television – Drobny beating Rosewall at Wimbledon and May and Cowdrey scoring 411 against Ramadhin and Valentine at Edgbaston. In the dark of our dormitory we began to talk incoherently about sex. We boys had vivid imaginations and we debated whether the headmaster's very pretty and much younger wife Anne was having an affair with the young and handsome English teacher Peter Huxtable (whatever an affair was); and whether John Watson was similarly involved with the beauteous matron.

Music was also important at Eagle House, though sadly, at that time, my contribution was limited. Billy Bean was a splendid music teacher and his carol concert every Christmas with the choir under the great stairs in the school hall was magical. How I longed to be the pretty treble singing the first verse of 'Once in Royal David's City'. This was not to be. My voice was breaking, very young. The result was that I was the only boy in the school in my last term who was told that I should wear long trousers. Not *could*, but *should*, as I was so large. Even more remarkably, in the early morning dip in the summer term, which the whole school took part in – one length of the pool, naked – it was suggested to me that I should cover myself up and wear a swimming costume. I was never sure exactly whom I was meant to be embarrassing. In one Easter term, during a particularly cold spell, the school lake froze over. We begged to be allowed to go on the ice and slide. Permission was given but only after Scott had been told to go on the ice by himself to test it. When I alone did not break the ice, the whole school was allowed on. Happily, my skin was thick and none of these episodes were humiliations. I obviously quite enjoyed being different.

With my father's career demanding that he be abroad much of the time it was inevitable that I would have to go to a boarding school after prep school, especially as my parents were now resident in Singapore. My only contribution to the debate of where to go next was that I insisted on going to a rugby school, not a soccer school. This eliminated my father's school, Charterhouse. My parents, who I discovered later were not mad about my grandmother's influence, thought that she would be too close for comfort if I went to Wellington. It was, therefore, decided that I should go to Haileybury.

In the almost three years that they were in Singapore I only saw them once for that Christmas holiday in 1956. In those days the government paid for one trip per tour per child, not like today when children travel to their parents for every holiday. So, it was well over a year since my mother had last seen me when she came to Liverpool Street to greet me off the school train. By now I was a large public schoolboy who shaved. She walked straight past me. I was five inches taller, much heavier and my voice had broken. She did not recognise the gruff 'Hello Mum' from a young man of thirteen stones that I offered her.

Haileybury stands just outside the City of Hertford and was built in 1806 as the East India College. It became one of the great centres of scholarship in

England in the first half of the nineteenth century and trained young men for service in India. It was apparently much tougher to get into than Oxbridge. In those days a job in the Indian Civil Service was regarded as enormously grand. Thomas Malthus was the Professor of History and the college offered the teaching of some forty languages. The college closed after the Mutiny in 1857, when the government took over the East India Company, and it reopened as a school for boys in 1862. In 1957 when I arrived it was still a school only for boys, aged from thirteen to eighteen. The Indian connections lived on. Houses were called Bartle Frere, Colvin, Lawrence, Kipling, Trevelyan, etc. New boys were called 'New Governors' in recognition of every newcomer's supposed ambition to end up as a governor of an Indian State. Still in 1957 at the end of your first month at the school you had to face an appalling written test, entirely administered by other, older boys about general history with a special emphasis on the history of British India. If you failed the test, your 'mentor', not you, was beaten by a prefect. I am not certain if that was true as my lot all passed. My first housemaster was the legendary Douglas 'Killer' Cook, so called for his apparent devotion to the cane. I have to say he never whacked me.

Haileybury's architect was William Wilkins, the architect of the National Gallery and Downing College, Cambridge. The design was based on a huge central quadrangle, said to be still the largest in Britain. Even I could see how beautiful the place was. But it was also incredibly cold with winds sweeping in over East Anglia from the Urals – or so we believed. In summer it was glorious with magnificent buildings set in magnificent grounds and woods. The school is still beautiful. Today it is co-ed with both boys and girls starting at the age of eleven. Apparently, the dormitories are now centrally heated. They most certainly were not in my day. Girls and warmth combined – very dangerous.

As well as undergoing the New Governors' test you were also introduced to the joys of fagging. This meant running errands and satisfying the whims of the House prefects. You also had one particular prefect to whom you were a kind of manservant. I fagged for the 1st XV rugby star Roger Godfrey who went into the Navy and played for the Combined Services. He ended up as General Secretary of the RFU. The oddity was that I was about four inches taller than him and two stone heavier. In fact, at thirteen I found out that I was the heaviest boy in the school in my first term. However, I still made Godfrey's rugger boots shine like patent leather. He was my god and I was his hulking slave.

I was in the top set of my year, usually about sixth or seventh out of thirty. I was in the Latin and Greek set. But I never really mastered Greek. I was clearly not academic. I peaked at O Level. I mastered Elementary Maths but put me in front of trigonometry papers and I was baffled. I was the ultimate 'jack of all trades'. Size, maturity and loudness, however, marked me out as one of the leaders of my intake. I did everything – I played every sport (enthusiastically, but still not very well), sang in the choir in my first term as a bass, acted and sang in lots of productions, became Head of the Cadet Corps. I spent an amazing afternoon looking after our most famous living Old Boy, the ex-Prime Minister Clement Attlee, making an unofficial visit to the school. He was a devoted Old Haileyburian rather competing with Winston Churchill and his famous devotion to Harrow. Right through the war he told me he would get the school sports results every Monday. He was particularly proud that Old Haileyburians almost ran the Royal Air Force during the war (Air Marshalls Slessor, Dickson, Baker, Leigh-Mallory, Brooke-Popham) and as a school Haileybury boasted the third highest number of VCs – seventeen. He told me that he and a group of friends were beaten by the Master for illegally going down the hill to Hertford to join the celebrations for the Relief of Mafeking in May 1900, against specific orders.

I became Head of my House. I stopped the beating of boys by boys – partly because I didn't like it and partly because I couldn't really do it! When I was called upon to do it for the first time, it involved me delivering three strokes of the cane with my friend Peter Fowkes delivering the other three on the very small backside of a very small boy draped over one of the baths in the main house bathroom. Peter and I had never done it before and were extremely nervous. We decided that we ought to practice on each other. My first attempt to beat Peter missed completely and went straight over his back. It was absurd and I swore never to do it again. After the pathetic punishment was meted out, I marched down to my housemaster and demanded that this primitive activity of a big boy beating a small boy must stop. I think he thought I was rather fine. I knew I was a coward.

I presume there was quite a lot of 'loving' between boys going on, but I never saw any evidence of it at all! The trouble with such behaviour is that it is secret and not the norm. Those boys who suffered from big bullies must have suffered dreadfully, their lives affected for ever. For the majority of us, plain, spotty and unattractive, we just sailed through. We all knew there were a few dodgy masters too and that must have been even more ghastly, if and when they chased the young. The average clot like me thought these masters were just jokes. There were, I suppose, love affairs between boys, and my gay Uncle

More Schools

Tim told me he was never so in love as he was at Gordonstoun in the 1930s. All I know is that I am no expert on the subject.

Like many others, I had a religious phase in my mid-teens. I loved Christmas but I found Easter especially moving, and one Good Friday I was certain that the sky darkened at 3pm. I clearly neglected the time difference between Hertford and Jerusalem. I 'served' at Communion on a Wednesday when one of my duties was to turn to the congregation, while the School Chaplain blessed the Host, to count the number of celebrants in chapel so that he knew how many wafers to prepare. The average Wednesday number was about fifteen. On one occasion it was very different. Every Lent we would have a guest priest stay at the school for a few weeks giving a nightly Lenten Address, making himself available to those who wanted to talk with him. One year we had an amazing Franciscan friar called Brother Edward in brown habit, sandals and a white rope around his waist. He was a member of the community at Cerne Abbas in Dorset. His addresses were astonishing. He had been an officer in a regiment which had liberated Belsen and had been one of the first to enter the camp. He had never recovered. When he left the Army he gave up everything to join the Franciscans. As a missionary to us heathens, he was brilliant. I cannot remember any visiting speaker making such an impact. His last day with us was a Wednesday and then he had to get back to Dorset. He and the School Chaplain shared the Communion Service on his last day. I was serving. When I came to do my quick count of the number in Chapel that morning I had to report that there were at least 300 out there, possibly more. School breakfast was late that day.

My favourite master by a mile was Basil Edwards, who never taught me, but who directed three of the plays I was in – *Coriolanus* (small part), Aeschylus' *Agamemnon* (middling part) and *King Lear* (the man himself). Playing Lear was a memorable experience and I can still remember whole chunks. An eighteen-year-old Lear sounds dreadful and the idea of three young boys playing Goneril, Regan and Cordelia sounds weird today. But a powerful memory it remains. I console myself with the line that Nevill Coghill gave me later at Oxford – this was a man who directed Peggy Ashcroft and Sybil Thorndike amongst others – 'the best Cleopatra I ever saw was a boy at Marlborough.'

I also sang in splendid – also boys only – productions of Gilbert and Sullivan. I was the immortal Private Willis in *Iolanthe* and Wilfred Shadbolt in *The Yeomen of the Guard*. This last was a special production because we performed it in the year that the G&S copyright ended. Our enterprising producer/teacher Hugh Sawbridge saw a chance to make a little history. He arranged for our production to tour to seven Danish towns and cities, which meant that the 1962 Haileybury *Yeomen* was the first G&S production to tour abroad that was not a D'Oyly Carte production. What the Danes made of *Yeomen* I cannot imagine, but they were always extremely polite. In each town we were hosted by the children of another school and it was always exciting to discover who you would be billeted with for the two days you were in the town. I remember falling in love with a smashing girl within our allotted forty-eight hours in Hans Christian Andersen's hometown of Odense. I remember her well but I am damned if I can remember her name. Our performance at the Theatre Royal in Holbaek was even televised. Boys playing girls must have roused the worst suspicions of the Danes about the English.

I had an entirely unexpected and exotic last term – the winter term 1962, which was Haileybury's Centenary Term with a planned royal visit from the Queen and the Duke of Edinburgh. I simply cannot believe it is sixty years ago. I had been meant to leave in the summer, having already got my place at Merton College, Oxford. Instead, the Master (the title of our Headmaster) changed all that in an extraordinary conversation at the start of what was meant to be my final term. The Master, Christopher Smith was a quiet man and pathologically shy. He didn't really like me a lot – I was too noisy and too full of myself. Anyway, he sought me out.

The conversation started by him calling me Robert, which startled me, and then he said that he had that morning talked on the phone to my father. This was even more startling than calling me by my Christian name, because by now my father and mother were in Salisbury, Southern Rhodesia. Sixty years ago, a phone call to Rhodesia from Hertford was unimaginable. 'I want you to be Head of the School next term. I have talked to your father, and he has agreed,' he said. 'But I am going up to Oxford in October, sir,' I stammered. 'Well, I have talked to your Tutor and he is happy to wait a year for you. I have also talked with your grandmother. Everyone is happy.' 'But why, sir?' I said, wanting to add, 'You don't even like me.' 'Well, you are the only boy I can think of who might be able to put the Queen at her ease, when she visits us next term to mark the Centenary. Oh, and I have told your father that there will be no fees for him to pay.' So, I became Head Boy, supposedly to make the Queen 'feel at home'. I had the Head Boy's study in College and another study in my House, Basil Edwards asked me to play King Lear, I played rugby, I smoked like a chimney, I was costing nothing and I had already got into Oxford. I was almost above the law and a new master once called me 'sir'. It helped that I looked like a portly forty-year-old accountant. I never was so grand.

The royal visit was memorable for us even though it must have been like a million others for the Queen and the Duke. The four senior prefects had to escort the royal pair around the college. We were given several bits of advice. We were told, 'When you bow, drop your eyes completely to the ground. If you keep your eyes up as you go down, her eyes will follow yours and she might become sick. Don't mention the fact that the main school colour is magenta – it is her least favourite colour. Most important of all, when you show her around Lawrence House (which was the chosen, typical House to show them on the walkabout), do not mention that Group Captain Peter Townsend had been a member of the House thirty years ago.' His famous relationship with Princess Margaret had been a huge story and she had married Tony Armstrong-Jones only two years before.

The Visit went well. The Duke endeared himself to us by telling us that he was pleased to see the sun was out, as it had been 'pissing down' in Luton, from where they had just come. We loved him for that. I was able to tell him that my Uncle Tim Scott had been his contemporary at Gordonstoun. He was genuinely pleased to hear of him. The Queen and the Duke had tea with the whole school in our magnificent dining hall and I had to say our lengthy Latin Grace. She complimented me for getting through it. My overwhelming memory of being with the Queen for a couple of hours was her smile and how beautiful she was. My best friend Dick Durden-Smith was just behind us with the Duke. It is an amazing thought that this visit took place in only the tenth year of her reign and Prince Edward had not yet been born.

I also remember my last Passing Out Parade well. This was when the whole school dressed in uniform as a Cadet Corps, pretending to be soldiers, sailors and airmen, and would parade in front of some military top brass. As the senior schoolboy there, the Company Sergeant Major, I had to give what seemed to be the longest Word of Command ever invented. 'Haileybury and Imperial Service College Contingent will march past in columns of three, Royal Naval Section leading – by the right – quick march!' Our 'top brass' in 1962 was a full-dress Major General. This splendid gentleman's control of the English language, however, was a little less sumptuous than his uniform and his conversation was constantly punctuated by the word 'jolly'. Indeed, the depth of his regard on any subject was marked by the number of 'jollys' he used. When we met, we conversed thus:

'So, you're Head of the Corps are you, Scott?'
'Yes, Sir.'
'Jolly good. And what are you going to do when you leave school?'
'I'm going up to Oxford, Sir.'
'Jolly, jolly good. And what will be studying there?'
'Classics, Sir. Latin and Greek.'
'Oh, jolly, jolly, jolly good. And then what will you do with your life, young man?'
'I'm hoping to go into the theatre, Sir.'
'Oh, jolly, jol… Good God!'

I loved Haileybury. By the time I left I was no longer bigger than everyone else. I had been well over six feet tall for years, but now many others had caught me up. I had a host of real friends. They were a special lot. My group of contemporaries all loved both sport and the arts. There were school prefects both in *King Lear* and the 1st XV. We were not thick and we were not precious. In five years I had risen up the school in regulation time and got past each hurdle. I did all kinds of things. As well as looking after the Queen and playing King Lear, I sang a solo on *Songs of Praise* on BBC TV. I went on Corps Camp on Salisbury Plain and we lived like soldiers for a week, I boxed for the school and got knocked out by a boy called Clark from Bedford, I captained the Third XI at cricket against St. Dunstan's, a school for the blind, and lost. The bell in the ball helped them but it completely fooled us. Hailey House, my House, drew with Allenby House in the Cock House rugby match as a result of my last-minute penalty. What larks.

It was now Christmas 1962 and there were eight months to fill before going up to Oxford. By now I was thrilled that I had this opportunity to do something special before starting at Oxford. My father had been posted to Salisbury as British Deputy High Commissioner to the Central African Federation made up of Southern Rhodesia (now Zimbabwe), Northern Rhodesia (now Zambia) and Nyasaland (now Malawi). Having seen so little of my parents for the past nine years and also because I could not get a Voluntary Service Overseas post for less than a full year, I decided to join them in Salisbury, if I could get a day job working with African children. I managed to get a paid job at one of only two African Secondary Schools in Salisbury, one of which was in Harare where I was going, and the other in Highfield, the two biggest, dustiest, most run-down, overcrowded townships outside Salisbury. After the full independence of Zimbabwe was declared eighteen years later, Salisbury was, of course, renamed Harare. My job was as one of the first-year form teachers. The staff was wholly European and the pupils wholly African. My salary was enough for me to buy a clapped-out open-top Morris Minor, which got me every day from one side of Salisbury (the white elegant side) to the other (the black township side). Meanwhile, my sister Diana, who was completing her London University degree in Salisbury, was becoming very friendly with the High Commissioner's Private Secretary, Brian Unwin, later to become her husband.

I grew up in those eight months in Rhodesia. I quickly became politically aware and what I saw and experienced forced me to rethink my old-fashioned British assumptions. My two terms at Harare African Secondary School taught me that things could not possibly go on as they were. The Central African Federation was on its last legs anyway and was dissolved three months after I left Salisbury. It had only been in existence for ten years and in a time of very rapid global decolonisation, Britain's efforts to try to slow down inevitable British departure were failing. Britain's declared effort was not to persevere with the Federation but somehow to manage a more gradual process towards majority African rule. It never worked. At that time the total population of the three countries was 8,000,000 Africans and 300,000 Europeans and the largest proportion of whites was in Southern Rhodesia. (Today the African population exceeds 50,000,000 and the European less than 100,000.) No wonder Robert Mugabe, Joshua Nkomo, Kenneth Kaunda and Hastings Banda wanted independence. After the Federation collapsed, Zambia and Malawi achieved independence and black rule quickly in 1964, even though Kaunda and Banda both spent time in British prisons before they each became presidents. The problem for Britain was essentially the thousands of whites in Southern Rhodesia, many of whom still called Britain 'home'.

It is hard for anyone under sixty to understand what a huge issue Rhodesia was and what a huge figure in the public mind Sir Roy Welensky was in 1963. Rhodesia and Welensky were in the UK press all the time. While Labour was fiercely pro majority rule, the Tory government was split and many on the right considered Welensky a hero. There was a great deal of talk about 'kith and kin'. He boasted that he was 50% Afrikaans, 50% Jewish and 100% British. But at the time I was there he was about to be out of a job when the Federation was dissolved and he protested violently. He claimed he loved Britain and had fought for it during the Second World War and now he was forced to fight against it at the end of his life. He insisted that he was no supporter of the

South African solution of apartheid. He constantly claimed that he admired Africans and was their friend but that they were simply not ready for power. He attempted to re-enter Southern Rhodesian politics in 1964 on a muddled, paternalistic ticket but it was far too late and he was reviled, if you can credit it, as a communist. There were new, far more right-wing leaders in power in Southern Rhodesia by now in the new dominant party, the Rhodesia Front. This party was first led by Winston Field and later by the intransigent Ian Smith, who was a highly controversial figure. Some saw him as a straight-talking realist who believed that only Europeans could maintain the country's economy while others saw him as an out-and-out racist.

To show how seriously the government took the future of the Federation, they appointed a minister, Lord Alport, to be High Commissioner. My father was his deputy. A year later, Harold Macmillan appointed the most important figure in his Cabinet, the First Secretary of State, RA Butler, to take responsibility for Central Africa. It was Butler who convened the famous Victoria Falls Conference but agreement proved impossible as the double British aim was to protect the white population and at the same time move towards majority rule. By 1965, Southern Rhodesia, under the leadership of Ian Smith, achieved independence but pledged to white rule. This led to the declaration of UDI, thus making the new government illegal. UDI led to sanctions and a complete severing of relations with Britain. Ultimately, Smith went to war with ZANU, resulting in over 30,000 deaths. For many years the British, the illegal regime and the African leaders, who did not get on well with each other either, stumbled from one appallingly messy compromise to another. First Macmillan, then Douglas-Home, then Wilson, then Heath and finally Thatcher grappled with the problem. You can make up your own mind about the process. Zimbabwe has survived, just. Please God it will prosper. But all those catastrophes, which were finally resolved at Lancaster House in 1980, came long after I had left.

I have never forgotten my first day at the Harare Secondary School in February 1963, the first day of the school year. When I arrived, I could see there was one dusty football pitch in the grounds and collected on it, sitting, was a crowd of over a thousand children, all waving papers and chanting that they wanted places at the school. The papers they were waving were their Standard VI Certificates, which they had just received at the end of their six years in Primary School. The desperate problem was that there were only two black Secondary Schools in the whole Salisbury region which they could go on to and there were nothing like enough places for everyone. So, the authorities had to make conditions. To get in, a child had to be under thirteen years old and had to have achieved either 1st or 2nd Grade in the Standard VI Exam. Only one hundred passed this test meaning that education for the vast majority of Salisbury's black youngsters was over. The horror was immediately apparent. These children could now read and write and had basic maths. They were on their way to being educated. Suddenly, it had come to a juddering halt. Without being able to go on to Secondary School they would now be condemned to manual work or domestic service or unemployment. It was a disaster. I could do nothing, of course, and just hoped that I could make a difference for those I taught.

That first day continued to be memorable. I was designated Form Teacher of Form 1A – the new intake. At the first lesson I had two duties apart from trying to get to know my pupils. As I called them to order I could not help noticing that there were some very mature thirteen-year-olds. There had obviously been a lot of lying about ages. I did not blame them. When I took my first register, there was the most wonderful list of first names. My class of forty included amongst the boys Clever, Golden, Porridge, Sixpence, Bicycle and my favourite, whose father had obvious tastes, was called Littlewoods Wimbledon. It has a certain ring! The girls had more standard names but all rather high-sounding Victorian ones like Louisa, Victoria, Elizabeth, Emmeline and Charlotte. My second task was to divide them into their religious groups – all Christian. Every Thursday morning at 10am priests of different denominations would arrive to take them for RE. Most of the Primary Schools had religious 'foundations', so the children all had fierce commitments to their churches. 'How many of you are Roman Catholics?' I asked. Six put up their hands. I took their names. 'How many Anglicans?' I asked. Eight more raised their hands. *Crikey.* I thought. *There are still twenty-six to go.* Rather meekly I asked the rest of them to tell me what they were. Mormons, Seventh Day Adventists, Methodists, Baptists, Particular Baptists, Congregationalists, Presbyterians and some others which I have forgotten. They hung on proudly to their denominations because of their loyalty to the Primary School they had come from. What rubbish they were taught each Thursday, I could only imagine, especially as the Bibles which I had to distribute had illustrations of Jesus as a white man who looked as if he came from the Cotswolds, and the devil as an evil black man.

I lived a schizophrenic existence. I lived at the Deputy High Commissioner's Residence and met all kinds of grand people like RA Butler, Lord Alport,

Winston Field and Sir Patrick Dean, Britain's Ambassador to the UN. At the same time I was teaching in what I soon discovered was the fairly tense pre-revolutionary atmosphere in Harare. I much preferred my kids to my colleagues, many of whom were unhappy Brits who had emigrated to Rhodesia for a better life after the war and were discovering that Rhodesia was not the dream they had imagined. The cost of living was high. There was tension between the quite impressive white pioneer settlers and the recent arrivals from the home counties. Worst of all for many of them, the place was swarming with blacks. The ratio was something like 25:1. The whites were clinging on and most of them knew it. But they dreaded going 'home'.

The story of Zimbabwe has been unbearably awful. It is the most beautiful country. It has everything – good land, minerals, coal, water, natural advantages, beauty, talented people, wonderful game parks. I am not well enough informed to know how much of the mess there can be attributed to the fault of the British or the locals. You can blame the Brits for a lot but not everything. I have a probably naive hunch that the worst people imaginable, from Rhodes through Smith to Mugabe, with several villains in between, fought vile battles to get control when all they and their supporters had been after was pillage of one sort or another. Perhaps Zimbabwe was doomed and would never have worked out well even if independence had come quickly. Maybe in a hundred years it will look different. I do not know, but in September 1963 I certainly left utterly gloomy about the country's prospects. Unlike most Rhodesian whites, I was happy to be going home.

3

ARRIVAL AT UNIVERSITY

An Unusual First Year at Oxford and in the West End

Oxford – Dick Durden-Smith – Hang Down Your Head And Die – theatres not libraries – vacation in the West End – important new friends David, Adele, Michael, John, Braham – reunions

I was thrilled to get to Oxford and, especially, to Merton College. It is a small, old, rich, beautiful college with a garden overlooking the Meadows and the oldest quadrangle in Oxford, the incomparable Mob Quad. Very quickly I discovered that your first loyalty was almost more to your College than to the University. The College had chosen you to come to Oxford. You ate and slept in the College for at least two years. Your Tutor was a Fellow of the College and you met with him in his rooms in College. Indeed, many students at Oxford did very little outside their College. However, if you wanted to do anything at a University level you also realised quickly that you would only be able to do one outside thing at a decent standard. My days as a schoolboy all-rounder were over. I gave up sport and debating and the cadet corps, everything, in fact, except singing and acting. Oh, and darts. I played darts almost every day in the Merton bar to a reasonable standard. Frankly, I behaved in a way unthinkable today. Today, I doubt I would have got in at all and I certainly would not have lasted three years.

Instinctively, I knew that I had hit my academic ceiling by just getting into Merton and consequently elected to do the minimum of work. Someone foolishly told me that anyone capable of getting into Oxford was capable of getting a second-class degree. 'Why prove it?' I asked myself. 'That is not why I am here.' I would have had to work hard to get a Second. *I am here,* I thought to myself, *in this beautiful place, with exciting new friends, enjoying historic buildings and institutions and traditions for just three years and for that short time the whole place belongs to me.*

I am sorry if I behaved badly. I suppose I must have kept out of the University a deserving, hard-working student. But I insist no one took fuller advantage of glorious Oxford. At least I did not waste my time. Also, when people hear that you went to Oxford they assume you got a degree without asking you. 'I read Classics and Law,' is a true statement. Mark you, since I left in 1966, I have never thrown off the guilt that I felt from my behaviour.

There were twelve in my Classics set in Merton with our Tutor, Robert Levens. After five terms we had to sit 'Mods', the slang for the fourteen three-hour papers we had to complete. The Merton twelve produced ten Firsts (a record, I believe), one Second and one Pass – me. Only two of us in the whole University got Passes, me and a girl from St. Hilda's who sat the exams at the Warneford, Oxford's main psychiatric institution, where she was a patient. But I did not fail! Happily, Robert, unlike most dons, loved the theatre and his wife, Daphne, was a rather good theatre director herself. He would greet me at my weekly tutorial by correctly suggesting I had probably not done enough to justify lengthy discussion. We would deal with my essay and then fall pretty quickly into chat about the state of Oxford theatre. He knew my fellow students would do him proud and with me he could investigate and encourage other things. And the other results show what a great teacher he was. Robert was the heaviest smoker I have ever known. He would get through a cigarette in about three pulls and when the smoke finally emerged from his chest, it seemed to come out not just from his mouth and nose but from the back of his collar and the cuffs of his jacket. Lovely man.

The three most memorable events of my first week at Oxford were two auditions and a ritualistic drunken session. I had arrived at Merton with my best friend, Dick Durden-Smith, from the same school, at the same College, reading the same subject. Also, we enjoyed the protection of Dick's older brother Jo, another Mertonian, who was a third-year Oxford figure to conjure with. He told us of the proposed Oxford University Dramatic Society (OUDS) major production of *Twelfth Night*, to be directed by Michael Rudman, and the Experimental Theatre Club's (ETC) intended capital punishment extravaganza, to be directed by Braham Murray, both scheduled for the following term. Dick and I immediately applied for the ETC auditions. I also sought an OUDS audition for *Twelfth Night*. The third event was on the first Wednesday of term known as the Freshers' Blind, an annual occasion when freshmen were amiably pressured by their elders, in the name of a Merton welcome, to become drunk. I passed all these tests. I have only been paralytically drunk twice in my life, the first time that October night in 1963 in the Merton JCR bar. The second was in January 1993 in a grand house in Santiago, Chile in the presence of the British Ambassador – but that is another story. Both auditions went well. I was offered the double parts of Antonio and the Sea Captain in *Twelfth Night* and a part in the company of 'Hang Down Your Head and Die' – no role as yet identified. My sense of glory lasted only a matter of hours until Jo sternly informed me that a part in both would be impossible – a freshman could either join the Murray court or the Rudman court but not both. Incidentally, my good friend, Michael Emrys-Jones, two years my senior and very grand in Oxford Theatre, did uniquely appear in both. But like me later, he left without a degree as well. As Jo was not a Rudmanite and anyway I had never heard of Antonio or a Sea Captain in *Twelfth Night*, I chose 'Hang' and to become a Murrayite. What a good decision. I owed Braham a great deal, not just at Oxford but in later life as a rookie theatre manager.

In truth, I remember very little of both the *Twelfth Night* audition and the Freshers Blind, but I remember the 'Hang' audition vividly. The auditions were held in a large hall in University College. You queued up outside and entered one by one from the back. You then walked the length of the hall to a large table at the end. Behind the table was a row of leather-jacketed, smoking, stubbled men who had apparently just got out of bed. 'Name? College? What have you done?' 'Well, I played the part of King Lear at school and also sang in Gilbert and Sullivan and…' (thinking to clinch matters!) 'I won a bronze medal in July in the Rhodesian Eisteddford for solo voices.' Groans of horror. 'Oh Christ! So, what are you going to do?' 'Well, I thought I could give you "Blow Winds and Crack your Cheeks". But perhaps I should stand a little way back as I have quite a big voice.' 'No, no, just get on with it.' 'OK.' (Big breath.) 'BLOW WINDS…' 'Christ. Yes, I think you better go back a bit.' I reckon I got in on volume and maybe got myself a juicy solo song in the show, *Sam Hall*, in that moment. More of that later. Anyway, I was in. The other joy was that Dick and

Jo also were chosen and it meant that Merton had three members of the cast, the largest representation by one college.

The first term went by in a flash. Rehearsals began. The concept of the show was explained to us. The subject was capital punishment. It was assumed that we were all dead against it. We were. The production would be set in a circus with each of us playing ringmasters, clowns, showgirls, strong men, jugglers, etc. Which exactly we would each be would be decided later. There was no sign of a draft script. The show would develop during rehearsals. Any ideas were encouraged and would be considered. Songs, either original or known, would be especially welcome. It was suggested we do some research. We improvised and talked and disagreed. The 'deviser in chief' was the gentle, rather beautiful, long-haired David Wright but, of course, our leader was clearly Braham Murray. The two of them would make the final decisions.

Although the show did finally emerge from this slightly baffling start, there was pain getting there. I still have a first script from December which bears little relationship to the show that would open the following February. To be frank, I never thought we were at the time a close-knit team. That has come later with anniversaries. There were seniors and juniors. There were soloists, duos, small groups. There was competition. There were threats of walkouts. There were calls for complete rewrites. Terry Jones was a figure alone, never content. Michael Palin and his pal Robert Hewison were a duo slightly by themselves. David Wood was a fierce competitor and contributor, but uniquely liked by all. Jo D-S and Michael E-J were the seniors, frequently absent, and they inevitably became the ringmasters. I was part of two pairs with my life-long friend Dick and my new friend David Wood. Clive Mitchell was private and this was somehow emphasised by his becoming the DJ'd Narrator and not a circus performer. Dickon Reed was known to none of us, was not an undergraduate, and was a slightly solitary figure. Roland Oliver was the Assistant Director and President of the ETC. Only the girls were a group, quietly led by the glamorous Hope McIntyre, partly because, with the glorious exception of Adele Weston (now Geras) and her voice, they were essentially cast as show ponies. The boys, on reflection, seemed to get all the plum bits. I do wonder whether very bright women like Viv Ault, Jane Sommerville and Sue Solomon really made the contribution they could have. It was 1963, remember. In no way was it war, but it was bitty at best and angry at worst. Perhaps the people who bound us together the best were the musical team. Everyone loved Iwan Williams, Hugh Davies and later John Gould. The band were also major contributors, especially Greg Stephens as a songwriter and guitarist.

Unlike the professional world, the rehearsal period was spasmodic. Everyone, well almost everyone, had studying to do. Meanwhile, Dick and I took part in Cuppers, the inter-College one-act play competition for freshmen. Merton's entry was a new play by David Ambrose, a four-hander with the two of us, Maria Aitken and a talented Irishman called Desmond Lapsley. I cannot remember the title, but I do remember Dick muttering, when we were asked for suggestions for a title in front of the author, that it might best be called *A Load of Old Rope*. Surprisingly, Merton won! Meanwhile Michael E-J was also rehearsing both Aguecheek in *Twelfth Night* and in Ionesco's *Rhinoceros*. He was certainly one of those not studying particularly hard! Many of the others had competing activities. But a core group soldiered on and sequences and songs began to emerge. A dreadful but somehow relevant interruption to the rehearsals was the assassination of President Kennedy on November 22nd. I heard the news in a hotel room in London putting on a DJ before taking one of Pussy Galore's pilots (sister of a school friend) to a ball at Grosvenor House. For the two days before Lee Harvey Oswald was himself gunned down, we reckoned that there might just be an historic Texan execution happening very shortly. Jack Ruby then shot Oswald dead and was condemned to death himself. But he died of cancer while his sentence was being appealed. It all felt horribly close to Hang. It was a bleak and troubling time.

Another altogether more jolly distraction from the rehearsal process was a series of ETC evenings with visiting glitterati from the theatre world. The Hang cast was expected to attend. Two stand out for me – an evening with Joan Littlewood and another with Bill Gaskill – two eminent directors. Joan Littlewood was especially relevant because of the debt Hang owed to *Oh What a Lovely War*. She was mesmerising. I had never heard such an endless stream of expletives in my life. The evening with Bill Gaskill was memorable for quite other reasons. The last part of the event was when the cast of Hang were split into pairs and each pair had to improvise the simple act of one person offering something to the other and the other accepting it. This would demonstrate the art of improvisation and Gaskill would then comment on each sixty-second encounter. David W and I were the final pair and totally cocked it up to hoots of derision. Gaskill laid into us to uproarious approval and we were required to have another 'redeeming' go. With no premeditated collusion David and I sent up ourselves, the audience, improvisation and Gaskill to new roars. I think my friendship with David dates from that night.

Another memorable night at about this time was the Merton Christmas dance. It took place on the evening of the day that the Beatles hit 'I Wanna Hold your Hand' was released. Oxford's great undergraduate band, the Four Beats, played that night, having learnt the song during the day. They played it over and over again. By the end of the night we were all word perfect. It is hard to convey now what the Beatles meant to us in 1963. We more than loved them. They were ours.

Even closer to Christmas, I had another good moment when Braham asked me to replace someone in a small part in his University College production of *Rhinoceros*, which had made the final selection for the National Union of Students Drama Festival sponsored by the *Sunday Times*. This involved rehearsals in Oxford and just one performance in Aberystwyth. My parents were abroad in India and were to remain all the way through the Hang saga, so I was delighted to be asked. The production was memorable largely because of two standout performances by Michael E-J (now Elwyn) and Michael Johnson (now York). They were the star actors of their year. We came second to Leeds University's *Three Sisters* although Harold Hobson, the *ST* critic and adjudicator, later said disingenuously that we should have won! What? The adjudication had been in his hands. I have a hunch he simply preferred Chekhov to Ionesco.

Back to Oxford and the mad rush to get Hang into final shape. In my case the singing was fine but the dancing very dodgy. However, I loved our dance sessions with Helen Belman, our choreographer, who was affectionate and beautiful. Her personal arranging of my incorrectly positioned arms and legs was bewitching. I remember the cold of our rehearsal hall in St. Margaret's Road. I remember drinking tea and eating sugar lumps at the Turl in noisy groups after rehearsals. I had come up to read Classics but I do not remember lectures or libraries. Meanwhile Dick had changed courses from Classics to English. Whatever we claimed to be reading we certainly did not allow ourselves to be deflected from a bit of fun. Our birthdays are close and we decided to share a twentieth birthday party at the end of January with a black tie/long dress champagne breakfast at a greasy spoon cafe, the Town and Gown, off the High. The invitations were sent out in the names of Richard Durden-Smith and Robert Hillyer-Scott and *Cherwell*, the student rag, was invited to send a reporter. The party went well but it came to the attention of the Proctors who charged us with organising an illegal term-time gathering. On false advice we attended our interview in full sub fusc (which, in fact, was not required) and to our surprise we were let off with a smiling, gentle rebuke. Apparently,

Arrival at University

our inquisitors saw us as perfectly harmless, if idiotic, chaps simply trying to restore the spirit of Zuleika Dobson.

Meanwhile Hang was facing a serious crisis. We had fallen foul of the Lord Chamberlain, an absurd figure who had amongst his duties the job of licensing every new play in the country before it could be offered to a paying public, i.e. he was the nation's censor. The role had been created by Sir Robert Walpole, in the reign of George the Second, when satire, songs and writings were scabrous especially when the plays and songs were aimed at the King or at him. Our script came back with several scenes blue-pencilled out. At the same time the University authorities had also banned our graphic poster of a hanged man 'modelled' by Michael Elwyn. We were appalled but the shock was turned to our advantage wonderfully. These episodes got national publicity in the hands of our ebullient PR man, James Burnett-Hitchcock. We managed to mobilise the next Lord Chancellor, the deeply distinguished Gerald Gardiner QC, to make protest about egregious censorship, claiming it was politically motivated. We got some concessions from his intervention.

We also turned one of the Lord Chamberlain's objections to our advantage. We were planning to mime the infamous electrocution of the Rosenbergs. This was refused. Instead, we were allowed simply to have the narrator read aloud, with the cast seated like reporters, a newspaper eyewitness account of the grisly event. When it came to the sentence that the first electric shock lasted fifty-seven seconds, the whole theatre went silent for fifty-seven seconds, made more chilling when the doctors, after examining the victim, could not confirm that he was dead and more volts were required. You could have heard a pin drop. One night a lady in the audience fainted. It was an extraordinary 'coup de theatre' and a great improvement on a group mime. I say 'we' did this but, of course, it was Braham and David Wright who plotted this response and all the very helpful attendant publicity. I am not sure how important the show was in furthering the abolition of capital punishment, but the Abolition Act was passed the very next year and Sydney Silverman MP, the sponsor of the Bill, gave us grateful credit. I also think we were very slightly responsible for removing the role of national censor from the duties of the Lord Chamberlain, which passed into law in 1968.

But I am moving ahead too fast. As the first night approached a great moment came when baskets of costumes arrived from Bertram Mills Circus, most of them exceedingly well worn. By then I had been designated a clown. It is a sign of the times that I accepted without question the role of the black-faced clown, which meant blacking up with a large painted white mouth and eyes like a Minstrel. A political career could be blighted today by such photographs! The ringmasters were terrific, the slim Dick D-S a not wholly convincing strong man and the girls very pretty in tiny skirts, fishnet tights and high heels. I was glad I had not been allotted Dickon's frilly top as the juggler. The stage was pushed forward with the band up above and behind us, in Michael Ackland's clever design. Technically, for a student production, the show was complicated, with endless sound and lighting cues, but we were blessed by a great team led by Tony Summers, Val Myers, Peter Wiles, Tim Godden and David Plowright. The show opened with the grand parade which finished with David Wood, the chief clown, sprinting across the stage, leaping like a trout, to be caught by me. We must have looked like Little and Large. The first night at the Playhouse on February 18th was tremendous. We received excellent press, and Terry Jones and David, as the condemned man and the manic chief clown, emerged as the stars of the show, with a Highly Commended for Adele. The show was to play for a fortnight in Oxford and then that would be that.

I am not sure who knew – I certainly didn't – but at an early performance Michael Codron, an eminent West End producer of that period, came to see the show and sat down with Braham the next morning. We regarded him as a godlike figure but, in fact, he had been at Oxford only ten years before us. He admired the show and asked Braham if we might like to take it to London. Immediately and without consulting us, Braham said 'yes' but Codron sadly imposed one condition. He wanted a cast change. Susan Solomon would have to stand down. It was no fault of hers, and she later became a successful barrister, but I think she knew she was not really a show pony. I was not in the theatre when Braham had to tell Susan but those who were there found it a distressing moment. The rest of us did not behave very well. We should have refused to agree. She could easily have been accommodated as another kind of circus performer and not as a showgirl. However, it was unnegotiable and in due course Jasmina Hamzavi, who was excellent, took her place. We were now approaching the end of February and the invitation to the cast was to play a limited run of the six weeks of the spring vacation at the Comedy Theatre in the West End opening on March 19th. There were exams to be sat, dubious dons to be quietened, Actors Equity to be squared, but no one said that they could not make it. I am not sure if it was a unique event, a student production moving lock, stock and barrel straight from a University to London's West End, but it certainly would feel very special indeed.

Arrival at University

There was one more delicious diversion for the cast, who began tightening up the show for the London opening less than a month away. I have never known who arranged it – it may just have been dreamt up as a pre-West End try-out of the new changes – but, however it occurred, we found ourselves invited to Stratford upon Avon to give a week of performances at the Royal Shakespeare Theatre for a week in early March. This would be heaven for us – to be on those famous boards. However, the good burghers of Stratford failed to turn out in great numbers to see a group of students turning executions and hangings into a grand circus act. I remember a serious debate before the mid-week matinee about whether we had to perform at all if there were fewer people in the audience than there were on stage. Well, perform we did, although we lost Jo D-S and Michael E for that week. Their tutors put their feet down at last. They were replaced by Michael York (not a bad understudy) and Paul Collins on his way to becoming a Judge. Michael E and Michael Y were roughly the same size and the costume fitted fine. Paul, a good foot shorter than Jo, rather swam in Jo's tailcoat. A bus took us to Stratford and back each night and we loved swanning it to the Dirty Duck before and after the show.

London was even more exciting than we expected. We had money in our pockets, not much, £12 a week each for expenses, if I remember correctly. The Comedy was the perfect theatre for the show, although I was rather shocked by the state of the backstage areas. Even that added to the mystique. The first night was astonishing. Curtain calls galore and a party on stage after the audience had departed. We then wandered the streets waiting for the first editions to come out. We expected to be patronised. Instead, we were seriously applauded. Bernard Levin's review in the *Mail* had a one-word headline – Brilliant. *The Times*, the *Guardian*, the *FT*, the *Telegraph* were not only terrific, they were also respectful. The Sundays were just as fulsome. For Braham and David Wright, it was a major achievement. David Wood and Terry were again universally acclaimed. We were very happy but curiously quite cool. I suppose we were too young to be humbled. What is more, we were fashionable. Each night, it seemed, someone famous would be out front. One such night I rather blotted my copybook. Princess Margaret and Lord Snowdon were in the front row. My big moment in the show was a ferocious folk song about a murderer called Sam Hall and I stood to sing it at the front of the forestage with the cast miming and humming in the background. I was standing right over the Royal couple. I fear I tend to spit when I sing and there were a lot of s's in Sam Hall. At one particularly violent point I sent a shower of spit over them. I can still see the

Princess swiftly raising her programme to her face either to protect herself or take down my name for punishment later.

We all, of course, had to make our own accommodation arrangements. Some eight people stayed in Martin Maudling's parents' flat while they lived in Number 11 Downing Street when his father Reginald was Chancellor of the Exchequer. This resulted in a very jolly early evening party at Chester Street where the drinks flowed. Braham was not there. He was waiting for our late arrival at the theatre, stone-cold sober and very angry. We thought we gave a terrific performance that night. Braham violently disagreed and gave us a serious bollocking. I wondered whether his reaction had been fuelled by the fact he had not been invited to the party. I stayed in the family house in Guildford while my parents were away, although I would occasionally cadge a bed from Dick's mother in town when yet another party claimed us. Some people were still doing battle with examiners and had to commute to and from Oxford. With my parents away I invited everyone to Guildford for a Sunday party. A lot came and a lot missed their trains back home. In the early hours I was distributing bodies to beds and floors around the house and finally made my way to my attic room and a celibate stall. As I tried to go to sleep it suddenly dawned on me that our lovely family cleaning lady was due in at 9am sharp that same Monday morning. I leapt out of bed to alert everyone. My only problem was that the glamorous couple of Michael E and Juliet A were tucked up in my parents' bed. They would have to be out at 8.50 with the bed made. I tentatively, even shyly, knocked on their door. 'Come in,' came Michael's clear tones. I went in expecting I knew not what. What I found were two people very much on each side of the bed contentedly reading. When I had delivered my message, Michael boomed a cheery 'right-ho' and returned to his book.

What an amazing way to spend the first seven months of a university life. The whole experience was dreamlike after a post-war austerity childhood. The dreaming spires were astonishing enough but the West End as well, and in a hit. I loved the Haymarket and Panton Street and I ate regularly at the Stockpot. We went free to matinees of other London shows if there were seats available. Dick was so immersed in a movie matinee one afternoon that it was not until his name was urgently flashed up on the screen that he realised he was missing his own matinee. Braham, who had to go on in his place for the first half, and Codron were not amused.

In February 2004, 2014 and 2019 we have had three anniversary Sunday lunches in private rooms at the Ivy, Joe Allen's and Brown's, beautifully organised by David. At the last one he suggested we send in potted biogs to report how we had passed the time since 1964. Universally cheerful stories came back. Marriages, children, grandchildren were all reported. It emerged that the show had produced successful actors, writers, lawyers, academics, producers, critics, administrators, TV and radio execs, businessmen with some serious stars amongst us, Palin, Jones and York to name just three. My favourite biog came from our last recruit – Jasmina. Her story included fabulous items… 'Spent six months teaching the French Army to scuba dive in Martinique… RGS Expedition to Pitcairn Island… Married second husband on expedition in Torres Straits… Made juggling film in Fiji and Tonga… Became Grenadian citizen.' Of course, at each lunch we discovered our numbers had reduced. Of the original forty-five involved in all sides of the production, twelve have left the stage, including our leaders Braham and David Wright. But there are still lots of us for the sixtieth anniversary in two years' time. And I fancy we will go on meeting until there are only two of us left.

4

UNIVERSITY CONTINUES

More Oxford Follies and Burton and Taylor

Oxford continues – holiday in Delhi – funeral of Winston Churchill – Dr. Faustus with Richard Burton and Elizabeth Taylor for 3 weeks – exam fiasco – Four Degrees Over in Edinburgh and London – now what?

At the end of this unusual first year I spent most of the 1964 long summer vacation with my diplomat parents in India. The British High Commission in Delhi is huge and virtually the entire staff lives in a special diplomatic compound. I could see that, unless I was very careful, I would just be meeting Brits and I would never meet Indians or even see much of India. I did the great sights of the city and we made a day trip to Agra to see the Taj but the country was on alert and travel was restricted because war had broken out between India and Pakistan. In Delhi the war was not exactly intense. The only incident I remember was the non-appearance of a Pakistani reconnaissance plane a hundred miles west of the city, which had crashed when it ran out of fuel. Apparently, it was lost. The Indian papers were full of articles comparing the brave people of Delhi with the plucky people of London who had endured the Blitz with similar courage.

University Continues

My mother, God bless her, discovered that a group of students at Delhi University were doing a play and they were having problems and perhaps I could help. I made my way to the theatre where rehearsals were under way and I sat at the back and watched. Two things struck me. First the play was wildly unsuitable for an Indian cast. It was a silly, very English comedy called *Mad About Men*, set in a Cornish fishing village, in which the lead part is Miranda, a mermaid. Indian students as Cornish policemen were a sight to behold. The second thing was that the girl playing Miranda was ravishing. And I suppose a sari is as good a dress as any for a mermaid. By the end of the rehearsal I had become the director and by the end of the run I was hopelessly in love with Miranda, Brinda Das. She and I remained close for a year or so, especially when she came over to London to work for a while at Air India, before we drifted apart. Now, all these years later, she is a celebrated Indian politician, under her married name of Brinda Karat, prominent in the Communist Party of India, the first woman ever to be a member of the CPI Politburo. I confess I did not see that coming! A political life maybe, but not a communist one. Sadly, our correspondence stopped more than fifty years ago.

On another memorable day at the end of January 1965, I was transfixed by Sir Winston Churchill's funeral. He was not a particular hero at home, but I knew his death was the end of an era. I wonder if there has ever been another figure in British history quite like him: such a mixture of boldness, heroism, oratory and mistakes. I watched the BBC coverage all day – the gun carriage with the flag-draped coffin pulled by the slow-marching sailors, the huge silent crowds, bowing their heads, the Service at St. Paul's, the coffin on the Royal Barge and the cranes dipping – right up to the moment that the funeral train left Waterloo and the cameras stopped rolling because the burial at Bladon, near Blenheim, was private. In fact, I had been so impressed that at 11pm I went back to the Merton Junior Common Room to watch the TV highlights. In the armchair next to mine was a stranger. We talked. He turned out to be a New Zealander postgraduate who had had an extraordinary day.

The previous afternoon he had gone up to London with a sleeping bag and sweaters to camp out on the Strand to get himself a good viewing spot. But before he took up his place he had gone for supper to a family friend, who was no less than the Canon in Residence at St. Paul's, also a New Zealander, who was to read the lesson in the Service. Extraordinarily, the Canon said that he had a spare seat for the service in the Cathedral because of illness. 'Would you like it?' The problem was that the boy was wearing jeans and a sweater. My new friend, whose name I never discovered, calculated that he had enough time to get the last train back to Oxford, grab his suit and be back on the first train up to London that morning and be in his seat on time. He made it. The experience, he said, had been amazing. He could almost touch the casket, the music was overwhelming, the world was present. The only downside was that, by sitting in St. Paul's, he had seen nothing of the procession, the crowds, the solemn bands – the whole experience on the streets – and, although he was exhausted, he had come to watch the highlights to see what he had missed.

We watched in silence and it really was terrific. At about 1am it was over and we stood up to say goodnight. Then I had a thought. 'Listen,' I said, 'I have a dirty little A35 van. I don't know exactly where the village of Bladon is, but I know it is near Woodstock and I am sure we can find it. To finish your day properly why don't we join what I imagine will be crowds who have gone to see the grave?' He was thrilled, so off we set. We got to the tiny church at about 2am, I suppose. To our astonishment, the only sign of human life at the church was an elderly constable in his helmet, wearing a cape, leaning on a pushbike, standing by the porch. 'Would it be possible for us to see the grave?' we asked. 'Of course, boys. You'll have it to yourselves. Don't touch anything.' We knew immediately where the grave was by the overpowering scent of the fresh flowers, especially the freesias. There was a single spotlight crudely rigged up over the flowers and cards and the newly cut turf. We read the messages from 'Elizabeth R' and 'Clemmie'. We gazed and reflected and then drove back to Oxford without seeing another soul.

If my first year was exciting and unusual, so was my third. At the start of my last year I had reached the dizzy heights of being elected President of the Oxford University Dramatic Society (OUDS), a venerable institution founded in 1885. At least I hoped that my elevation might bring my neglected College a little comfort. Now the main privilege, if you are President and an aspiring actor, is to choose what is called the OUDS Major Production in the Lent term and give yourself the plum part. You know the sort of thing – Hamlet, Macbeth, Prospero, King Lear. My secret desire was to turn Orson Welles's wonderful film *Chimes at Midnight* into a stage production and take the part of Falstaff, which Welles culled from three Shakespeare plays. My dreaming was irresistibly interrupted by Professor Nevill Coghill, the great Chaucerian and formidable theatre figure. He told me that he had persuaded Richard Burton, whom he had known well during Burton's six months at Oxford during the war, to come back to his 'alma mater' to play Marlowe's *Doctor Faustus*. Profits from the production would go towards extending the Playhouse. It had also been agreed that his wife, Elizabeth Taylor, might be entrusted with the non-speaking role of Helen of Troy! The rest of the large cast would be students. The only time he could come was in February 1966. This would emphatically make *Doctor Faustus* the OUDS Major. 'Would I be so noble as to step aside from my presidential rights,' asked Nevill, 'and agree to understudy Burton and play the Chorus?' How, as they say, could I say no? Their arrival was an international news story. 'The most famous showbiz couple in the world to appear in a play with students.' Surely a fantasy.

My understudying role was tougher than might be imagined. It felt like the cart pulling the horse. The Burtons were originally coming for four weeks' rehearsal, then it was three, then it was two, then it was ten days. Hovering over this timetable was that it might be 'never'. How delighted the audience would have been, I thought, if just before the play began a man in a dinner jacket would come to the front of the stage and announce that, 'Owing to the unfortunate indisposition of Mr Richard Burton, the part of Doctor Faustus at tonight's performance would be taken by Mr Robert Scott.' We got our ten days' rehearsal, but it is a bloody big part and, frankly, any actor – including Richard Burton – needed longer. As preparation, Coghill decided to rehearse it solidly for a month with me in the part and then on the Burtons' first day in Oxford we would perform it to them in its entirety to show him what was wanted. 'Oh great! Thanks a bunch.' Well, we did our special run-through in the gym of the old Oxford Police Station to this audience of two. We then proceeded to his rehearsals proper and then we did a week of performances. I probably learnt by heart two-thirds of the play because the Chorus has quite a lot to say too! Richard always struggled with the lines, but there were glimpses of magic. And, of course, there was the voice.

There are so many memories from that crazy two and a half weeks with two of the most famous people on the planet. Literally the first thing that was organised, even before the first run-through – essentially to get it out of the way – was a press conference at the Playhouse. It was massive: TV crews, journalists, photographers from all over the world. Sheila Dawson, my friend David W's very pretty first wife (I was their best man), understudied Elizabeth in her non-speaking role (not as demanding as my job) and became briefly famous. The conference was meant to be run by Nevill and the Burtons' London agent, John Heyman, father of David, later the producer of the Harry Potter films. Just as it started, Nevill decided he was too old and too shy to take charge. Then

John decided, after he had got the show on the road, that he was too deaf and calmly suggested, 'Bob, will you take over?' The whole event was interminable with asinine questions and we were desperate to get to the first rehearsal. Terry Coleman writing in the *Guardian* was brutal. 'Mr Bob Scott, President of the Oxford University Dramatic Society, set about running things his way. "Only one more minute" he admonished photographers. They glowered. An agency man said he'd had less trouble at Buck House. The general opinion was that Mr Scott should go far, the farther the better.'

The rehearsals went fine, at least I cannot really remember big problems. The big set pieces with the Angels, the Pope, the Emperor and the Deadly Sins, Richard just had to be slotted into. The major scenes with Mephistopheles needed a lot of time and Andreas Teuber, an American postgraduate, was superb and was a worthy foil. Richard told funny stories, some of them rather often. Elizabeth was hugely popular. By the way, you did not call them Dick or Liz. They were definitely Richard and Elizabeth. They were doing a huge favour to Nevill, whom they loved, and this affection was clearly the big driver, but Richard enjoyed being lionised by Oxford. Elizabeth was fascinated by the history and the old buildings and loved being with the young. They stayed at the Bull in Woodstock and drove in and out of Oxford each day in their Rolls chauffeured by the faithful Gaston. Elizabeth was so determined to be 'ordinary' that once she asked me where she could buy tights. I suggested M&S. 'Will you come with me, Bob?' Although Marks is only round the corner from the theatre, I wondered if we would be mobbed? 'No, no. That's what I love about England,' Elizabeth said. 'If they recognise me, they usually turn their backs and pretend that they haven't seen me. Unlike Americans.' That's exactly what happened. We ventured out, Elizabeth in headscarf and dark glasses, made it to the store where she was both recognised and deliberately ignored. The young shop assistant did not know who she was dealing with.

The first night was predictably memorable. As Chorus, Nevill had the idea that I should stand downstage right, at the front of the stage to start the play. The opening speech is quite long and Nevill's second bright idea was that halfway through my speech and in dark shadow, Burton, as Faustus, should enter backstage left into his study. There he would start perusing his great books of magic and alchemy so that he could go straight into his famous opening speech as soon as the Chorus had finished. It was Burton all right but he was very dimly lit while I as the Chorus rabbited on. A quiet whisper went round the audience: 'Is it him? I'm sure it is. It's Richard Burton. Well, I can't see properly. But I think so. Maybe it isn't. Not sure.' All I knew was that the 700 pairs of eyes which had been vaguely fixed on me when I began had left me for ever. I could have recited the telephone directory and no one would have noticed. Once I was out of the way the show seemed to go OK. Richard more or less knew his lines and Andreas was terrific as Mephistopheles. Elizabeth's entrance was stunning in a gown designed by Irene Sharaff – sensational and very revealing. The costumes must have been the most expensive ever made for a student production. My great friends Dick Durden-Smith and Maria Aitken looked extraordinary as the Evil and Good Angels. At the end the audience applauded loudly.

The reviews were dreadful. The truth is that it was not very good. With the exception of Andreas and one or two others the students looked extremely modest alongside Richard. Fresh-faced youths pretending to be either rapacious sheiks or shivering slaves, and nice ladies from Lady Margaret Hall pretending to be raddled prostitutes, were dire. And the Seven Deadly Sins were anything but. A friend consoled us that at least the reviews were very long and the coverage was on several pages of most of the papers. It was a major national event. I found Nevill at lunch and expressed my sympathy. He was wonderfully calm, just sad for Richard. He also gave me a line about critics I have used many times since. 'My dear boy, what do you expect from a pig but a grunt?' Happily, the audiences were not put off by the press and every night was an event. The gasps that greeted Elizabeth's only entrance and the kiss that ended the scene seemed to indicate that they had got their money's worth even if it was 10pm before she came on. Most nights there was a party at the Randolph Hotel, where they also had an apartment, after the performance. There was one very late, very Welsh night when Harry Secombe and Stanley Baker attended and we were treated to splendid quartets mostly of hymns sung by the three of them with Richard's brother Ivor who was in Oxford with his wife for the whole week. One morning during the run they laid on for the cast a private viewing in an Oxford cinema of their great movie *Who's Afraid of Virginia Woolf?*, which they had just finished. This was the first screening in the world apparently. It was sensational. Anyway, every ticket for every performance of *Faustus* was sold out and with very high prices the Playhouse made a handsome sum. The run of seven performances finished on Saturday February 19th. The next day the Burtons decamped from Woodstock to the Dorchester Hotel, and that should have been that.

There was an extraordinary postscript. On the Sunday night after the last performance Richard had agreed to make an LP of the play at a tiny private recording studio in the basement of a house in Putney. The six or so leading members of the student cast were also asked to come to the studio. We came up from Oxford for about 7pm in a minivan. We got there before Richard – we did not expect to see Elizabeth as she had no lines – and were astonished to find a camera crew from *24 Hours*, the *Newsnight* of those days, with the eminent interviewer Kenneth Alsop. They were waiting for both Burtons who had apparently promised to do a special joint interview for the BBC. As the 'senior' student there I stepped in and said that I was pretty sure that the Burtons had no memory of their promise. I was told to 'piss off' and keep out of the matter. The Burtons duly arrived, Elizabeth looking particularly sloppy in trousers and sweater and no make-up. She knew nothing of the interview and made it clear that she had only come along to say goodbye to us again.

Richard finally accepted that he had made some kind of commitment back at the original press conference to the interview, but he had an extremely tricky time persuading Elizabeth that he had made a commitment for her too. Not only did she not do these kinds of newsy interviews, she was looking a mess. Nevertheless, finally she agreed. She politely asked the wife of the record producer, whose house we were in, if she could borrow some basic make-up. Then she said to me, 'Get me a large vodka and tonic,' and 'Stay with me.' She was furious. We went up to the nice lady's very modest bathroom. Elizabeth and I perched on the side of the bath by the mirror, I fed her slugs of vodka and tonic and tried to keep her cheerful, while I watched her transform her face into the world's most beautiful woman. It was wondrous.

Down we went to the living room where the crew had set up. Elizabeth's one condition was that she could only be filmed head and shoulders, and she took her place on the sofa next to Richard. I sat on the floor at her feet, out of shot, with more vodka and tonic ready. The atmosphere was tense but the interview went fine. When it was over, Richard got to his feet and said fiercely 'Now fuck off. I am going down to the basement to start the recording.' 'OK,' said Alsop, 'but we just have to retake my questions, as we only have one camera.' By now Richard was out of the room, but Elizabeth looked at me and said, 'Let's just listen to this. I don't trust him.' It was one of those little houses with just one main room on each floor with a staircase connecting each level. So, we sat on the bottom stair outside the living room out of sight of the crew. They started to record Alsop's questions.

One of the questions to Elizabeth had been 'Miss Taylor, what is it like acting on stage with your husband?' On the retake of the question, Kenneth Alsop, exceedingly unprofessionally, asked, 'Miss Taylor, what is it like acting on stage with your fifth, or is it sixth, husband?' Elizabeth gripped my arm and whispered, 'He never asked that, did he?' 'He certainly did not,' I whispered back. Elizabeth smiled for the first time in more than an hour and said 'Right!' and went dancing down the stairs to the basement. A few moments later there was the subterranean roar of an angry bull. Burton came charging upstairs, picked up Kenneth Alsop by his lapels and roared into his face 'Alslop, Alslop, I shall be watching tomorrow night and if I do not like what I see, I will have you killed, Alslop.' Kenneth Alsop, who was not tall and had a wooden leg from the war, was extremely shaken. We all watched on Monday night and the question was never asked.

The next part of the *Faustus* saga I cannot describe. The cast, less David Wood and me, flew to Rome in the summer vacation to make a movie of the film. We had another engagement at the Edinburgh Festival. We were told we did not miss that much. Several of the student actors had their parts cut or their voices dubbed. On location the Burtons were apparently much more invisible than they had been in Oxford, although their generosity was as splendid as ever. Sadly, the film was even less successful than the stage play in critical terms and it did very badly at the box office.

There is even a postscript to the postscript. Two years later, in the summer of 1968, I was walking down St. Martin's Lane, with a particularly beautiful girl – Susie Caulcutt, the stage designer – and we dropped into the Salisbury Arms for a drink, only to discover Richard and a small entourage on the other side of the bar. Probably because he wanted to meet my companion he recognised me immediately. He then told us that he was bored with his film, that Elizabeth would never forgive him if she didn't see me as well, that he was now stopping work for the day, that Gaston was outside with the Rolls and we were going immediately to the Dorchester to see her. The film was *The Bofors Gun* directed by Jack Gold, which Richard was not enjoying. His departure from the shoot that afternoon was apparently one of the reasons why he was later replaced by Nicol Williamson. When we got to the Dorchester we were told that Elizabeth was still out shopping with Princess Elisabeth of Yugoslavia. *A good line*, I thought. Anyway, they soon arrived back and Elizabeth was as lovely as ever. She wanted to know about everyone. She then said, 'Bob, you haven't seen my ring.' This was the first famous diamond that Richard had very recently and publicly given her. The second was even bigger.

'You must look at the sun through it, the colours are amazing,' she said. We went out onto the balcony of their suite overlooking Park Lane. She gave me the ring and I admired it appropriately, but I could not help wondering what simply dropping it into the traffic of Park Lane would have achieved as a PR stunt.

I have guiltily calculated that I took part in fourteen productions in nine terms, some wonderful, some less so. Eight were at the Playhouse, the others were mostly open-air in College Gardens. I was also a Merton Chapel chorister and a member of the Kodaly Choir. We gave a wonderful concert to celebrate our 700th Anniversary as a College under the baton of Yehudi Menuhin, which included a specially commissioned Zoltan Kodaly premiere. The head of Merton music was a charismatic Czech ex-pupil of Kodaly called Laslo Heltai – hence the choir's name. We punted, we partied, we loved.

I did sit another exam at the end of my third year. Not, I am ashamed to say, my Finals for an Honours Degree, but the second leg of a Pass Degree, to which I was condemned by my showing in Classical Mods. This was Law, two papers on Contract and Tort. For the privilege of tutoring me in Law I was handed over to an eccentric Merton Fellow called John Barton, who thought I was a waste of space. I had a distinguished friend at Magdalen called Michael Beloff, who had just been made a don and who later became President of Trinity College. He gallantly agreed to take me on from Barton. Michael and I stumbled through a few tutorials and I actually did a bit of work for the two three-hour papers which were set for the 15th June 1966.

At about 1pm on Tuesday the 14th, I bumped into Barton at Merton Lodge – he was still theoretically my tutor. He aggressively asked me where I had been at 9am that morning. Smugly I told him I had been in the library. 'Well, you should have been at the Examination Schools, sitting your first exam.' 'No, no,' I cried. 'That's tomorrow.' 'It was today,' he replied. 'You missed it and you will be sent down this afternoon at the Meeting of the Warden and Fellows. I will enjoy seeing to that,' and marched off. I was devastated and slunk abjectly into the bar. I picked up a newspaper and, by chance, read the date – Tuesday 14th June. I remembered for certain that the published notice of the exam was for the 15th June, so I rushed round to the official noticeboard at the Examination Schools, which clearly stated that the Law Pass Exam was scheduled for Tuesday 15th June. But Tuesday was the 14th and while the authorities were working to the Tuesday, I was working to the 15th. A cock-up.

I hotfooted it to Barton to explain the mix-up. Barton loathed me but he loathed the University authorities more. Once he was convinced by my story he went into battle on my behalf with relish. After various meetings and phone calls that afternoon he called me to his rooms to say that I had been given special dispensation and I could sit the exams tomorrow (the 15th) after all. *Right*, I thought. *Now all I have to do is find someone who sat the papers today*. I searched and drew a complete blank. I discovered that I was the only person in the entire University sitting the Law Pass Exam. No wonder they have stopped Pass Degrees altogether now. Anyway, I sat the papers and got, for me, a distinguished Beta minus – that's a Pass in anyone's language. The irony of the story is that on the Tuesday afternoon, I later discovered, I was indeed sent down. The following Tuesday the Warden and Tutors formally reversed my sentence and reinstated me. However, on the previous Wednesday I had sat and passed an official Oxford University Examination while no longer a Member of the University. My Merton rehabilitation was complete when I was made President of the Merton Society for three years in 2008.

My last appearance on the boards of the Playhouse was in the summer of 1966 in the dishonestly titled musical revue *Four Degrees Over*. The other three – David Wood, Adele Weston and John Gould – had all crossed swords successfully with their examiners. I, of course, had not completed my battle. Anyway, we all knew each other extremely well. We had all been in Hang and several other shows. David, John and I had also made decent money in Oxford, Cambridge and London doing late-night cabaret: enough money at least to enable me to leave Oxford not only degree-free but, more importantly, debt-free. We three chaps asked Adele to join us in the revue, written by David and John, for the Edinburgh Festival Fringe. Doing the show, which had been arranged for some time, meant that David and I could not go to Rome to be in the film of *Doctor Faustus*. The Burtons, however, entirely understood and sweetly agreed to sponsor our revue with £250 (real money in those days) and enough to enable us to start at the Playhouse and go on a short tour before landing up in Edinburgh. By now all four of us had something of a reputation in Oxford and we played there in early July. We then took the show on a short tour before Edinburgh in August.

On the 30th July we found ourselves doing an afternoon performance at the King's Lynn Festival. We were astonished to play to a full house. Not only were we completely unknown in King's Lynn, but our performance coincided exactly with the famous England–Germany World Cup Final at Wembley. At the start I told the audience, rather to the irritation of my three companions whose interest in sport was roughly zero, that I would religiously keep them abreast of the score. When the score got to 2–2 and extra-time was needed, the place was abuzz. The end of the show in Kings Lynn and extra-time at Wembley coincided. When I was able to announce a 4–2 victory, there were several audience members who thought I was having them on.

By the time we got to Edinburgh, Michael Codron told us that he wanted to bring the show to the Fortune, the perfect London theatre for us, where Beyond the Fringe and Flanders and Swann before them had triumphed. But he wanted some new material, a proper stage design and a proper director. John Cox, a rising force in opera, became our director, Barry Kay our designer and David and John had to write some more. Codron worked very hard for us. Norman Parkinson photographed us for *Vogue*, we did *Late Night Line Up* and it was decided that an LP be made from the best of the first live performances in London. The producer, who was engaged by Parlophone to make us sound better than we were, was none other than George Martin. He was a master at adding applause and laughter to the live performance he recorded when there wasn't any. We were thrilled. And, remember, in 1966 he was still producing the Beatles. There is a sad little ending to the story of our LP. A few years later, I was in Lewis's in Manchester in the record department and, as was my wont, I flicked through the albums in the Shows section. To my amazement, I found a copy of the *Four Degrees Over* LP. The price of £1.19.6d was printed on the top right-hand corner. Only by now there were a series of little stickers on top of the price about a quarter of an inch thick. The price had declined, sticker by sticker, and now was 6d. I picked the record up, paid over my 6d and put it out of its misery. But at least we can claim that we only ever made one LP together and George Martin produced it.

We weren't a flop and we weren't a hit. Our reviews did not compare with the Hang notices. We got some pleasant ones, the weekends were full and we ran about twelve weeks. I doubt the investors got all their money back, but they would not have lost all of it, I would guess. It was an experience for all of us but in different ways. By now we were ex-students (I left without finishing my Pass Degree) and thinking about the future. John Higgins, the *FT* Drama Critic, described Adele as a stocky brunette (while warmly praising her voice) and she was furious – 'I am not going to go through life with strange men allowed to call me stocky in public journals'. She gave up being a brilliant songstress to become a successful author under her married name of Adele Geras.

John and David, separately and together, went on to make excellent lives in the business. John both composed and performed. For a while he was quite famous, appearing on the Esther Rantzen show. He used to say that there was only one tune ever written – 'Ten Green Bottles' – and then prove it by playing Bach or the Beatles, always allowing the melody to dwindle imperceptibly into 'Ten Green Bottles'. He was so clever and lovely but, very sadly, died some time ago. David has blossomed, mostly as a superb writer of children's plays. He is an OBE and has been the winner of an Olivier Award. *The Times* dubbed him 'the National Children's Dramatist'. His CV is wonderful as an actor, a producer, a magician, a singer as well as a writer. He is a special person, immensely energetic and thoughtful. He remains a close friend.

But what about my future? Was I now a singer/actor? I suggested to John that I was thinking of trying to become a proper baritone/bass. He sat me down and gently pointed out that I was fine as long as I just did our jolly stuff but actually I didn't really sing reliably in tune and that my sense of rhythm was dodgy. This came as a bit of a rude shock and persuaded me that probably I would not be the next Fischer-Dieskau, my ambition. I was having other doubts anyway. I was living in Guildford when we were doing the show, going up to London at 5pm and coming back after 11pm. I noticed that my trains up to town were empty and the trains going the other way were packed. For some reason I felt I should be in the full trains. Also, I wanted my Saturdays to myself. During the run I hated refusing invitations. Finally, I got bored doing the same thing night after night. Even bank clerks change their words each day. I loved rehearsing and short runs but the thought of a year's run of anything horrified me. But what to do?

5

A GRANDMOTHER

An Amazing Friend and Lady

Amazing lady – in loco parentis – loved and not – a big influence – extraordinary talks – sport and theatre – generous and mean, serious and funny – letter-writer – dies at 95

There had been times in the nineteenth century when most families, including mine, boasted multitudes of great aunts and uncles. I only saw the tail end of those fertile Victorian times, which tragically, because of the Boer Wars and the First World War, produced hundreds of thousands of elderly maiden aunts and widows. We certainly had ours – Constance, Winifred, May, Edith, Helen, Agatha to name a few. Unusually, all four of my grandparents were alive until I was a teenager but each pair only produced two children: my father David and his younger brother Tim on one side and my mother Vera and her older brother Eric on the other. Eric had a daughter by a first marriage but I do not remember her. Tim was cheerfully gay and unproductive. My sister, brother and I were, therefore, effectively cousin-free. In later life I had a special friendship with my Uncle Tim but my key relationship in the family right up to my forties was with my Granny Scott. In particular, she got me through my schools and University and we emerged the other side of my education as close friends. I had an intimacy with her that I never really had with my parents. Up to her death in 1991 I saw a lot more of her than of them simply because of their long postings abroad.

In the 1950s British diplomatic children either travelled with their parents or, more commonly, went to boarding schools back at home. Someone, usually a grandparent, had to be 'in loco parentis'. My sister Diana got my mother's mother, I got my father's mother. In my view my sister definitely got the worse deal. I am afraid I found Granny Ibbitson boring and usually miserable. Granny Scott was none of these things. Quite simply, I adored her. We seemed to love the same things and we talked and talked. However, mine was not the universal view. Whether it was as Granny Scott at home, or as Mrs Scott in the village, or as Councillor Barbara Scott on several Local Authorities and public bodies, she divided the world. Some found her bossy, aggressive, impatient, full of herself. Others found her spirited, funny, serious, surprising, interested in everybody and everything. My father and mother, I reckon, fell into Category One. My Uncle Tim and I fell into Category Two. I do not at all condemn my parents. Gran was almost certainly a much better grandmother than a mother-in-law and my father was perilously poised between a fierce mother and a powerful wife. My special place in Gran's affections were recognised when my father and uncle, for different reasons, asked me to give the eulogy at her packed funeral – Father demurred, because he did not trust himself to praise her sufficiently; Uncle opted out, because he was sure he would break down.

My grandmother was very much aware that she had lived a very long life, almost a hundred years, through an extraordinary period of history. She was born at the end of the nineteenth century. She had her appendix removed in an operation on the kitchen table in the night nursery at home, with straw on the street outside the house to deaden the noise of the horses and metal wheels. She lived through the grimmest, bloodiest two wars in our history, with a husband in one and two sons in the other. Telephones, cars, aeroplanes, television, the nuclear bomb were invented before her eyes. She watched men walking on the moon. All the same, in the 1980s as she approached one hundred she definitely did not want to die. She was a regular churchgoer, but her religious faith was essentially pragmatic, I reckoned. She pointed out, 'The church is opposite my house, I am naturally an early riser and I love the King James Bible. It's a sort of insurance policy, I suppose. I am not at all sure about an afterlife but I will feel such a fool discovering that St. Peter is actually there waiting for me, extremely cross that I had not made the effort to join in, especially when it was so easy.' Nevertheless, she definitely raged against the dying of the light. 'There is still so much to do, so many books to read.' But she was not scared.

The longest period of her life was spent at Wellington College (almost seventy years), for much of it as the enthusiastic and involved wife of a senior housemaster. Her 'boys' were at the centre of her life. She had an amazing connection with young people, especially boys. She always talked to young people as grown-ups. She was interested in their views, in their experiences, in their hopes. And the more 'difficult' the boy, the more she took them seriously and talked with them. Later in life – unsurprisingly, with one son an Ambassador and the other in the British Council – she developed a taste for foreign travel. She never stayed in a hotel. Everywhere she wanted to go there was an Old Wellingtonian (or five) urging her to stay with him.

Having put a great deal into grand-mothering she took to great-grand-mothering as well. Fortunately, one of the eight of them, my eldest son David, begged her to write down the story of her life and she started. Unfortunately, she only got to page 30. It never even got to her marriage – indeed it does not get to men – or the First World War. What she recorded are confined to memories from childhood. She writes of a bizarre home education regime with governesses engaged by her mother. She writes of long happy summer holidays in Suffolk and Cornwall. She remembers slightly dull friends from Kensington and what she calls 'ancient' Victorian aunts who were years younger than she was when she came to write about them. In particular, she remembers her parents and her sister, who died at seventeen.

She was rather pleased and almost proud to have been born in another century – in 1896 to be precise. A few short extracts give a flavour of her childhood and her character. Remember she is in her late eighties and is writing to an eight-year-old boy.

On Queen Victoria:

> *The story always remembered against me is of my seeing Queen Victoria in her carriage in High Street Kensington complete with coloured attendant [presumably the famous Abdel Karim, her private secretary, known as the Munshi] high up on the Box next to the Coachman and of rushing home in high excitement exclaiming 'Mother, mother, I have seen the Queen and she's a black man.'*

A Grandmother

On her father:

I adored my father and loved my mother. There is a difference. During my early childhood I lived in dread that something would befall him. Just as Queen Victoria is a dim memory, so is the Boer War. I had a horror that he would become involved in it, that he might be sent to South Africa and would inevitably be killed.

On shyness:

My sister Elisabeth, 15 months younger than me, completed the party. We were good friends. I was nervous but never shy. She was rather shy but more philosophic and equable. I can remember a short-lived attempt to cultivate shyness. It seemed to be an attractive trait admired by grown-up people. How well I recall an occasion in a bus when Mother was joined by a friend and I deliberately became shy and as I thought very sweet. It seemed to go excellently but it was such a frightful effort that after a few further attempts I gave up.

On money:

Our pocket money started at 1 penny a week and went gradually over the years to its pinnacle of a shilling a week. It never occurred to either of us girls that we might overspend. The effect on me of this thrift is that never once in my life have I been overdrawn at the bank and never in possession of an unpaid bill. For this I am endlessly grateful but I am regretful that as a result I am incapable of spending money freely, happily or light-heartedly.

On grief:

My mother and Elisabeth were very close and looking back I know she meant more to Mother than I did. Certainly, her death at 17 of measles was a grief from which my mother never completely recovered. I will never forget the sound of Mother's uncontrollable sobbing which went on for days behind her closed bedroom door. 'At least I'm alive,' I thought. But it was no consolation.

On formal education:

> *The only serious regret I have for myself when young is that I was never allowed to face the competition inevitably provided at a good school. I was taught entirely at home. It would have cut me to size and I needed that.*

Yes, she was penny pinching and I suffered quite a bit from it when she took me in hand. For instance, the telephone was definitely for incoming calls only. Her own phone was one of the old black Bakelite ones with a circular metal dial on the front except that her dial was broken at the 0 and if you tried to dial 0, which was how all long-distance calls began, you were likely to end up with a cut finger. As for her education she was right that she was denied good formal teaching but, boy, she made up for it. She regarded it as some kind of crime not to have a book always on the go. 'What are you reading?' would always be one of her first questions. She loved being read to and also to read aloud to others. Great-Granny Jackson, her mother, who was going blind and with whom she had a brittle relationship, lived with her for years and years and she read to her almost every day. I remember Great-Granny quite well, a tiny twinkling lady who played patience endlessly, an obsession I have inherited.

Gran's first major responsibility towards me was getting me to my new prep school – Eagle House – in the next village, in September 1953 when we came back from South Africa. I was to be a boarder there for four years. I was a large and enthusiastic nine-year-old and I was panting to get there, apparently all dressed up in my uniform ready to leave four hours early. I later discovered that I embarrassed Gran on that very first day. The first person we met was the cheerful but portly music master called Billy Bean who greeted me with the words 'My goodness, you're a chubby chap, Scott.' It is said that I replied, 'Well, you're not so slim yourself, are you, Sir?' Poor Gran!

In truth, at Eagle House my grandmother added to my sense of feeling rather different. As I have already said, she was known for being tight with money when she could be. She considered the official school uniform as supplied by Messrs Swan and Edgar of Piccadilly Circus as ridiculously expensive. She bought my shorts and shirts from Woolworths, she tracked down a second-hand blazer from an Old Boy, but, worst of all, she herself knitted my sweater and my long socks, which were roughly the correct colour, but they were just not right. And when I finally made it into the First XI cricket team, at that moment when one was, for the first time, gloriously required to

A Grandmother

wear long white trousers, I was condemned to my grandfather's old cricket flannels which were nearer yellow than white. 'Perfect!' said Gran. Also, at this rather posh school on Sunday Exeats, parents would arrive in their Jaguars and Rovers to collect their little Clives and Christophers. Gran arrived on her push bike and we would walk the couple of miles home to Crowthorne for lunch. I longed to have my own copy of the *Eagle* comic, to have my own private supply of chocolate and to be collected by parents with a posh car. But most of all I longed to have the regulation machine-knitted sweater and socks and not my grandmother's strange hand-knitted versions.

Gran adored the theatre, especially plays, and at a boys' boarding school like Wellington there were endless play-readings. As the housemaster's wife she was in the perfect position to get the best female parts. One of her Old Boys was Michael Meyer, the eminent translator and biographer of Ibsen and Strindberg. I knew him well in my years in the theatre. He was astonished to discover that I was Barbara Scott's grandson. 'I did not much like Wellington but your grandparents were very important to me.' (I think he was one of their 'difficult' pupils.) 'You know, the first time I ever encountered Ibsen was at a play-reading at Wellington one Sunday night of *A Doll's House*. Your grandmother, of course, read the part of Nora.' Gran was thrilled when I told her. Indeed, I think she was entitled to be. But you can see why the world was always divided about her.

The extremely distinguished military historian Sir Michael Howard, OM CH was a beloved Old Boy and, like so many, stayed in touch with her all her life. He definitely fell into the category of 'admirer' and in his autobiography *Soldier Professor* he talks affectionately and at some length of the early influence of both my grandparents. However, as a close friend of Sir Michael's mother, Gran was deeply shocked to discover from the affectionate passage about her in his book that the boys' nickname for her was Napoleon. I think she rather assumed it might have been Cordelia or Rosalind.

Gran never undertook a minute of housework in her life. Hoovers, washing machines, ovens and irons were foreign objects to her. There were at least four servants in her childhood home in London. There was an army of servants, inside and outside the House at Wellington all my grandfather's working life. And when he retired, they took with them Kate, their kitchen maid, who had already been with them forty years. My deeply competent and intelligent Gran was a disaster in the kitchen and the only words I dreaded hearing when I came to stay, which I did endlessly, was 'Kate's off tonight'. Gran could not even warm up food that had been left fully prepared. I loved Kate but her life was a complete mystery to me. She had her own room in the house which I never saw into. Two newspapers arrived every morning – *The Times* and the *Daily Express*, which was always referred to as 'Kate's paper' and which Grandpa and I used guiltily to read. Kate very rarely left the house and when I asked her why she had never married, she said that at eighteen she had had an understanding with a young man, but she refused to see him again after some friend had seen him coming out of a pub. She lived, eyeball to eyeball, with Gran for nearly seventy years but they had no intimacy at all; indeed, I would say that they disliked each other.

It cannot be denied that there was a dark side to Gran's attitudes and energy. It never touched me but it showed itself sadly in my grandfather's last years. She was years younger than him in every sense. He was anyway twelve years older than her, but he died at the age of sixty-nine, looking and moving like an old man. At the time she was only fifty-seven, full of life and destined to live to ninety-five. It was in these years that I got to know her so well. And there is no doubt that her impatience led to my grandfather's last years being miserable. She knew it, she confessed to it and as an eleven-year-old I witnessed it. He felt the cold dreadfully and I remember, one freezing day, sitting with him in front of a gas fire. He was wearing three cricket sweaters. We were secretly congratulating ourselves that at last the room was almost warm. My grandmother burst in and complained of the dreadful fug in the room, turned off the gas and threw up the window. 'That's better,' she said. My grandfather's shivers returned.

Their life together had not been well synchronised. She was to have a long life alone – thirty-eight years – after his death, more years as a widow than they had had together as a couple. Their marriage seemed made in heaven at the beginning, even though she always believed her in-laws did not approve of her. They had been very attracted to each other and her sexual enthusiasm seems to have matched Queen Victoria's. I know this for two reasons: one, because she actually told me so in the amazing, frank talks that we had over the years. Secondly, because I found and read a packet of letters in the attic of her house which they had sent each other to and from the trenches during the First War after they had been married for only a few months. I saw the letters only once and remember chiefly that they were vividly descriptive of their best moments of sex together, which they called their 'wars'. Even though it was not yet 1963 at least I learnt that Philip Larkin's poem was wrong about the date of

A Grandmother

the invention of sex! Both of them were clearly reliving the vivid experiences of their young sexual love, knowing that they might have only memories to live on. I never found them again. I suppose she might have discovered that they had been disturbed. Even Uncle Tim, who was much closer to her than I was, knew nothing of them.

Of course, I never talked to Gran about the letters but she was extremely anxious in our talks that I should know how deeply in love she had been with Grandpa. She wanted to erase the memory of the last pathetic years of his life. After the First War ended, the marriage apparently became less electric and more predictable. She got angry and jealous with his endless cricket and golf weekends. His years as a Housemaster were good to them both but she wanted him to be more ambitious and try to become a Headmaster. She wanted to be the wife of a Malim or a Birley. Indeed, I had a sense the marriage went gently but steadily downhill. She was constantly impatient with him and as he became vaguer and quieter, she became tougher but lonelier. She had her two boys, but they were not enough. She wanted to live. She also had a daughter, who died in infancy, and who like her seventeen-year-old sister who died, was called Elisabeth.

Through ambition and determination her own life was becoming fuller. She first became a Parish Councillor and Chair of the Women's Institute, then a member of the Easthampstead Rural District Council and quickly its Chair and in that role she played a leading part in the creation of Bracknell, which virtually removed Easthampstead from the face of the earth. Moving ever onwards and upwards she then stood for election onto Berkshire County Council in Reading and eventually became Chair of the Education Committee, responsible for a huge budget. She relished her lack of schooling for the job. As the years passed, put quite simply, Gran rose and thrived while Grandpa declined and died. She became Chair of innumerable Boards of School Governors. She was, of course, a Conservative but an independent one. She was a sympathetic Magistrate who greatly approved of Roy Jenkins' social reforms in the 70s. One of her frequent comments was 'There but for the grace of God go I!' She was a visitor at Broadmoor, round the corner from her house. She often said how much she looked forward to seeing her murderers and wanted to understand them. She was fond of a famous poisoner called Thompson. She was everywhere and it was a scandal that she never received even a measly MBE, which she would have loved.

But it was not for her appointments or public work that I loved her. As I have said, we had the most amazing talks while she sat in her drawing room embroidering wonderful tapestry chair seats. She was always, always busy, even when she was supposedly doing nothing. Once in my late teens, I asked her what she admired most in a human being. After serious thought, she said she honoured physical courage and she talked of dead and injured friends and relations from the First War. I think she combined courage with beauty. She usually described her heroes as 'frightfully good-looking'.

On another occasion I asked her what she disliked most about herself. She put down her square of canvas and her needle, took off her half-rimmed spectacles and quickly replied, almost without thinking, 'my sexual jealousy'. I was stunned. I am almost certain that she was faithful to my grandfather, but as we talked, I realised that she clearly fell in love fairly regularly, if secretly. She even told me of a few men who had meant so much to her, but none of them meant anything to me. Some of them were young masters at Wellington. The effect of the feelings, she confessed, was that she hated the wife or partner of the adored object with murderous passion. Once she admitted to devising slow and painful deaths in her head. But, even though she might have had a more than vivid imagination, I am pretty sure that she viewed faithfulness as she viewed thrift – unnegotiable. Nevertheless, I have no doubt that her sexuality outlasted her husband's by many years. Who will ever know? All I am certain of is that they were pretty exciting chats for a seventeen-year-old schoolboy to have with his formidable sixty-five-year-old grandmother. And she looked sixty-five. She was not remotely beautiful, nor flirtatious. She was short and pretty square. But she was fit and rode a bicycle into her eighties. She dressed in what looked like Oxfam cast-offs. As she said, she hated spending money.

Her influence on me was certainly not sartorial, but it was, at least partly, from my grandmother that I developed the two passions that have dominated my life – the theatre and sport. We went to the theatre together a lot and to all sorts of theatre. There was the annual visit to the Windsor pantomime. She took me to the Old Vic to see Richard Burton in *Henry V* with Gran insisting that instead of my having a smart new suit, which had been promised, I was required to sport a baggy, ancient blue herringbone suit belonging to my now deceased grandfather, which he had certainly worn out, and which equally certainly did not fit me, just like the yellow cricket 'whites'. *Henry V* made a great impression on me, although I relished Esmond Knight's Fluellen almost as vividly as Burton's Henry.

Not to get above ourselves, we went to see *Cranford* (with an all-female cast) at the local Women's Institute and to see plays at Wellington (with all-

A Grandmother

male schoolboy casts). I still remember seeing the immensely tall Peter Snow as Richard of Bordeaux who was very good. Then there was the Bradfield College Greek Play in Greek and an open-air performance of *Much Ado About Nothing* in the garden of a country house. Later, more than once, she took my sister and me to Glyndebourne. Sadly, she always slightly spoiled the occasion by producing a dreadful picnic – soft hard-boiled eggs, Ryvita with Marmite, which I detest, and sardine sandwiches. This was especially hard on my sister who could not eat fish. We read Shakespeare and Dickens and Dumas aloud. She loved classical music and I can still see her sitting in her upright, wing-backed armchair listening to the Bach St. Matthew Passion with her head in her hands and her eyes closed, frequently sighing loudly with pleasure.

At the same time she loved all types of sport. We both followed cricket with a passion. Her team was Surrey, so mine was too. Not a hard choice in those days – they won everything. She would follow all the Wellington College sports and was very expert about the success of the school teams. One of the reasons she loved to talk sport with me was because her two sons hardly knew the difference between a bat and a ball and cared not a jot. She also loved horse racing and her absolutely favourite sportsman was Lester Piggott. She always had a tiny bet on him in the Derby. To demonstrate love, rather than to make money, I reckoned. She thought he was the sexiest thing on two legs. Later, I suggested to her that she had clearly never heard him speak in that dreadful high-pitched whine. 'Don't spoil it now. Be quiet,' she said.

As I grew older and we became closer, I loved to make her laugh. Tears would well up and then roll down her cheeks. When we were together, she insisted that I tell her what I was up to and what I thought of this and that and I would try to recount the funny bits. 'Stop it, Rob. Stop it, Rob,' she would plead, as she dabbed her eyes with her handkerchief. Towards the end of her life when she was in her nineties I visited her in hospital after she had had a bad fall. I took with me a letter from the Vice-Chancellor of Manchester University. 'What have you got there?' she demanded. 'Well, you remember how I left Oxford without completing my degree?' 'Remember?' she exploded. 'I have never been so angry in my life. You let me down. You let yourself down. You let your college down. It was disgraceful.' 'Now calm down and read this,' I suggested. It was a letter inviting me to accept an Honorary Degree from Manchester. She laughed so much her teeth fell out on the bedspread. When she recovered, she was impressed to hear that I was receiving my Honour in company with Billy Beaumont, the England Rugby Captain.

Gran was a wonderful letter writer. She wrote voluminously to my Uncle Tim, who was in the British Council in various posts in Africa and Asia. Sadly, Tim destroyed the lot. I am pretty sure it was because they both enjoyed being rude about members of the family. She wrote to me as well, not nearly so frequently, nor so indiscreetly, but always beautifully. I kept many of hers and to my surprise she kept my inadequate outpourings. In the summer of 1966 she included a marvellous little tale:

Dearest Rob,

One day last week I went to one of my favourite places on earth, Glyndebourne. Mozart, thank God. All the best tunes. You know my habit of wanting to kill as many birds with as few stones as possible. Well, I discovered that the funeral of an old friend, not known to you, was taking place in a village near Haywards Heath on the same day at 2.30pm. So, I thought I could take in the obsequies before I took in the opera. I knew, of course, that my attire was entirely inappropriate for a funeral and I brought with me a black coat which I put on over my bright dress. As I approached the church from the car park I realised to my horror that I had on my head a jolly summer hat covered with colourful artificial flowers. I whipped it off and put it on the bench in the church porch and made my way to a seat in suitably sombre mood.

Imagine my surprise, when the coffin was borne down the aisle and there amongst the floral tributes on the lid was my hat. I must tell you that, as I knelt to pray, my mind was not properly on either my dear departed chum or the hereafter. I could think only of how to retrieve my hat. Alas, we are separated for ever. When I finally got back to the porch in the queue of mourners, the hearse was pulling away; taking not only the coffin but also my hat to their final destinations.'

Dear Gran. I always loved 'Imagine my surprise...' She was my special influence. She was, I admit, intolerant. She was capable of being unkind. I heard her say some fearfully snobbish things. She was as dreadful a driver as she was a cook. She seemed to regard the white line down the middle of the road as a guideline for your wheels on each side. Of course, she never had to take a test. Then she would reveal her impatience at zebra crossings, waiting for a woman half her age to cross, by frequently muttering under her breath, 'Better dead'. But I can't help it, I adored her. She was so alive, so modern, so serious, so funny.

A Grandmother

I think my final story about her reveals something essential. At the party after her huge funeral in 1991 a man I did not know came up to me and introduced himself as the Headmaster of a special school for educationally challenged teenagers of both sexes. Gran was Chair of Governors when she was well past eighty, but he assured me she was superb at it. Like many others he was one of the 'admirer' lot. The problem his staff had been facing was that it was very apparent that the strapping pupils, who were now surviving much more frequently into adulthood, needed sex education. 'How do we discuss this with the Governors and especially with Mrs Scott?' a member of the staff asked the Head. 'Don't you worry about Mrs Scott. She will not only approve, she will want to know every detail.' How right he was. She insisted on attending an early session and sat there silently as the lesson unfolded. After a long and painstaking presentation, the teacher asked if there were any questions. 'Yes,' slowly said a large boy. 'Are you saying that if I take a girl I like into the woods for a walk with me, holding hands, she might end up having a baby?' Quick as a flash, apparently, Gran intervened from the floor. 'Not if you keep walking,' she advised.

When Tim died in 2012 I had to accept that she had finally left the stage. She always came into our conversations because we were the two who specially loved her. One of the things we laughed about was Gran's flat refusal to accept that Tim would never be bringing home a pretty young woman for her to meet as a prospective wife. For years Tim had had a Nepalese lover who had been a Gurkha and who had then become his servant in Singapore when he was there with the British Council and whom later, after Gran had died, he married. To Gran, Pasang was Tim's servant and that was all. Mark you, Pasang always preferred to be in the background in company and chose never to eat with Tim and Gran or with any of Tim's guests. He was a brilliant cook and seemed to want to be seen as that. I cannot work out if this was a serious flaw in her. Gran was thoroughly modern and knew all about homosexuality. Many of her Old Boys whom she had befriended through the years had suffered through the years of illegality and not being able to come out. But for some reason she never believed that this could be the case with her beloved Tim.

There is hardly a day when I don't miss her. I am reminded of her all the time. What a force. What a life!

6

ARRIVAL IN MANCHESTER

The Road to the Royal Exchange Theatre

Arts Council bursary – Manchester – Administrator, 69 Theatre Company – big stars, big success – London transfers – leads to building Royal Exchange Theatre – LS Lowry and JB Priestley – Princess Alexandra – Michael Elliott

Leaving university without a degree in 1966 was an interesting moment. The Sixties were in full swing even though the Carnaby Street side of it seemed to have nothing to do with me. I was the wrong shape. Nor, despite my Rhodesian experience, did the radical politics of the time grab me, I confess. I hated the Vietnam War but I was never moved to protest and *'les événements'* were a couple of years off. Frankly, for me Oxford had been much more Brideshead than Black Panther. But one sensed times were changing, especially for the young, and the future seemed to be all about music, the theatre, movies, entertainment. Professional sport was blossoming.

Stuffy, bowler-hatted Britain never occurred to me as a world to enter. The Beatles, the Stones, the Who on the one hand, David Hockney, Jonathan Miller, Albert Finney on the other were my heroes. Trevor Nunn, Tom Stoppard, Tom Allen were my admired contemporaries, Audrey Hepburn, Jeanne Moreau,

Arrival in Manchester

Julie Christie my pin-ups. There must be a place for me, I felt, somewhere in the world they shone in. Happily, my overwhelming instinct was fearlessness. It never occurred to me that I would not find a niche. The current terror of unemployment simply was not a factor. Not having a degree meant a few possible worlds like a BBC General Traineeship were closed to me but the Arts seemed the place to be. What I did not realise was that these were the early days of a golden age when the talents of inventive Britons would conquer the world. I just wanted to get into the world which the people I admired inhabited. The pleasant surprise was that it was a world that was expanding at a great rate. It was a big open world, not a small closed one. World-class performances, exhibitions, buildings, movies were on their way. I just felt lucky. I knew roughly where I wanted to be.

For three solid years at Oxford and beyond I had acted, but in truth, as I had already discovered, I much preferred rehearsing to performing, which I found repetitive. My instinct was somehow to stay in the theatre but not on the boards. It seemed that I would have to make the move either to directing or to management. I actually directed two plays: firstly, the silly farce in Delhi, then later I was invited to direct the biannual Cambridge Greek play – *Hippolytus* by Euripides (in ancient Greek, I'll have you know). They both happened and that was something. But neither experience worked for me, except that I fell in love with the leading lady on both occasions. Sadly, I knew that I did not really have the creative drive or self-belief to be a director. However, I still quite fancied the idea of being in charge.

Management seemed the possible answer. Even Richard Burton, I realised, had to wait for people to offer him parts. Even he did not entirely control his own career. After *Doctor Faustus*, Richard's agent, John Heyman, offered me a job and I spent a trial three weeks in his posh offices in Brook Street, Mayfair, running errands, but what little I saw of that glossy world did not grab me. One little task was to drive John's Jag to Heathrow with a box of pills for Elizabeth T which had to be given personally to a BA pilot inside the terminal who was about to fly to Rome. I had no idea what was in the box but I rather doubted John's description of them as Elizabeth's special contraception pills. Perhaps, but why the subterfuge? All in all I preferred the idea of being the employer rather than the employee. I wrote lots of letters and had a few interviews but they did not come to much.

Then, in early 1967 I discovered the Arts Council of Great Britain, an institution with which I would become extremely familiar over the next twenty years or so. As I was floundering around, sure that I belonged in the theatre but not as an actor, a friend told me the Council ran an Arts Administration Bursary scheme. If you were chosen, for the first six months you would be attached to an Arts body, a theatre or orchestra or gallery, and then spend the second six months on much shorter attachments around the country spending a fortnight or so at each place. One of the interviewing panel members was Reginald Salberg, the very amiable director of the Salisbury Playhouse. Somewhat irregularly, he phoned me on the evening of the interview, saying that I had been successful and that he would like me to come and spend the first six months with him. The value of the bursary was £14 a week for twelve months, which was fine.

So off I went to Salisbury. From Reggie's point of view I was free and a willing pair of hands; for me I could learn all about box offices, front of house duties, budgets, artists' contracts, running bars, publicity, marketing, etc. After the heady days of Oxford, the Burtons and the West End, it was very down to earth and probably just what I needed. Salisbury was an old-fashioned Rep in a tumble-down old building – now replaced. There was a resident company of actors doing a different play every fortnight. Stephanie Cole was our leading lady and Christopher Biggins our somewhat unusual assistant stage manager. I loved it and learnt a great deal. I did everything. I even once played a butler.

My second six months worked out extremely well too but, as always, unusually. I was warned that the institutions you were offered to did not particularly enjoy having 'student administrators' dumped on them for a fortnight. You just took up their time and energy and gave nothing back in return. So I asked the man at the Arts Council, who was frankly lazy, if I could organise my own 'tour'. This suited him fine. 'Just keep in touch and tell me where you are,' he said. My first visit set my life for years to come. The director of Hang Down Your Head and Die, Braham Murray, was by then the artistic director of Century Theatre, which had a double-headed operation, partly at the University Theatre in Manchester and partly in a touring mobile theatre, constructed on three huge trailers, at that moment playing a summer season in a car park in Keswick.

The role of Century in Manchester was essentially to fill those twenty or so weeks a year at the small but superb University Theatre which the student societies did not want. The theatre had a very modest seating capacity of under 300 on three sides of a flexible and large stage, designed by the important designer/director Stephen Joseph. The companies in the two places were quite distinct and Braham was usually in Manchester while his general manager, Ruari McNeil, was in Keswick. They were hardly on speaking terms. When I offered myself to Braham, he said 'Great. You can help me in Manchester and you can help Ruari in Keswick.' What this meant was that with a bit of luck they would not have to talk directly to each other at all. This went on for six weeks, with me shuttling happily between Manchester and Keswick in my beaten-up Austin A35 van. When I was in Manchester I briefly met Michael Elliott, who, as a guest director at Century, was rehearsing Tom Courtenay in *The Playboy of the Western World*. This was a great thrill. Tom was a big star and Michael a distinguished director. What I did not know then was that secret conversations were going on between Michael, Braham and others to form a new theatre company to replace the Century weeks at the University Theatre the following year.

The six weeks passed. I left Keswick for Glasgow, Lincoln, Bristol, Sadlers Wells and the National Theatre at the Old Vic in London. I tried to see as much of as many operations in different buildings as I could. While at the National I managed to blag my way into the first meeting and read-through of Seneca's *Oedipus*, which Peter Brook was directing. Sir John Gielgud was Oedipus and Irene Worth Jocasta. The meeting began with a very long and bewildering introductory talk by Peter Brook. Like the members of the cast I sat there in respectful and, I reckoned, mostly uncomprehending silence. At the end of the speech there was a long and awkward pause after Brook asked for questions. Sir John finally broke the silence by saying very gently, 'Peter, I wonder what you would think if in the play I wore a pair of those National Health spectacles, you know the rimless ones with bendy, metal arms which wrap around your ears. I would find them so helpful.' Peter Brook looked baffled. It was an exquisite moment and I had no clue whether Sir John was being mischievous or entirely serious.

Just before Christmas I got a call in Lincoln from Braham asking me if I would be interested in coming to London to meet Michael Elliott and Casper Wrede. These three were the chief plotters of the scheme, I discovered, to replace Century at the University Theatre. They would be the leaders of a new company as the joint artistic directors. They interviewed me about joining this new venture as soon as possible in Manchester as their administrator. I felt deeply 'umble and unqualified. I discovered later that they deliberately chose someone without experience. They wanted an uncontaminated servant administrator not an old hand, set in his ways. It was a flattering offer. I already knew that Michael Elliott was a major player in the British theatre. I knew that Braham was a rising star. I did not know Casper at all. I asked the man at the Arts Council if I could spend the last three months of my bursary not touring around the country but helping to set up this new theatre company, which was already on the Arts Council's radar. I got his permission and I completed my trainee year preparing a bid for funds for a new theatre company. We were told that it must be a low-budget affair. I remember doing draft costings which included an allowance for actors' travel from London to Manchester. I made a rough calculation of how many would come in a full year to and from London. The price then was £4 16s for a second-class return ticket and I budgeted £5 a head – a crafty way to have a few quid up my sleeve at four bob a head. A couple of years in Manchester, I thought, helping to set up a new project with high-class colleagues, would be a good career start. As it turned out, I would be in Manchester for twenty-seven years.

The company was to be called the 69 Theatre Company, even though we were still then only just into 1968. The name was chosen because many of the group who were coming together for this new venture had worked together in the 59 Theatre Company, which had mounted a season of plays in 1959 at the Lyric, Hammersmith, to considerable critical praise, but massive financial loss. In the years since then the group had worked together informally and occasionally both on theatre and television productions. For instance, the last season at the Old Vic, before it became the temporary home of the National Theatre in 1963, included Michael Elliott's famous production of *Peer Gynt* with Leo McKern, which had a distinct ring of '59' about it. Similarly, Michael's equally admired production of *As You Like It* with Vanessa Redgrave at Stratford in 1961 was a chip off the '59' block. Nevertheless, Manchester would be the first formal manifestation of the group, with some additions, since 1959. With the exception of Braham, very few of the members of the group had any feeling for Manchester at all. The best thing about Manchester was that it was not London. They were turning their backs on the metropolis with greater conviction than they turned their eyes northwards.

Traditionally, in truth virtually always, theatres are led by one person. Of course, each one would likely have a team of trusted lieutenants. But the buck usually stops with one boss. 69 was to be different, perhaps unique. This was to be a directorial triumvirate: Casper Wrede, Michael Elliott, Braham Murray. Of these three, Casper was the senior partner, almost the 'guru', Michael was the 'star' partner with the glittering reputation, Braham was the gifted 'junior member' with the local connections. I respected Casper a lot but I never really knew him. He was a Finnish director who met Michael at Oxford. He spoke carefully and at length and would then add 'you know' at the end of each sentence. Frankly, I rarely did. He spent his time with the other artistic directors and hardly with the staff, unless he was directing his own production. Nevertheless, he was a key figure even though they were to be equal.

Richard Pilbrow joined the Gang of Three but he was different from the others. He was a great lighting designer who also ran a big, technical operation in London called Theatre Projects. He admired Michael hugely, but like many others he was really a member of the wider group of actors, designers, and writers who had launched their careers with 59 and who now were keen to be involved with 69 in Manchester merely on a coming-and-going basis. They were all based in London and they were hired for one production at a time. Richard's clout was that he had real London cred.

Probably like all my successors as administrators or executive directors of this now fifty-four-year-old and still thriving project, I worked out that my main role in those early days was to discover who held the leadership baton at any moment and to work to him. I never challenged the group ethic – indeed it was essential to our functioning – but I worked out quickly that one artistic director was 'dominant' at any given moment. My main problem, apart from the fact that I was on a steep learning curve, was that they were none of them resident in Manchester and would keep disappearing for weeks or months on end on their other projects. After an absence they would return to the fold, often outraged at what had happened while they were away. Inevitably, they were interested in their own work more than another's, but they always fought to keep the sense of a group enterprise alive. Cosy, however, it was not.

This wider group of people who wanted to sail in this unique craft captained jointly by Casper, Michael and Braham was very distinguished. The mark of a group member was that they would always make themselves available to a production for pitifully little money, diary permitting. If you study the programmes of the 69 and early Royal Exchange years, the same names keep cropping up. Tom Courtenay, Albert Finney, Vanessa Redgrave, Trevor Peacock, Dilys Hamlett, Edward Fox and Brian Cox stand out among the actors. James Maxwell acted, directed and wrote for the group. Michael Meyer, Ronald Harwood and Gerard McLarnon led the writers. Richard Negri, Malcolm Pride and Johanna Bryant were the most regular designers. Eric Thompson, father of Emma and Sophie and the legendary voice behind

The Magic Roundabout, directed his first play for 69. Jack Good, a real TV pop legend, came and went like a firework. The list was impressive and some in the British theatre regarded the group as exclusive, over-serious and self-regarding. All I can say, writing as someone who was, as the administrator, both inside and outside the group, is that Manchester was blessed to have them.

The company opened with a bang – at the Edinburgh Festival in August 1968 at the Assembly Hall. We presented *Hamlet* with Tom Courtenay directed by Casper, which was not greatly liked by the critics but sold out, and Michael Elliott's production of Ibsen's *When We Dead Awaken* with Wendy Hiller and Alexander Knox, which was extravagantly praised but did not sell out. From Edinburgh both productions came south to the University Theatre to begin our life there. The Ibsen was also televised. Another early standout moment was Michael's production of George Eliot's *Daniel Deronda* with Vanessa Redgrave. I still carry the picture in my mind's eye of her standing looking at herself almost shyly in front of a full-length mirror in a shimmering gown and then suddenly twirling around with a knowing laugh. Her performance as Gwendolen Harleth, moving from innocent to haughty to tragic, in a performance that lasted four hours, was shattering.

Casper had got to know André Previn and through him was able to suggest to his wife Mia Farrow that Peyton Place and movies and TV were great, but what about the theatre? Casper and Braham chose a very clever play to display her 'other worldly' qualities. Manchester could not believe that *the* Mia Farrow was coming to play *Mary Rose* by JM Barrie. She did and she was ethereal, as was the music John Tavener wrote for it. When we brought *Mary Rose* and Mia down to London for a short season, we hired the famous Nobby Clark to take the photos. He joked that, try as he could, he could never take a bad picture of her. She was unalterably beautiful.

The best production of a Shakespeare play I have ever seen was *The Tempest* with James Maxwell as Prospero and Michael Feast as Ariel. Michael E directed, Richard Negri designed and Richard Pilbrow lit the production – the same team that produced Ibsen's *Brand* for 59 and *As You Like It* at Stratford in 1961. The whole stage was a sandy beach with a giant tree trunk lying diagonally across the sand. At the start of the play with Richard P's fabulous lighting the tree was like a phantom ship in a terrible storm. The back wall was a huge sky either on a baking, sunlit day or a starry black night. It haunted me then and it still does today.

Eric Thompson's first ever production was of *Journey's End* by RC Sherriff. It was a terrific cast led by James Maxwell and Peter Egan. Each generation seems to mount its own defining production of this play. Eric's was certainly the production of the 70s and it triumphantly transferred to the Mermaid and then the Cambridge Theatre in London. The day before the first night the actor playing Trotter collapsed and could not go on. He was replaced at literally twenty-four hours' notice by Colin Prockter who learnt the part and his moves in that time. An amazing achievement. He fainted after the curtain calls. Eric's wretchedly early death was very sad.

Jack Good came to the 69 party late in the day – in 1973. He had been a legendary figure in developing first pop and then rock music programmes for TV. His BBC series of such shows as *Six-Five Special* and *Oh Boy!* invented a whole new genre. Surprisingly for a man with his reputation he had been an Oxford friend of Michael and Casper and had been obsessed all his life with *Othello*. Finally, he put his literary obsession together with his rock music genius into *Catch My Soul*. The University Theatre will never see such money spent on its stage ever again. 'Spectacular' hardly does it justice. With artists like Lance Legault, PJ Proby and Emil Dean Zogby on stage, it was not a question of saying 'No smoking' in the theatre. It was rather 'What in God's name is that stuff you are smoking on the set?' The rather shy theatre fireman almost had a heart attack at every performance. Again, it was transferred to the West End and caused quite a stir at the Prince of Wales Theatre.

The show that saved our financial lives was Braham's production of *She Stoops to Conquer* with Tom Courtenay and Juliet Mills. It also featured great performances of Tony Lumpkin by Trevor Peacock and Mrs Hardcastle by Rosalind Knight. After its run in Manchester it transferred to the Garrick Theatre in London and made us quite a lot of much-needed cash. Later it was redirected for television by Michael. The transfer of some productions to London was backed by a team of Manchester 'angels' and both they and Richard, as the London producer, were very generous in reducing their share of the profits in our favour. We lived permanently on a financial knife edge and these transfers saved our bacon.

We occasionally did manage to have a bit of fun! During the last week of rehearsals for *She Stoops* in Manchester I managed to arrange a trip to Old Trafford for the cast to go to a mid-week evening match of Manchester United versus Queens Park Rangers. We were all invited to the players' lounge after the game, which was a great celebration because United had won 8–2, with even Nobby Stiles scoring. I remember introducing Tom Courtenay to George Best, which was an extraordinary meeting of the famous and the shy. They seemed thrilled to meet each other but they could hardly exchange a word.

The first years in Manchester were exciting but as I was the resident glue of the operation for fifty-two weeks a year I would get my head bitten off a lot. It was the most intense and least light-hearted period of my working life. The standards were fantastically high. Richard P and our wonderfully supportive chairman, Laurence Harbottle, kept my spirits up. No theatre company outside London at that time was making such an impact, even though the numbers of people who came to see us were very small in such a tiny theatre. There was no concession to our miniscule budgets. One journalist judged the new company to be 'as eminent as the Hallé is in the musical world.' However, most productions were rehearsed in London and in those four years there were only four full-time members of staff living in Manchester. The artistic directors were not paid properly – Michael and Casper hardly at all. Almost everybody working for us was subsidising us.

The whole tone of the operation was on the one hand wildly ambitious and on the other limited. In those first years at the University Theatre it all felt like a trial marriage. 'Do we want to stay together and do we want to be based in Manchester?' The answer to both questions was finally 'yes'. It was, however, obvious that this meant finding a new and bigger home in the city as we had clearly outgrown the University Theatre. Also, the drama students at Manchester University, with whom we shared the theatre, were unfriendly to us and thought we were both too elitist and too commercial, which was a bad joke. We were resolutely neither. The result was that we wanted out and they were pleased to see us go. We considered temporary and permanent solutions.

In 1972 the company began tentative talks with the City Council and the Arts Council about a possible new theatre building on a city centre site. We thought of adapting a derelict warehouse or even building a steel and glass Manchester Playhouse on the lines of the new Nottingham Playhouse, if you like, only better. The conversations were quite promising but we were a long way from a solution and we now had given notice to get out of the University Theatre.

One of the main reasons why we survived into a new life was because we had formed very strong and important links with not only a grateful audience but with a wonderfully supportive group of businessmen and, of course, their influential wives. With both the artistic directors and the chairman being London-based, much of the responsibility for organising this support rested with me. Alongside the board of directors we created a council of influential local figures who gave us credit with the City Council, credibility with City institutions, entrance into Manchester and Cheshire society, and many of them gave us money. They guaranteed our overdraft when it became daunting, they backed our West End transfers and gave us part of the profits and they ran fundraising events. There was a terrific local Jewish community, who supported the Arts and were always ready to help. The first chairman of the council was a stockbroker called Peter Henriques and until his sudden death in 1974 was our best friend. I loved him dearly and spent almost as much time in his office as in my own. It was he who, by having a sudden idea in his bath in 1972, took us from the University Theatre to our own home.

At exactly the same time that the company arrived in Manchester in 1968, one of the city's iconic buildings was changing hands. Its essential function had ceased and it was now considered by its new owners to be a large and difficult piece of real estate. The building was the Manchester Royal Exchange. The story of the Exchange from its modest beginning at the start of the eighteenth century to its glory days in the second half of the nineteenth culminating in its post-1945 decline was the story of Manchester. There had been four Exchange buildings in the city centre since the first in 1729. The final, present one was vast and built in two stages, the last being completed in 1921. It made a decent return in rental income from the shops and offices, but the property had a yawning absurdity – the now deserted Great Hall, three-quarters of an acre of mock Victorian splendour under three great domes. It had actually been twice as big with six domes but a Luftwaffe incendiary bomb had neatly demolished half the building in 1941 and it was the offices which had been built within the space of that destroyed half that made the money. It was truly serendipitous that while we were looking for a new home, the Royal Exchange owners were looking for a new use of the cavernous Great Hall.

When Peter Henriques first took us to see the Royal Exchange we were blown away but, to be honest, it did not occur to us that it could be a long-term solution. But it might be a workable space for a year or two. If we could camp briefly in the Exchange, we reasoned, we could simultaneously pursue our dream of a new permanent building on a city centre site. The Exchange solution was short-term perhaps, but a proper one, nevertheless. By now the Royal Exchange building belonged to the Prudential and they certainly did not see us as a long-term occupant but they thought a few months' tenancy might give the building some marketing publicity. The first negotiations were for a lease at a peppercorn for six months for a temporary structure.

The more we thought about it, however, the more we realised what a brilliant place it would be to build properly. Also, the rules for Arts Council capital grants at the time did not include help for temporary buildings. Very quickly we began to think 'long-term'. Three-quarters of parquet floor above Boots, opposite Marks & Spencer, and on a direct line between Piccadilly and Victoria Stations was, by any calculation, city centre. But it was on the first floor, it was a listed building and how did you value it? The Pru, not used to dealing with a troupe of rogues and vagabonds, insisted that if we wanted a proper lease, they would have to demand a substantial rent guarantor.

The City Council was the only acceptable candidate and, somewhat warily, they joined the discussions. Harry Ogden, the city's town clerk, and the canny Labour leader, Sir Bob Thomas, who were both quite keen to support us, began to think that a theatre structure in the Exchange might be a good deal cheaper than a concrete-and-glass edifice in Piccadilly Gardens. At first the Pru offered a five-year lease. We said it had to be twenty-five. The Pru wanted £1 a square foot rental. In the name of the city we proposed a peppercorn. I shuttled back and forth between the parties, always keeping the Arts Council informed. Frankly, we did not care what the price was because someone else had to pay it. We just wanted an agreement. In the end we came to the fairly obvious deal. The parties settled on 50p a square foot, we got our twenty-five years and the city agreed to act as guarantor.

Now we had to complete the design of the theatre, establish a credible capital cost budget and raise the money. Crucially, we also had to persuade our various public sector partners that they would support a fifty-two-week operation. Michael Elliott and I headed those financial and operational negotiations. We were successful and on November 9th 1972, we launched the concept publicly. I remember the date exactly, because my eldest child, David, was born the following day. Very nervously, I had to persuade my wife Su and her obstetrician to delay inducing the birth for twenty-four hours for my work reasons. I just about got away with it. All the pictures were of Richard Negri's pen-and-ink design concept, for the good reason that we had not yet appointed architects. But Manchester would now have a new theatre. It was costed at £400,000. Initially, the city and the Arts Council promised £100,000 each and substantial but unspecified revenue support. We launched an Appeal for £200,000. Optimistically, we said that the new theatre would take only a year or so to build.

Meanwhile, we had a big stroke of good luck. In April 1973 the Greater Manchester Council, made up of ten metropolitan boroughs, was to be born and they wanted to celebrate their own arrival. An arts festival, with a budget, was announced for that May. We went to work and managed to attract a small grant of £8,000 to run a three-week season in a 'tent' on the Exchange floor. A tent theatre with 430 seats, designed by Laurie Dennett and realised by our production manager Michael Williams, was erected. It was an open structure made of scaffolding with timber walls which were actually old railway sleepers standing upright. The floor was the floor of the Exchange itself. The roof was made from old canvas stage-cloths from Covent Garden. The seats were intercepted on their way from the Usher Hall in Edinburgh to the knacker's yard. And then the whole structure was draped in several hundred metres of fireproofed colourful fabric donated by the Manchester based textiles giant Tootal.

Having been built to last three weeks the tent stayed up for ten months. When winter arrived we handed out blankets to the audience to ward off the bitter cold. There was no heating in the Hall at all. It was all incredibly successful. Tom Courtenay and Brian Cox were terrific in James Maxwell's production of *Arms and the Man*. Edward Fox was magnificent in Michael's superb production of TS Eliot's *The Family Reunion*. Dame Edith Evans and Albert Finney performed in it. Elisabeth Söderström and Tom Allen sang in it. Ballet Rambert danced in it. Braham directed a wonderful production of JB Priestley's play *Time and the Conways*. I spent an afternoon looking after Mr Priestley and his wife Jacquetta Hawkes, the archaeologist. He was an impressive man with his pipe and famous radio voice. I found myself pathetically asking him naive questions like, 'What is the best thing you ever did in the theatre?' meaning I suppose that I wanted him to name his favourite play. Instead, he disarmingly said, 'My greatest achievement was, I think, that I am the only playwright who successfully demanded a share of the bar profits while my play was being performed. Without me, I told them, there would be no bar sales and I always give you two intervals.' A splendid Yorkshire response which put me beautifully in my place as the theatre manager.

James Maxwell had become an important member of the group and was made an artistic director in place of Richard Pilbrow. I never hit it off with Max. He was a wonderful actor. For 69 he was sensational as Prospero and in *Journey's End*. When he started directing he became an irritable martinet, at least to lowlifes like administrators. We always messed up. I consoled myself that he was unhappy. He seemed always on the edge of volcanic anger. He did not like me.

The tent season proved, as no amount of words could, that putting a permanent theatre in the Exchange was not only possible, it was brilliant. Putting up a building within another building would reduce costs, with no need for foundations or a weather shell. The Hall itself would provide the biggest foyer in the world, undreamt of public space within a new building. It could be a theatre for today. It would not have to justify itself by being there in a hundred years' time. This was in contrast to the new National Theatre rising on the South Bank at that moment at a cost of untold millions, which would only be justified by a very long life. Michael made the excellent point that new theatres were needed today because we did not want to be forced to play in Victorian proscenium arch buildings any longer. We were building for ourselves, not for our grandchildren. In short, it might only last twenty years, but that was good and properly sustainable. Our grandchildren should be free to design and build their own theatres. Ironically, in 2026 the Royal Exchange Theatre will be fifty years old! Shades of the Eiffel Tower. Get it right and your grandchildren will want to keep it.

Before I ever arrived in Manchester the only connection I had with the city was a splendid oil painting by LS Lowry, which my grandparents owned, of a typical street scene, given them as a present by some Wellington boys in the mid-1930s. The boys had raised £35 and asked my grandfather whether he wanted the money or for them to buy something as a present. Very properly he preferred a present. A clever boy found a wonderful large Lowry oil for exactly £35! I always loved it hanging over the fireplace in their drawing room.

In the early 70s we bought another cottage in Derbyshire and my daily drive into Manchester took me through the village of Mottram in Longdendale where Lowry lived. One day I spotted him in his famous beaten-up overcoat and strange hat. I thought, *I must say hello. If I don't do it now, I never will.* I quickly parked and ran after him. 'Mr Lowry, Mr Lowry,' I called. He turned on me ferociously. 'I'm not a meal ticket, you know,' he snarled. As best I could, I explained my vague connection. He softened and we started chatting. He was amused at the price the boys had paid for his painting. He asked me what I did. I told him that I was very involved in putting a new theatre into the Royal Exchange. Currently we had the tent up. 'Oh yes,' he said. 'I know that building well. It is near my old insurance office, where I was a clerk. The old Members of the Exchange will be turning in their graves at the idea of a theatre in their sacred building. Actually, I have heard a bit about your plans. I wouldn't mind seeing the place one day. I've never been inside.'

Arrival in Manchester

Instantly, I offered to take him and we fixed a date. When I went to pick him up he opened his front door with a suitcase in his hand and the same fierce frown that I had encountered when we first met. 'Oh, it's you, is it?' he said. 'OK, let's be off.' 'Do you need a suitcase?' I asked. 'No, no. I always do that when someone comes to the door. I get too many visitors. I tell them I am going to get the bus for my holidays. I keep the case by the door as proof. I just walk round the block.' The visit to the Exchange was a success and he liked the whole idea. By the time the proper theatre opened Lowry had sadly died a few months before. But to celebrate the day, my good friend, the Salford artist Harold Riley, who knew Lowry well and who inherited many of his pencil sketches, generously gave me an original Lowry drawing of the old Exchange, with figures outside, signed and dated 1927. It is a prized possession. My grandmother's big Lowry is gone. She became rather alarmed to own a Lowry in her own house and sold hers for £40,000 in the late 70s. It must be worth seven figures now.

Once the tent came down we had to concentrate on the new building. We also had to keep the company's name alive. The preparations for building the new theatre and running the company were split and I became the administrator of the trust committed to getting the building up and paid for. It was mutually agreed that I would not run the new building when it finally opened. After nearly ten years we had had enough of each other. An old Oxford friend of mine and at that time general manager of Ballet Rambert, Tim Mason, joined the project to prepare for the running of the permanent full-time operation as the administrator. He found the going tough and did not last long.

Time was passing and it was important we did not disappear from sight. So we took out to the towns around Manchester a show called *Rogues and Vagabonds*, a cunning entertainment telling the story of English theatre, devised by Michael Meyer, with a different celebrity cast of four for each performance – it was clever, informative and jolly. It was not easy to think of Michael Meyer as a scholar. He was rustic in appearance with a big white beard in later years. He had dreadful table manners, grunted a lot and was very greedy. If he saw something good on your plate he would stretch across and bag it. He also had a lascivious eye. Put him next to a pretty girl and in front of a delicious plateful together at a table and it was wonderful to behold his confusion as to which he would attend to. Yet this was the same man who knew more of the gloom and intensity of Ibsen and Strindberg than any man alive. Michael knew everyone and he was able to corral all kinds of people to take part in the different performances – Albert Finney, Eleanor Bron, Tom Courtenay, Diana Rigg, Brian Cox, Edith Evans, Michael Flanders, Edward Fox, Polly James, Frank Muir, Wendy Hiller and Michael York were some.

We also mounted occasional plays in Manchester Cathedral, including Christopher Fry's *Murder in the Cathedral*, TS Eliot's *The Cocktail Party*, Shakespeare's *Much Ado About Nothing* and Robert Bolt's *A Man for All Seasons* with great performances from James Maxwell as Thomas More and Bob Hoskins as the Common Man. They were all excellent productions but Hilary Mantel's wonderful Thomas Cromwell trilogy has rather done for Robert Bolt in my view. His saintly portrait of Thomas More, while very dramatic, just does not cut it anymore. It is fascinating how history is being continuously rewritten even from centuries ago.

The design of the permanent theatre was proceeding, led by Richard Negri working with our now chosen architects Levitt, Bernstein Associates and Engineers Ove Arup Associates. But now our unbroken good luck changed – for the worse. The engineers reported that a fully equipped, three-level theatre with 700 people in their seats would not be able to stand on the Exchange floor. The calculations were that it would sink majestically into the Danish Food Centre and Boots below. It really was 'back to the drawing board'. The startling solution of suspending the whole structure from the four main columns, although magnificently successful, put up the costs dramatically and meant delays of over a year. In the end the building cost £1.2 million, but the task of putting a highly sophisticated theatre 'module' into a mock Victorian pile, with all the problems of engineering, acoustics and heating during one of the worst inflationary periods in the country's history, was never likely to be plain sailing.

Completing the new design was one problem. Another was getting hold of the steel required to bear the weight of the structure. In 1974–5 steel was readily available. All steel, that is, except tubular steel, which was needed for the huge new North Sea oil rigs. This was precisely the steel needed in the theatre design. The problem was solved by the estimable Sir William Mather, chairman of the mighty Mather and Platt, and one of our Manchester trustees, who successfully pleaded with the chairman of British Steel to reduce delivery from eighteen months to six weeks. Once that was solved we were incredibly fortunate to have met very few other problems during the construction period. Weather, of course, was not an issue. Building started in April 1975 and was completed in early August 1976. The City, the new Metropolitan County Council and the Arts Council all contributed handsomely to the new costs.

Arrival in Manchester

We had several major fundraising events, as well as making the obvious approaches to trusts, foundations and major companies. One Sunday night while the 'tent' theatre was still functioning we held a fundraising dinner in the Piccadilly Hotel with about twenty tables with twelve people at each table, where there were a combination of established givers on the one hand and 'targets' on the other. There was also an empty seat at every table. Enter Albert Finney, the 'host' of the evening, who proceeded to introduce an extraordinary group of major theatre and TV stars who went one by one, each introduced by Albert, to the empty seat at each table. All properly briefed, they then worked with our supporters on the 'targets'. Anouk Aimee, Rupert Davies, Geoffrey Keen, Frank Windsor, Robert Powell, Polly James, Coral Atkins, Edward Woodward, Patrick Allen, Gerald Harper, Tom Courtenay, Eleanor Bron, Trevor Peacock, Jenny Agutter added tremendous glamour and punch to the occasion. We managed to hire an extra, exclusive first-class carriage on the train up from Euston, which meant our stars arrived in good heart. In one night we raised £36,000, which was a huge sum then. The theatre was officially opened by Laurence Olivier on September 15th 1976, with a rousing speech followed by Braham's production of Sheridan's *The Rivals* with a cast including Tom Courtenay and Patricia Routledge.

We held a major event on the first Saturday of the run of *The Rivals*. We sold 400 expensive combined 'show and dinner' tickets and after the performance fed and watered them at a dinner at special tables laid out in the Hall around the theatre with the cast and with our Royal Visitor, Princess Alexandra. The Princess was with us for about six hours. She received a bouquet from Michael's younger daughter, Marianne, then aged eight, and now a major theatre director herself. The Princess seemed to have a good time. Certainly, she stayed longer than she said she could. Apparently, however, we made little impact on her. In his role as chairman of the Royal Overseas League in London, my father sat next to her – she was the president – at a dinner a few years later and, as you do, told her that she had once met his son at a performance of *The Rivals* in Manchester in 1976. She told him he was mistaken. When he gently persisted, 'You know, the opening of the Royal Exchange Theatre with Tom Courtenay and Patricia Routledge in *The Rivals*.' She replied quite tartly that she thought she would remember if she had ever been to the theatre in Manchester. She insisted she never had. My father considered saying that he had the photos as proof but decided not to.

The Royal Exchange Theatre staff by now had grown to 150, a little different from our 69 days, eight years before, of just four staff in our grubby

Oxford Road offices. As in any artistic group there were lots of tensions. Braham Murray's autobiography *The Worst It Can Be Is A Disaster* describes the relationships in vivid and gory detail. Some of his revelations even shocked me and for several years I was as close to the action as anyone. With all the ups and downs, and battles and feuds, the group artistic directorate concept lasted over thirty years, at least in a form which I recognised, but with many changes of personnel. Something similar exists today but perhaps not in the abrasive form it did earlier on.

At its best, when Michael Elliott was still alive (he died horrendously young in 1985 of kidney failure at the age of fifty-seven), the Royal Exchange Theatre was utterly brilliant and all the strengths of a group initiative shone through. For me, if not for Braham, Michael was a great man. He was an important, if demanding, friend and mentor. He had his oddities – he was as thin and tall as a heron. His long nose made the comparison all the more real. When he sat he would cross his right long leg so high up his left thigh it looked as if he was wrapping one leg round the other twice. He liked the occasional cigarette, which he always cadged off you. I never knew him to have a packet of his own. He maintained he was a non-smoker. He would make lists and run you through them, and often was critical that you did not have your own in response. I often wondered if I made the grade with him even though he could suddenly be very loving. He had girlfriends. He was blissfully sure they were secret and that no one knew. I must have been introduced ten times to one, who will be nameless, as if for the first time.

His productions were the standout events of the years I spent with the group. Actors, including distinguished and difficult ones, almost worshipped him. Designers did their best work with him. For me his productions of *The Tempest* at the University Theatre, *The Family Reunion* by TS Eliot in the tent and Ibsen's *The Lady from the Sea* in the Exchange Theatre proper were sublime. The birth and realisation of the theatre was truly a group effort. Several people played key roles. But it can only be said of Michael Elliott that without him the theatre would never have happened.

The opening of the Royal Exchange Theatre was one of many great artistic events in the country in the 70s. The flowering of Britain's cultural life caught fire in the 60s and was later greatly assisted by the phenomenal success of the National Lottery. If any one individual can be identified as the instigator of this golden period, it is probably Jennie Lee, Harold Wilson's formidable Arts Minister from 1964 to 1970. She was close to Wilson and managed to persuade him to take the Arts much more seriously. The Arts Council was reconstituted, considerable new funding was found, the developments of the South Bank were greatly boosted. These were some of the things she was directly responsible for. But more than that, from her days onwards the political power of the Arts changed gear and Britain's nineteenth-century reputation in Germany for being 'a country without music', never entirely accurate, was killed forever. The repertory theatre movement was reborn. Local Authorities, well at least some of them, were beginning to understand that an investment in the Arts could contribute to the revival of communities. The universities were increasingly drawn into making their 'offer' more exciting either by developing arts-based courses or by improving facilities. Drama schools, art colleges, music conservatoires were entering the Further Education sector with their own degree-awarding powers. It really was a revolution.

London, inevitably, has been the main beneficiary and is now properly regarded as one of the great cultural capitals of the world, if not the greatest. The regions have, frankly, benefitted rather less – for instance, there is still no permanent symphony orchestra east of the Pennines. But national opera companies in Wales and Glasgow were created and Opera North began in Leeds as an offshoot of the ENO in London. Important dance companies have flourished in Birmingham, Manchester – later moved to Leeds – and Glasgow. Galleries and museums have been created or extended in every corner of the country. Birmingham, Manchester, Nottingham, Newcastle have new concert halls which London envies. Audiences have increased massively. Generally, people are confident that the crowds and the quality will return after the pandemic retreats. Arts education has been transformed and the Digital Revolution has made every child, nationwide, a potential player. Children have been encouraged to act, sing, dance, play instruments and paint in ways that were unimaginable before the war. The spin-off in movies and TV has been astonishing. British actors, directors, artists, composers, writers, designers, technicians lead the world. No one who works in the Arts is ever content with the government support they receive, but it is now totally accepted that the Arts are a major net contributor to GDP, and the soft cultural power the country exerts worldwide is colossal.

Today, most of our national human treasures, it seems, come from the Arts. Compare the list of Orders of Merit and Companions of Honour from the 50s. In those days most of the OMs and CHs were either aristocrats, politicians or academics. Today the list is filled by the likes of Janet Baker, Tom Stoppard,

Paul McCartney, Simon Rattle, Melvyn Bragg, Elton John, Judi Dench, David Hockney, Ian McKellen, Mark Elder, Neil MacGregor, Maggie Smith, JK Rowling. No wonder parents are very happy to see their children today taking up jobs which were once not thought serious.

By Christmas 1976 my job at the Royal Exchange Theatre was done and I was ready to leave the group. Crucially, the new theatre was paid for. I remained a non-executive director of the company for many years, keeping closely in touch, but I was no longer a senior full-time employee. It had been exhilarating and stressful. Laughter and jollity have always been a big part of my life, but with this group, with the wonderful exception of Trevor Peacock whom I adored, I remember mostly seriousness and hard words. Not a lot of laughs.

I was with the group for almost ten years. I was incredibly fortunate to have played a leading part in starting this amazing project, which looks and feels today as splendid in 2022 as it did in 1976. Michael Elliott was and remains one of the great influences on my life. Of course, virtually all the original group members are now dead. In 1996 the theatre suffered badly from the IRA bomb at the Manchester Arndale Centre. Happily, it was perfectly restored – ironically, at roughly thirty times what it cost to build. The Royal Exchange Theatre is truly one of Britain's great theatrical treasures and playing my part in its concept and birth remains the proudest memory of my working life.

7

MANCHESTER THEATRES PART TWO

The Palace Theatre Revived

Raymond Slater – Palace Theatre – Royal Opera House connections – hair-raising Royal Gala Opening – debt to Andrew Lloyd Webber – full houses – excitements with Nureyev, Olivier, Rex Harrison, Cosi Fan Tutti, Pavarotti and a horse

For the first three months of 1977 I mulled, increasingly fretfully, over my future. For the first time I was unemployed. I was not sure at all what to do and whether to stay in Manchester. In the end, it was a member of the Royal Exchange Theatre Trust who provided the solution. Raymond Slater was a big, tough (some called him rough) Manchester property man. Unlike many businessmen who dabble in the arts for social reasons, he really took them seriously, especially opera and classical music. I was impressed one day, when driving with him in his huge Mercedes, to discover Bruckner symphonies on his car tape machine. Like many others he was distressed to see the state of neglect that the two huge lyric theatres of Manchester, the Opera House and the Palace, had fallen into. Unlike the others, however, he decided to do something about it and he asked me to join him. We agreed that we needed to form a small charitable trust company as the vehicle which at the start he would have to fund. We discussed a way forward and agreed that he would be the chairman and I would be the managing director.

As new life and money began to be pumped into the repertory movement around the country in the 60s and 70s with new medium-sized theatres opening in Nottingham, Manchester, Stoke, Sheffield, Liverpool, Leicester, Southampton, Leeds, Bolton and Salisbury, to name a few, the big old lyric theatres in the large cities were in dire straits. They were mostly owned by two large commercial companies which were run as chains and were losing money. Most had had glorious pasts but were now drab and unloved. More seriously, popular entertainment had migrated to television. Also acting styles had changed from larger-than-life performances in the cavernous spaces of the 2,000-seater theatres, striving to reach the back of the gods, to the intimate murmurings required for kitchen-sink dramas on the screen. Occasional weeks of opera and ballet and shortened seasons of modest variety programmes and pantomimes did not fill a year. The few musicals which toured were cut-down versions of their West End originals with flimsy sets which wobbled. These big theatres were on death row.

Manchester was unusual in having two such theatres and it was generally believed that at best only one of the two could be saved. Many believed they were both doomed. Raymond was determined but he was motivated only by opera while I knew that opera alone would only fill a few weeks in the year. One of my main jobs would be to build up the rest of the programme. Our first task was to decide which theatre to go for – the Palace with 2,150 seats and a grim 1950s exterior or the Opera House with 1,920 seats and a much finer colonnaded front. The commercial owners of both theatres were keen to sell. The Palace was owned by the Moss Empires, the Opera House by Howard and Wyndham. Our assumption was that it would be the Opera House, which had a larger orchestra pit, was in better repair, looked better outside and had the name. We opened discussions with the owners. Raymond put in an offer. They said they would consider it.

We also consulted the Arts Council and the opera companies and, suddenly, new advice was forthcoming. Yes, the exterior of the Palace was an eyesore and had been the home of variety and pantomime, but it had a wider stage, a better relationship between stage and auditorium and altogether was a finer interior. In short, it was a great Bertie Crewe theatre. More important, it was a less confined site than the Opera House with potential, albeit tricky, for stage extension. Raymond and I also thought that the pub next door, which was also owned by Moss Empires, could be incorporated into the theatre front of house areas. So, we quickly moved to longer-term thinking and started preliminary discussions with Covent Garden about one day persuading both the Royal Opera and Royal Ballet to visit Manchester and even perhaps make the city their second home.

Sir John Tooley, the general director, made it clear to us that, while there was a possibility of making the Palace capable of receiving both Royal Companies if a great deal of money was spent, there was just no way that the Opera House could cope with their demands, however much money was available. The site was simply not large enough to extend the Opera House stage. 'Well, make up your minds, but OK,' said Raymond. 'I'll buy the Palace then.' We immediately went to see Louis Benjamin, the MD of Moss Empires, and in just one meeting Raymond agreed a figure of £150,000 for the freehold of the Palace and the pub next door. It was a snip. Just in time he remembered to break off negotiations with the Opera House people. They were furious and, as quickly as they could, sold their theatre to Mecca to be turned into a bingo hall.

Raymond now had the bit between his teeth and we began serious conversations with Covent Garden, the Arts Council and the Local Authorities. Our new trust company approved his actions, basically because he was paying. There was one enormous problem. To extend the stage backwards to the critical sixty feet of depth, we would have to build on land next door to the Palace owned by Standard Life Assurance, and our new back wall would block off the light to one whole side of their building. So, what does Raymond do? He asks to see the Standard Life people in Edinburgh, takes me up to see them with him and, again, in what seemed the twinkling of an eye, he agrees to buy the whole Standard Life estate of five huge buildings in Whitworth Street just to get the extra twenty feet we needed for the stage extension. They were not prepared to sell off the small piece of land we needed. It had to be the whole estate or nothing and the price was £2.75 million. 'I reckon I will be able to make it all work with some judicious selling and development.' Like all successful developers he much preferred buying to selling. He said it was easier. We returned to Manchester from a freezing Edinburgh with me in a daze and a new sheepskin coat which he bought for me because looking at me in just my suit made him feel cold.

There were three very different reasons why I thought we had a real chance of making a success of running one of these great theatres, working on the assumption that the other one would close. Firstly, the glorious restoration of an important but neglected building with a dedicated local team would create enthusiasm, pride and loyalty in the city. Secondly, modern sound technology, although still in its infancy then, would be able to bring the whole stage sound of music and voices to all parts of the auditorium, not just a handful of people in the best seats. The third reason can best be expressed in one name – Andrew Lloyd Webber. He was a phenomenon. His shows and his management skills had transformed the popularity of commercial theatres both in London and New York. He was Sullivan, D'Oyly Carte and a bit of Gilbert in one man. He was to the West End and commercial theatre even more important than Jennie Lee was to the British subsidised arts world. His shows, and the others by other writers and producers that his success spawned, would all be available to tour the regions over the next few years. What we, as managers of the largest regional theatre in the country, had to ensure was that the standards of the touring versions were up to the standards of the West End. If we could do that, we believed we could bring back the audience.

Planning negotiations were complicated and the £4m building works were massive. Following the requirements of the Royal Opera House the stage, the orchestra pit and backstage areas were completely rebuilt with dressing room spaces for 150 artists. The fly tower was lifted fifteen feet and the stage made deeper by twenty feet. An orchestra pit for a hundred players was dug out with half of it under the stage. The auditorium was painted, re-gilded, re-carpeted, re-seated. We knocked through to the pub next door and new bars were created. It all took four years to organise and complete. The Palace finally reopened in March 1981 with *Jesus Christ Superstar*, which had just closed after eight years in London. By agreement with Bob Swash, the executive producer, this was the real thing, the full production from the West End. This was no cheap touring version and we charged West End prices. It ran eight weeks and was totally sold out. We argued that a Marks & Spencer suit cost the same in Manchester as it did in London. They were the same suit.

Superstar was followed immediately by five weeks of opera by the Royal Opera including the famous Zeffirelli production of *Tosca* with Grace Bumbry, Sir Colin Davis in the pit for *Otello* and Elijah Moshinsky's production of *Lohengrin* in the season. Festival Ballet came next and a sold-out two months of the musical *Annie* after that. It was altogether a sensational start to the new Palace. We sold out night after night. We had struck gold. Producers wanted to play longer seasons – Bill Kenwright wanted a month of *Joseph and his Amazing*

Technicolour Dreamcoat, not the usual single week. The stars discovered they could make real money in Manchester. With producer Paul Elliott we re-established the biggest pantomime in Britain and had one record-breaking season after another with Danny La Rue, Ken Dodd, Cannon and Ball, Russ Abbott and Les Dawson headlining.

In our opening week we almost overreached ourselves. *Jesus Christ Superstar* opened on a Wednesday. On the Sunday, just four days later, we had the bright idea of mounting a Royal Gala. This would be a special performance with major stars. Prince Charles had accepted our invitation to attend and we would charge fancy seat prices to boost the Appeal. Granada agreed to televise it. The fact that there was a performance of *Jesus Christ Superstar* on the Saturday night was a small problem which we could overcome easily. We thought. The cast list for the Gala included the Royal Ballet, led by Anthony Dowell and Antoinette Sibley, the cast of *Evita* led by Marti Webb, both companies coming up from London for the day. We had the Chorus of Opera North over from Leeds. We had Kiri Te Kanawa and Tom Allen (representing opera), Paul Scofield (representing drama), Danny La Rue and friends (representing variety), 10CC (representing pop music), Lynn Seymour and the Famous Mothers Club (representing modern dance) all with the full Hallé Orchestra in the new orchestra pit. John Copley from Covent Garden was the director and Nicholas Hytner his assistant. The aim was to demonstrate in one show all the different kinds of attractions the new Palace would be offering.

The idea was fine perhaps with a week of rehearsal on a clear stage. Instead, we had just twenty-one hours. I left the Palace at midnight on Saturday as the *Superstar* set was being struck and arrived back at 8am the next morning. Part of the *Superstar* set was still there. There was no sign of the Gala set and we were thirteen hours from the start of the Gala itself. We had planned to have rehearsals, then a television rehearsal with cameras, then the show. Impossible. We had to do everything together. Nothing can describe that day. The hanging around, the disbelief, the naked fear of artists, the show director and the TV producer, the wrath of conductors (there were five of them for different items), the exhaustion of the technical team was searing. We were only two-thirds of the way into the so-called TV run-through when news came that Prince Charles's car was drawing up outside the theatre. At least by then, I had my DJ on.

Astonishingly, the first half went well. No one was relaxing because most of the second half was uncharted territory. John Copley in high excitement during the interval sought me out. 'Listen, darling, there is no way we can get from Lynn Seymour and the Little Motherfuckers [he did not like the band!] to *Evita* without a four-minute technical changeover. We will have to bring the curtain down and raise it again when we are ready. Now, you got us into this fucking mess, so you have to get us out of it. Four minutes, remember, probably six.' With that he disappeared. I asked James Loughran if the Hallé could play an extra overture or something. They did not have the music scores for anything else. I asked Danny La Rue, who had three spots in the show, if he could do a fourth. 'Listen, sweetheart, I bought three frocks for three spots. What do you expect me to do? Go out there bollock-naked and sing a song?' I asked Paul Scofield, who was extraordinarily nervous anyway, if he could read a poem or tell a story, but I got the 'You must be joking' look.

There was no alternative. I would have to do something myself. I decided I would go through the curtains and thank everyone very slowly. Then I would tell a joke, which Michael Meyer had told me, of an event that took place at the Opera House in Manchester before the War. I decided to lie and pretend that the event had taken place at the Palace instead of the Opera House. It had taken place on the second night of an Old Vic production of *Richard II*, which happened to have in the cast two very distinguished actors, Wilfred Lawson playing John of Gaunt, who was in the opening scene, and Trevor Howard playing the Earl of Northumberland, who does not appear until the fourth Act. Now these great men shone as actors but they also starred as boozers. The first night on Monday had not gone well and a member of the Manchester Watch Committee happened to be present. He was so shocked that he demanded that his colleagues should attend the second night to see for themselves and decide on action. They agreed to be there on Tuesday.

The play opened with King Richard addressing his court thus:

> *Old John of Gaunt, time-honoured Lancaster:*
> *Hast thou, according to thy oath and bond,*
> *Brought hither Henry Hereford thy bold son*
> *Against the Duke of Norfolk, Thomas Mowbray?*

To which John of Gaunt is meant simply to say:

> *I have, my liege.*

Silence. Nothing. The King desperately improvises:

The flower of England's youth, the nation's pride, hast thou brought him?

Again silence. The King leaves his throne walks to Gaunt and shouts in his face:

Have you brought your son?

A flicker of understanding.

He's here somewhere, Gaunt mutters.

At which point the Watch Committee man says in an audible whisper to his colleagues:

What did I tell you? He's drunk.

This is taken up by a wag in the Gallery who shouts out:

Drunk, did you say? He's bloody pissed.

At this, the swaying John of Gaunt comes sharply and furiously to life and wheels on the audience. Outraged he roars back:

Pissed, am I? Pissed? You wait till you see the Earl of Northumberland.

Though I say it myself, the tale went a treat. And I was able to express my genuinely heartfelt thanks to all the long-suffering participants. Somehow, we got to the end of the show. Neither the stars nor the TV people from Granada were too unhappy. Even the wonderful John Copley forgave me. Prince Charles expressed his pleasure and was seen to talk afterwards at some length with Kiri Te Kanawa. Later we speculated that he was signing her up to sing at his wedding to Princess Diana four months later. It had certainly gone better than we all thought it could. For me it was twenty-four hours that finally laid the ghost of the Royal Exchange agony and ecstasy. My new life had finally, properly begun and the journey from one theatre to the other was now honourably completed.

So, what was it like to manage a large touring theatre, one of the very biggest in the land? The permanent staff was quite small, about twenty-five. It was quite different from the Exchange where every show was specially created. At the Palace we imported all our shows. It was really like running several theatres. As the boss it was my job to get the best shows on the best terms. The secret to programming is to ring the changes and not become too dependent on one section of the audience. The audiences for opera and pantomime and musicals are very different and the auditorium feels quite different whether it is full of screaming children or solemn middle-class classical music lovers or families hooting at a comedian. It shows by the way you stock the bars – is it going to be a gin and tonic audience or a coffee audience or a Coca-Cola audience? I offer one hint for aspiring theatre managers. Aim your marketing much more at women than men. Every audience is usually more female than male – ballet audiences, for instance, are over 80% female. Even more importantly, it is often the women who decide when the family or the couple goes to the theatre. Women make the key ticket-buying decisions. Also, to track our audience we put in the first computerised box office in the country. We had a brilliant publicity and marketing team under the legendary Forbes Cameron.

The theatre had a very small resident backstage staff. The shows brought their own technical teams with them. Our staff was there to help and liaise. Our stage manager was a lovely, chubby, efficient, very camp man called Jamie. He was thrilled when I told them that Rudolf Nureyev and the Boston Ballet were coming for a week in June 1983 with their production of *Don Quixote*. Now I am not going to beat about the bush. By 1983 Nureyev was not the dancer he had been. He had lost his leap and was frankly earthbound. But a major star he still was and he took a curtain call better than anyone on earth. At this time Nureyev went everywhere with a Vietnamese dresser, who looked after his every need. One of his jobs was to stand at the side of the stage just before Nureyev made his first entrance and take some heavy punches in the stomach to get the great man's adrenalin flowing. On our first night, for some reason, the dresser was not in position, but Jamie was and he got the punches instead.

At the interval I was summoned to see a very angry Jamie who said that unless he got a fulsome apology from Rudi immediately there would be no second half. Jamie had the authority to do that kind of thing. He commanded the stage area. I went to see Nureyev and begged him to say sorry to Jamie. 'No way. Why you ask? You are joking. He has job because of me. I not remember anyway.' I was a bit concerned, to say the least. I sought out Jamie and lied nakedly on behalf of 2,000 Manchester balletomanes. 'Jamie, Rudi is so embarrassed and ashamed. He simply cannot look you in the eye and say sorry. He has pleaded with me to do it for him.' Jamie sniffed and shook his curls, but he did take up the curtain on Act Two.

At the first-night party later that night at Coco's, my favourite Italian restaurant, Rudi suddenly asked me, 'Is true you have magnificent moors up here? I wish to see them.' After an awkward second when I thought he was referring to beautiful black men, I suddenly realised he was talking about Derbyshire. I said that indeed we did and that I would be delighted to take him there on a non-matinee day. I drove him to glorious Millers Dale and other bits of the Peak District and he loved it. As we had time on our hands I asked if he liked historic old buildings because we were only a few miles from Bakewell and glorious Haddon Hall, surely the finest fifteenth-century house in the country. He was keen to see it. It was quiet when we got there but as we were exploring the wonderful rooms, a busload of visiting Soroptimists also arrived. At one point we encountered a small group of very respectable ladies and Rudi, in his trademark leather trousers, boots and cap with a cape thrown over his shoulder, politely stood back to let them pass. I witnessed the best double-take ever. 'Rudolph Nureyev!' He was one of the most famous figures on the planet in his full gear and the word went round the whole bus group in seconds. We managed to get away within an inch of our lives as this posse of grey-haired ladies in hats pursued us to the car park. We made our way back to Manchester with Rudi fast asleep on my shoulder. It was a memorable day out. He was great company and he adored Haddon. We had a wonderful little moment with an elderly male attendant who had no idea who Rudi was. In answer to our question as to how the house was still so perfect and somehow untouched by the centuries, he lowered his voice conspiratorially and explained that in the seventeenth/eighteenth centuries there had been at least three unmarried dukes. 'So there weren't all those women making improvements.'

On another occasion we had two Dames of the British Empire in a Restoration Comedy for a packed week. I would be seeing the ladies after the first performance but just before 'curtain up' I saw Jamie and asked if everything was OK and how our illustrious ladies were. 'All right, I suppose,' he said, 'but one drinks and the other's a bitch.' 'Oh lord,' I said. Then I thought. 'Tell me, Jamie, which is which?' 'Does it matter?' was his mordant reply.

Not everything worked perfectly. I learnt that the Royal Shakespeare Company was taking their award-winning and fabulous production of *Nicholas Nickleby* – the eight-hour version over two performances – from Stratford-upon-Avon to Los Angeles and they had a six-week gap between dates. A deal had been done with the actors, so the company was not looking to fill the weeks. I was such a fan that I begged David Brierley, the RSC administrator, to bring the productions to Manchester. He agreed but I would have to pay full whack – namely a guarantee of £300,000 – because he could not take any risks. I did my figures and reckoned I could take £600,000 at capacity. I argued to myself that 50% was a good risk for us. Fortunately, I convinced Raymond and the board as well. Indeed, I thought it was a great deal for such a fabulous experience. And it *was* fabulous, one of the best things I have ever seen in any theatre. The problem was that in total we took £157,000. I misread the appeal of the show and the difficulty of selling one show over two nights. Somehow it confused the punters. I had simply struck the worst deal of my career.

One of the things I avoided like the plague was getting involved with actors' accommodation, especially the stars. You could never win. Some wanted flats, some wanted hotels. Either the location or the decoration or the price was wrong. Once, however, we had one of my real heroes (whom I had never met) coming to star in Bernard Shaw's *Heartbreak House*. This was Rex Harrison whom I had worshipped as a teenager in the greatest show of them all, *My Fair Lady*. I decided to beg the Midland Hotel to let him have their best suite – then the best hotel room in Manchester – at a knock-down price. I was successful and walked with him to the hotel to make sure he was happy. Fortunately, he loved the suite and was very grateful as well. We avoided the main lifts and made our way out via the single lift, which few know about, at the side of the hotel. We pressed the button. Up came the lift. The doors opened and there all alone was Laurence Olivier. He happened to be in Manchester recording *King Lear* for Granada TV.

They fell into each other's arms. 'My darling, how are you?' 'No, how are you? I know you have not been well.' 'I'm fine.' 'Isn't it awful about darling Ralphie?' 'How's Joanie?' 'Have you seen Johnnie?' 'Where exactly are you living now, darling?' So it went on for what seemed like several minutes. I stood awkwardly to one side, gawping at two of the living legends of the stage and movies, hugging and kissing and catching up. I thought it was wonderful. Then Olivier said, 'Listen, darling, I must go. I was late anyway, now I am posthumous. They are waiting for me upstairs.' 'No, of course, you must go.

Go. But please, please – keep in touch.' Olivier stepped back into the lift and pressed the button. The doors closed. Harrison looked at the doors, then at me and spluttered 'What a cunt.' He launched into an expletive-laden diatribe against Olivier and his absurd knighthood and his even more preposterous elevation to the House of Lords. I do not know how much of his wrath was fuelled by jealousy, but I was amused to see that he was belatedly made Sir Rex some five years later, only a few months before his death.

Another activity I tried to avoid was coming into the theatre on a Saturday night. One week, however, I could not get out of it. It was the last night of an Opera North season and the sponsors were there in force. The opera was *Cosi Fan Tutti*. There was a reception in the bar at the interval and I was dutifully 'mixing'. Suddenly, there was a rather desperate voice on the PA system. 'Would Bob Scott come immediately to the prompt corner.' This is the name for the stage manager's hidden position in the wings at the front of the stage. I had to walk through the stalls and there was a crowd of people looking up at the front of the dress circle, which was in a cloud of dust or smoke. It turned out that during the interval a large chunk of decorative plasterwork on the underside of the gallery above had fallen onto the front row of the circle. By unbelievable luck, no one had been struck because they had all left their seats for the bar. When I got to the stage we had to decide what to do. Nick Payne, the Opera North general manager, said it was my theatre and therefore my call. It was clear that we could not go on since we did not know how serious the damage was or what had caused it.

It was decided that we would raise the curtain, bring on the cast, and I would announce that that, sadly, was that. I told them what had happened and that we could not guarantee the audience's safety. The performance could not proceed, they must go home and their tickets would be refunded. There were groans but people were polite, like good Brits. The cast stepped forward, made their bows to generous applause and the theatre began to empty. I stood in the foyer saying 'sorry' and 'goodnight'. There was a nice moment right at the end when a Hooray Henry from deepest Cheshire approached me and asked if I had been 'that chappie on the stage saying that the show was over, that we should all leave now and that we would get our money back.' I sadly admitted that I was. 'You mean,' he said. 'I can go now and get a decent meal and I don't have to listen to any more of that stuff? And I'll get my money back?' 'Yes, that's right,' I said. 'My good chap, what a perfectly splendid evening.' He scooped up Arabella and off they tottered into the night.

Very occasionally lovely surprises happened. Only a few months after the theatre had reopened I received a phone call from an eminent music agent called John Coast. I knew his name but I had never met him. He asked me whether on a certain Sunday in October 1981 the theatre was free. I looked at my wallchart and said that it was indeed available. 'Excellent,' he said. 'Would you like to have a recital by Luciano Pavarotti?' I was thunderstruck. Admittedly this was before the Three Tenors and the stadium performances but he was a huge star. 'Er, yes,' I stammered. 'What's the catch?' 'There's only one condition. Luciano must be able to take £15,000 away for himself.' This was a massive fee in those days, but, as we were speaking, I did some quick calculations. I reckoned we could charge £50 for the best seats. We could sell expensive programmes. We could have a long interval and run a champagne bar. We could take £25,000 easily. 'Done,' I said. We did a very simple letter contract and announced the concert. We spent not one penny on advertising and we sold out in a morning after stories appeared in the local press and on TV. I got a furious phone call from John Tooley at Covent Garden. 'Is it true that you have booked Pavarotti for a recital and you are paying him £10,000? This would be a disaster for us. We only pay £5,000 for a recital, top whack.' 'Don't worry,' I said without blinking. 'I promise you we are not paying him £10,000.' 'Thank God!' he said and put the phone down.

A few weeks later, when the only thing left to do was put on the concert itself, at the end of a phone conversation I asked John Coast, 'Thanks a million and all that. But why us? Why the Manchester Palace?' By then I knew this was the only Pavarotti concert in Britain in 1981. 'It's a rather strange story,' said John. 'You know Luciano loves horses.' I admitted that I didn't. *Strong horse*, I thought. 'Well, back at home in Modena, he had one special horse and this horse got sick. Vets attended, advice was taken but the horse got sicker. Indeed, the horse was dying. Then, someone told Pavarotti that there was a horse magician in England – a farmer, who lived in a village outside Warrington. 'Bring him over immediately,' was the response. He came, he saw, he cured. Pavarotti was deeply impressed and grateful. He told the farmer that if he ever saw another horse which would suit him, he would buy it. Our farmer was not a fool and in no time he had found a suitable horse and rang Pavarotti who asked how much it would cost. The answer was £20,000. Pavarotti was a little taken aback but he agreed. The horse was taken to Manchester Airport, put on board a special transport plane and flown to Pisa, the nearest airport to Modena. Pavarotti went to Pisa to meet the plane. The plane landed, a ramp was let down at the back of the plane, the horse trotted down the ramp to the tarmac and fell dead at Pavarotti's feet.

After an awkward pause, understandably, Pavarotti said that he did not think he would be paying anything. The carcass was winched back onto the plane and flown back to Manchester, where it was presumably turned into Kitekat. Weeks passed and Pavarotti's conscience began to prick him. He phoned John Coast to ask him how much he thought the farmer had paid for the horse. John was no expert but guessed that it would probably have been no more than £10,000. 'Right, I tell you what I will do,' said Pavarotti. 'I will do a concert in Warrington. I'll want £15,000 from it, ten for the farmer and five for me. 'Warrington does not have a theatre,' said John. 'Well, near Warrington then,' said the great man. 'That's why you got lucky,' said John to me. The concert took place. All went wonderfully well and that should have been the end of the story. But I did hear a few months later that Pavarotti and the farmer had fallen out and no money had changed hands. That was all I knew.

It was twenty-two years later that I heard what eventually happened. In 2003 I was deeply involved in Liverpool's early preparations to be European Capital of Culture in 2008. Liverpool had won a fierce competition and we were making senior appointments. We hired a very nice lady called Heather Newill to help us – she was perhaps the best search consultant for Arts executives in the country. She was married to the ex-chairman of the London Philharmonic Orchestra. One evening Heather and I shared a train journey from Liverpool to London and we gossiped about the worlds we moved in, in the course of which I revealed that I had a good Pavarotti story. 'Oh! So do I. Mine involves a horse,' said Heather proudly. I could not believe my ears. Nor could she. I told my story first and she then revealed how her story completed mine. Back in the mid 80s her husband had been organising a big charity concert with Pavarotti and the LPO at the Albert Hall before a totally sold-out audience and the Queen Mother. A few days before the concert the LPO was rung up to be told that Pavarotti sadly would not be able to be there. They were appalled and protested that that was impossible. However, the LPO was told that if Luciano Pavarotti landed at Heathrow he would be arrested for non-payment of a debt of £10,000. It seemed it was all about a horse that had changed hands up North somewhere but had not been paid for. Clearly this was our horse. However, the LPO was told that if they wanted to meet the cost of the horse in the next few days then the gala could go ahead. After agonising discussion they agreed and Luciano sang. Now, at last, my Pavarotti story was completed.

For three years, the Palace could do no wrong and we were making a very decent profit. With no really large theatre in Yorkshire we were attracting large audiences, particularly for our musicals, from across the Pennines as well as from Lancashire and Cheshire. The Palace was now easily the highest-earning theatre outside London. We realised that we could be giving the big hit shows much longer runs than three or four weeks. Even quite small plays, which could look rather lost on the great open spaces of our stage, did double or treble the business they were doing elsewhere on their tours. For instance, we put on a week of John Wells' satirical piece about the Thatchers called *Anyone for Denis?* and we took £47,000. The rest of the tour had been grossing about £15,000 per week. As luck would have it, a few weeks later I was in London and went to J Sheekey's restaurant for dinner, where John Wells by chance was also dining. As I was leaving, I decided to say hello although we had never met. He was not best pleased to have his meal interrupted. Indeed, he scowled. When I told him who I was and how much we had enjoyed having his play in Manchester, he fell on his knees, grabbed mine and said, 'Thank you, thank you, thank you – you are a wonderful man.' Apparently, his author's royalties cheque from Manchester had just arrived and was three times the amount he had ever received before! It was probably paying for the meal.

In short, the Palace was doing unbelievably well and now I came up with a new 'cunning plan'.

8

MANCHESTER THEATRES PART THREE

Bingo Hall back to Opera House

Take over Manchester Opera House – Michael Crawford in Barnum – Topol in Fiddler on the Roof – Evita and Lloyd Webber again – more stars – first trip to USA – Cornerhouse – Raymond Slater in trouble – theatres sold

One of my 'pro bono' jobs in Manchester was (and still is in 2022) as a member of the Granada Foundation. We always used to meet in the penthouse flat on top of the old Granada building on Quay Street (now demolished) and from the windows of the dining room there was a good view of the front of the Opera House. In 1979 it had finally given up the ghost as a theatre and had been reduced to the status of a Mecca bingo hall. At a Foundation meeting in 1983, while the Palace basked in its success, I looked down and could see that only a trickle of people was going into the Opera House for the afternoon bingo session. *Obviously not working*, I thought.

I made a couple of enquiries and learnt that Mecca were very downhearted and wanted out. Partly because of the phenomenal business we were doing at the Palace and partly because I was nervous that another operator might want to take over the Opera House and set up in competition with us, I approached

Raymond Slater and put the idea to him that we could run the two theatres in harness. It was costing us about £15,000 a week to run the Palace and I calculated that we could run the two for £20,000 with one administration, one box office and one technical team for the two buildings.

The central idea would be to put some of the big musicals from the Palace into the Opera House for months rather than weeks. We did not need the same facilities or size of stage that we had been forced to provide for the Covent Garden companies at the Palace. If we could get shows in for twelve to fifteen weeks each, rather than six, we would only need four shows a year. I was sure certain producers would be very interested, but I warned Raymond we might have to mount productions ourselves sometimes, so there would be risks. Raymond loved the idea but millions for capital works were out of the question. 'We are in good shape. We will need to raise some money but only a fraction of what we needed for the Palace,' I said. 'I calculate we can buy it and reopen it for less than £600,000 all in.' We were right to be nervous of opposition. We heard that Apollo Leisure had offered £300,000 for the building. In his inimitable way Raymond instantly told me to put in an offer of £315,000 and we got it. We had to do some minor reconstruction especially around the boxes and the orchestra pit and redecoration of the auditorium. We took out the bingo tables and re-seated, re-carpeted and repainted the interior. The Palace was red and gold, the Opera House would be green and silver.

As soon as it was known what we were up to, one of London's most colourful and tricky producers, Harold Fielding, was on the phone to me suggesting that we needed a big show to reopen the Opera House and he had the perfect vehicle – Michael Crawford in *Barnum* – and he was prepared to have a go at eighteen weeks. Fielding was an extraordinary little man. When times were hard he would answer his own phone and put on the voice of his cleaning lady to say that Mr Fielding was out. When I did business with him he was doing very well on the back of his two stars – Michael Crawford and Tommy Steele. He assured them both that each was his only star and he had two sets of posters and photos and statuettes of them in his office which he would quickly swap round when one or other came to see him in Mount Street. His wife Maisie was virtually his only staff but he was a demon negotiator. Negotiations for *Barnum* were indeed tricky but we got there. The show opened in October 1984 and ran to the end of January. This was not going to be the start of a tour, but a stand-alone Manchester season. It was the perfect way for the Opera House to reopen and for the two theatres to play the Christmas season 'against' each other. *Barnum* at the Opera House did not compete with the pantomime at the Palace. Both theatres were packed.

It was a heady time. On the Saturday after Christmas, with three shows of *Aladdin* with Les Dawson and two of *Barnum*, we sold 6,231 ice creams, and there is a very good mark-up on ice creams, much better than beer. On the last Wednesday of the run of *Barnum*, Michael Crawford asked me to come to his dressing room at the Opera House after the matinee, a summons which always alarmed me a bit as he could be very cross when he wanted. I never resented his search for perfection. He always gave a stunning performance at every show, unlike others I could name. At 4.30 I walked down from my office at the Palace to the Opera House to see him. It was a filthy, sleety, dark, cold January late afternoon. As I approached the theatre I could see, lined up outside the Opera House, five identically liveried coaches waiting for some 200 people to come out to start their journeys home. *Where were they from?* I wondered. They were from East Kilbride. *Crikey*, I thought. *If we can get 200 people from East Kilbride to a show in January, we have a catchment area of half the country.* Happily, all Michael wanted to talk about was the 'end of show' party.

The main problem we faced was that ready-made shows of that quality were not always available. As I had anticipated, we would have to start producing shows ourselves, while we waited for the Andrew Lloyd Webber or Cameron Mackintosh shows to be ready to come. Producing is expensive and risky and a totally different skill from merely running a theatre building. We were cautious and chose shows which had track records and usually we chose shows which had succeeded in the West End and where the sets and costumes still existed and could be hired. Frankly, we were not a serious creative force at all. But neither were we satisfied with cut-down tours with wobbly sets and stars who no longer shone. We co-produced these shows with the excellent Andrew Treagus doing the work but with us taking the risk. We had four big successes working this way and they looked wonderful in the 'new' Opera House.

The first was the irreverent Joe Papp New York production of *The Pirates of Penzance*. This was a real test of my theories. We assembled a very talented cast with Paul Nicholas, Bonnie Langford, Victor Spinetti and, making his first professional appearance, a young, slim Michael Ball. He was a brilliant Frederick, who had the virtue also of putting a kick up Paul's backside, who was very talented but a notorious coaster. The show opened to respectable advance bookings but I was nervous of fifteen weeks. To my huge relief people loved it and came in droves. The second show, which was leased to us by

Cameron Mackintosh, was my beloved *My Fair Lady* with the excellent Liz Robertson playing Eliza. Denis Quilley was a splendid Professor Higgins and the wonderful Norman Rossington was Alfred P Doolittle. It did extremely well, as it usually does. The third was *Hello Dolly!* and I persuaded lovely, mad Dora Bryan to star and that too did well. They all had roughly three- or four-month runs.

The fourth show we produced ourselves was *Fiddler on the Roof*. The London sets and costumes were sitting in store available at an amazingly good price. But the problem with *Fiddler* was that the part of Tevye was so identified with the great Chaim Topol that in those days if you did not have him, you were somehow playing a second eleven. Topol was the show. So, I did a thing I had never done: I stalked him. I tried his agent, I rang his flat in London, I rang his home in Tel Aviv. I got nowhere. I then discovered he was going to be at an awards dinner at Grosvenor House. I gatecrashed the event and watched his every move across the great room. At some point he got up from his table and made for an exit. I followed him. We were in quite a small corridor probably on the way to the Gents. To his retreating back I called 'Mr Topol, Mr Topol, please will you talk to me?' He stopped but did not turn round. 'What do you want?' 'Mr Topol, would you consider playing Tevye at the Manchester Opera House for thirteen weeks?' Again, he did not turn round. 'You must be fucking joking,' and moved off. 'If you do, I will pay you £15,000 a week.' He stopped and slowly turned round. 'What are you doing tomorrow?' he asked. 'I am meeting you to talk about playing Tevye in Manchester.' 'Good. Meet me at 1pm. You can give me lunch.'

We ate, we talked, we walked. We walked for miles, it seemed, with a small green companion between us, called Topol's greed. He simply could not accept that the taxman should have a cut. We looked at the matter this way and that. Finally, we came to an agreement that others would have to work through. All completely legal, I promise. What I remember most about that walk through North London that afternoon was the number of Jewish people we met who wanted to talk to him. 'Chaim, Chaim, what an honour, what a privilege, you are my hero, please kiss my boy...' The nearest I came to it was walking with George Best once down Deansgate in Manchester.

The interesting thing about Topol's attitude to *Fiddler* is his love–hate relationship with the part. He began playing the part of this senior citizen at the age of thirty-one and he played it on and off for forty-three years. On the one hand he is rich and famous because of the part, both on stage and in the movie. On the other he has never been equally famous or rich in any other role. He is a great actor, he has a fabulous voice and presence but he could never get the part of Tevye off his back. To get through it he grumbled and was difficult, boy was he difficult, from first rehearsal to last performance. One of his ways of coping was to keep me on my toes with a series of demands. I learnt a useful lesson. Once one problem was solved, another would quickly take its place. He decided one of his daughters was hopeless, then his dressing room was a disgrace, then the programme had mistakes in it and would have to be reprinted, etc.

After painstakingly solving problems one to six, I decided that there was no point in solving problem seven. We would just move on to problem eight and so on. Problem seven was that the musical director had to be sacked. 'Yes,' I said. 'Of course, let's talk about it.' But he never went. In truth, he was fine. We fought about it. That took a week. After another week Topol could not believe he was still in the pit. 'The new one is coming, I promise,' I lied. A few days later I had to report, 'Oh lord, the new one has just got sick, so we have to start the search again…' We survived on problem seven for the last eight weeks and the musical director stayed. But as with Michael Crawford, who could also be both difficult and demanding, I admired Topol. Unlike some stars they were always magnificent and they were paying our wages. And Topol has some very funny Jewish jokes.

In early 1986 *Evita* finally closed in London. Bob Swash, the executive producer of both *Jesus Christ Superstar* and *Evita* and who had been so important to us in launching the new Palace, went one better with *Evita* and the Opera House. He offered to bring the full production straight from London, but this time for an unlimited run. We would open the production for a four-month season but then if the business justified it, he would keep the production running for as long as it made sense. As far as I was aware, this was the first open-ended run of a musical ever to be tried outside London. In all it ran eight months at the Opera House and broke all box office records at the time for an out-of-London show. At that point the production was trimmed down and started its tour.

I was fascinated to see the legendary director Hal Prince at work. As the original director of *Evita* he received a basic creator's royalty for every production worldwide but he had the right to choose to direct any revivals himself for an increased fee and royalty and he had been tipped off that Manchester would take good money. He decided to exercise his option. He took things fairly easy and at the last stage rehearsal he gave the cast detailed notes and wished them luck. He then sought me out and said he wanted to go back to my little Italian restaurant which he loved. 'Shall I book a table for after you have given your notes at the end of the show?' I asked. 'No, no, we'll go now. I'll get back for the final scene. I know what they will get right and what they will get wrong.' We got back for the last ten minutes, he consulted his assistant, and at the end he solemnly gave detailed notes of the rehearsal he had not witnessed.

The first night of *Evita* in Manchester was a big occasion for us, although it included an Andrew Lloyd Webber moment. I have known Andrew since his one term at Oxford and we have met many times since. He is truly an amazing talent. Just think how many times you have heard one of his melodies playing in a hotel lobby in some foreign city. Andrew, with Sarah Brightman, already in rehearsal for *Phantom of the Opera*, both agreed to attend the first night of *Evita* as did Tim Rice. The show was opening at 7.30pm and we had organised a press call for Andrew and Tim at 6pm in the bar of the theatre. At 6pm, no Andrew, at 6.30, still no Andrew, so Tim manfully represented them both. Just before 7pm a panic-stricken front-of-house usher finds me to say that ALW is on the phone and that he is very angry. I go to the phone. 'Hi,' I say calmly. 'Where are you?' 'What the fuck is going on?' shouts Andrew. 'Well, we're all here at the theatre wondering where you are.' 'I am in the foyer of the hotel waiting for my taxi.' 'Andrew, it has been at the door since 5.45, as I arranged with you. Have you been outside to look for him?' To which he made a remarkable response. 'Do you expect me to go outside on the pavement looking for my taxi? Don't you know what happened to John Lennon?' Well, maybe…

For five years or so the two theatres ran in tandem very smoothly and successfully. We lost the Royal Opera Company at the Palace after only two visits, one in 1981 and one in 1983. Admittedly they were fabulously expensive seasons but the Palace had been designated Covent Garden's second home and that kind of expense is apparently acceptable in London. At least in Manchester the operas would be performed before entirely British taxpaying audiences unlike the very mixed audiences at the Garden. And it is the British taxpayer who pays the piper who plays the tune, I believe. I mean, are these national or merely London companies? Also, we (or in truth Raymond Slater) had spent millions in fulfilling the brief laid down by the Royal Opera House. Two visits and that was it. I did not blame John Tooley who was a supporter and fought to maintain the relationship but I remain furious that Manchester was treated so badly by the Covent Garden board and the Arts Council. But I was determined to bring great opera and ballet to the Palace and I started fishing expeditions abroad to see what alternatives I could attract.

My very first visit to the US was both exciting and rather scary. American Ballet Theatre was playing in Washington at the Kennedy Center and I was invited by the dance producer, Rhoda Grauer, to come over and meet with Mikhail Baryshnikov, Natalia Makarova and Twyla Tharp, the famous choreographer – truly American Ballet royalty. I was invited to their show at the Kennedy Center and to dine with them afterwards. I was not at all sure what Manchester could offer but I was certainly keen to meet. I left it tight and got into Dulles Airport about three hours before the start of the show. I only had hand luggage. I rushed to the taxi rank and jumped in the first one. The driver was an Indian from Mumbai and within a hundred yards I realised he was extremely drunk.

We wove our way onto the turnpike and I started shouting at the man. Suddenly, he did a violent U-turn across the oncoming six lanes and stopped on the verge. He ordered me out and sped off. It was dark but below me down from the verge I could see a built-up area and the lights of a garage. I clambered down. I told my sad little story to the manager who fortunately believed it and called me another cab. I was staying at a hotel in the Watergate building and made it to the theatre with about five minutes to spare. Dinner was thrilling. I sat between Twyla Tharp and Natalia Makarova who had been dancing in the triple bill. Their idea was that the company might like to come to Manchester to film Twyla's latest piece, *The Catherine Wheel*. They wanted a big stage but mostly they wanted a British director (Brian Large) and a British crew and so the largest British stage then available seemed a solution. As 'payment' they would also play a short season for the public. Sadly, nothing came of it in the end, although Rhoda and Twyla, two fabulously feisty ladies, made a recce visit to Manchester. I remember them falling in love with the old junk shops in the Stockport Road. The trip to Washington is still a vivid memory. Trips to Russia to land the Bolshoi or the Kirov were more productive. They come later in a chapter devoted to adventures in Russia.

We continued to have some success with plays with major stars just for a high-earning week. Lauren Bacall appeared in Tennessee Williams' *Sweet Bird of Youth* before a season at London's Haymarket. She was extraordinarily nice but I failed to persuade her out to dinner. Shame. Another good example of this was *The Caine Mutiny Court-Martial* with Charlton Heston as the disciplinarian Captain Queeg. He was a colossal star and his press call in

Manchester was huge. He handled it as the considerable actor and Republican spokesman that he was. He was also the director of the play. With him in the cast was Ben Cross, who had had such a success in *Chariots of Fire*, as the attorney Greenwald. At the press conference Heston was asked why he had thought to cast Cross. 'I am really glad you asked that,' he said. 'Actually, it was my son, Fraser, who first had the idea. We were at home watching *Chariots of Fire* and my son suddenly turned to me and suggested that Ben would make a perfect Greenwald. There was a quality of quiet but youthful authority in Ben that… etc.' Excellent full answer. That night I took him and his wife Lydia with my wife Su to dinner and she asked him how he came to cast Ben Cross in the play. 'I am really glad you asked that. Actually, it was my son, Fraser, who first had the idea. We were at home watching *Chariots of Fire*…' Word for word as he had answered the press question that morning. A real politician's trick. Work out your answer, then stick to it!

We also staged very early performances of two plays written by Jeffrey Archer. *Beyond Reasonable Doubt* with Frank Finlay and *Exclusive* with Paul Scofield. They both had courtroom themes. *Beyond Reasonable Doubt* was successful and played a year in London but *Exclusive* was a flop. I was at Oxford with Jeffrey and we knew each other a bit, mostly because he wanted an introduction to the Burtons when he was a great fundraiser. His energy and self-belief are, of course, well known as are other sides of him, but he was hard to resist. He was also unbelievably famous. I used to take to dinner at Coco's Italian restaurant many of the stars who came to the theatres. The wonderful Alfiero, who ran Coco's like a bantam cock, looked after Pavarotti, Nureyev, Ustinov, Heston, Topol, and many others beautifully. It suited me as I knew he would be a perfect host and it suited him because he got the reputation of serving the famous. What fascinated me was that of all these A-listers nobody made a greater impression on entrance than Jeffrey. The restaurant went silent at his entrance and then burst into applause. On top of everything he has a terrific wife in Mary, a major force in her own right.

One of the pleasures of big theatre management was fitting in the occasional one-night show when the schedule allowed. Two were memorable. I am mad about cricket and there was a splendid man called John Huntley who had an amazing collection of nitrate film of the old greats like WG Grace, Don Bradman, Harold Larwood, Ranjitsinhji, etc., which he would run between live chat between more current legends. It was a light-hearted show for cricket nuts like me chaired by the great commentator Brian Johnson. For our evening he had assembled Tom Graveney, Jim Laker, Raymond Illingworth and Clive Lloyd. I had the thrill of joining my heroes at the interval in the dressing room where the discussion was almost wholly devoted to Geoffrey Boycott about whom they all had strong views. For me it was magic. Another was a Monday during the run of the Russ Abbot pantomime in 1981/2. The cast had Mondays off and I was able to slip in a performance of a particularly filthy but hilarious alternative comedy show called *Who Dares Wins*. It included one sketch with a nude Tony Robinson – later Baldrick. I was in the foyer at the interval when an elderly couple of ladies approached me to ask if Russ Abbott would be appearing in the second half. They thought they had just sat through the first half of *Robin Hood and His Merrie Men*!

My final memory of my Opera House/Palace days was a co-production with an Irishman called Noel Pearson. In those days he was a Dublin-based theatre producer who could not pay his bills, but later he became a major film producer with gems like *My Left Foot* and *The Field* under his belt. A day or two in Dublin staying at the Shelbourne Hotel with Noel as your companion is a serious treat. He proposed a souped-up (by which he meant extremely camp) version of *HMS Pinafore* starting at the Dublin Gaiety, coming to the Opera House and then hopefully going on to London. It was mostly an Irish cast and it was hilarious. I love my G & S and I think Gilbert would have approved. I am not so sure about Sullivan. The actor chosen to play Sir Joseph Porter KCB was a well-known Irish actor/boozer who simply could not get his tongue around the words of the famous patter song 'I am the Ruler of the Queen's Navee'. He tried and tried but one memorable night at the Gaiety, he finally gave up in the middle of the song. He roared at the band to stop and announced to the audience 'Oi cain't focking do this', jumped off the stage in full regalia, looking like Nelson, marched down the middle aisle, into the foyer, out into the street and into the pub next door, from where nobody could persuade him to budge. The news of his departure was an international story. Speedily, Victor Spinetti gloriously replaced him.

After Dublin, *Pinafore* played six weeks at the Opera House, then six more at the Old Vic, then on to Australia. I went down to one of the last shows in London and had a conversation with our splendid motherly company manager, Carol Spraggs. 'Tell me,' I asked, 'about the chorus of sailors.' 'Oh gawd,' she said, 'what do you want to know?' 'Well, at the risk of being incorrect,' I said, 'How many of them are actually gay?' 'Do you mean now or when we started rehearsals?' 'Crikey!' I said. 'I didn't know you could change that easily.' 'Well,' she said, 'I would guess about 50% when we started and about 90% now.' So, at least I helped to bring into being a production which changed a few lives.

By the end of the 80s, the golden theatre years were coming to an end. Raymond Slater was now in financial difficulties and had to get out. This would involve the difficult business of wrapping up the trust company and then selling the theatres on. By 1989, frankly, I was getting bored with the management of show after show. I had been involved with these two great theatres for over twelve years and I had discovered that that was beyond the limit of my attention span. Once you have produced six major musicals the seventh feels to me just to be another. I have always genuinely admired the way Cameron Mackintosh can mount seventy or eighty different productions of *Les Misérables* around the world and treat each one as unique and special. I could not do that.

Raymond Slater's name in Manchester has faded almost to zero. Certainly, there were no awards nor plaques anywhere which bear his name. But he was colossal. He bought the Palace and enabled the huge stage extension by the purchase of buildings he did not want. The rebuilding of the Palace cost over £4 million and although we got serious help from the Arts Council and the Greater Manchester Council, totalling nearly £1m, essentially, he funded the work. It was thanks to him that the full Royal Opera ventured out of London, twice, for the first time in decades. I was not really close to Raymond. I was not one of his chums. But we got on well. He was happy to let me lead in the areas where he was not confident. I knew the theatre adventure was important to him and I represented a part of his life which had nothing to do with the rest of it. Now he was in Guernsey without opera or Manchester United, his two passions. Very sad!

His third, less heralded but crucial, contribution to Manchester's cultural life was to help me found Cornerhouse, opposite the Palace, in a crumbling old furniture store called Shaw's on Oxford Road. In those days the city had a major gap in the contemporary arts – no modern art gallery and no art film house. I was asked to help tackle this shortcoming and after an examination of several sites we chose Shaw's. I went to Raymond and explained how it could be done but we had to buy the building. 'How much do they want?' '£250,000.' 'Bollocks!' he said. 'I tell you what I'll do. I'll lend you £300,000 at 5% [which was incredibly low then], you get the price down and you can use the balance to start the Appeal for the other costs. And you can take me out for the original sum whenever you want.' I agreed £195,000 for both Shaw's and the Adult Movie House on the Station Approach and Cornerhouse was born. I was chairman until I left Manchester. My nephew at Manchester University said Cornerhouse was much more important to him with its three galleries and three cinemas and bar than the two theatres combined! Even Eric Cantona thanked me for helping him see French movies! Another major debt to Raymond. We sold the freehold to the city and Raymond got back his loan. Cornerhouse was so successful that its larger and more ambitious successor HOME is a new jewel in Manchester's cultural crown.

Now it feels as if Raymond hardly existed. For me, the extraordinary thing about him is best demonstrated by a moment we shared in 1992 when he was on a visit from exile to Manchester. I stood with him at the Oxford Street/Whitworth Street junction where you could see all the buildings he had either owned or funded for the good of the city. He said to me, 'I did alright, didn't I?' 'My God, Raymond, you did fantastically.' 'Actually,' he said. 'I did better than people realise. I was fucking skint at the time.' He died in 2018.

The theatres were now for sale, having been changed utterly. At that time there was only one contender, namely Apollo Leisure, whom we had thwarted in the purchase of the Opera House back in 1984. Apollo was buying up theatres all over the country. They were very keen to get their hands on the Manchester double-headed operation to be their provincial flagship. If anyone needed evidence of our phenomenal success, this was it. After twelve years two huge theatres, whose combined freeholds had cost £465,000, were sold for £7 million. Paul Gregg, the Apollo boss, asked me to stay on as a consultant. I gratefully agreed because I needed a salary.

By then I was in truth part-time, immersed in a completely new dream, which had taken over my life. A new life, effectively, but wholly unpaid! My days as a theatre manager were over.

9

MANCHESTER AND ABROAD PART ONE

Olympic Flights of Fancy Landing in Tokyo

Olympic dreams – Olympic journey begins 21/2/85 – committee formed – Graham Stringer – slow start – great team of volunteers – visit Los Angeles –attend Calgary (Eddie the Eagle) and Seoul (Ben Johnson) in 1988 – Duke of Westminster – Mrs. Thatcher – team and Princess Anne in Puerto Rico – IOC Members – lose in Tokyo

> It is necessary to issue a word of warning about the next three chapters which cover my years before the Olympic Bidding mast. For almost seventy unbroken years the Olympic Games, from Helsinki in 1952 to Tokyo in 2020, were awarded through a competitive process between cities which became fiercer and fiercer and more and more expensive. Finally, it led to a general belief that the process had become disreputable and corrupt. I became involved when it was probably at its fiercest and, by implication, most corrupt. Bidding had itself become an Olympic sport, except that there was only one medal awarded every four years – a gold one. Against de Coubertin's mantra, it was not a sport where 'taking part' was the motivation, it was entirely about 'winning'! Everything is now changed. The next three Summer Olympics have been awarded by

negotiation. In 2017 Paris and Los Angeles fought each other for 2024 and the International Olympic Committee (IOC) decided to present two Gold Medals – to Paris for 2024 and to Los Angeles for 2028. In July 2021, with no competition from other cities, Brisbane was simply awarded the Games of 2032. The following three chapters cover a very different era and one that will probably never return. The experience was exciting but today (2022) my weird Olympic bidding world is part of history.

I can take you to the exact place where it all began – in a lay-by on the A45 just east of Bury St. Edmunds. And I can tell you the date – Saturday 28th July 1984. That's when I caught the Olympic virus. Very mildly at first. It was the busiest Saturday of the year on the roads and I was driving my three children, David, Tom and Anna, to Suffolk for our annual summer holiday in Thorpeness. Su, my wife, was not with us; she was coming on later. The engine blew and I limped into the lay-by and phoned the AA. It was about 5pm. They warned me they were very busy but would be with us as soon as possible. The breakdown truck finally came at about 11pm.

Terry Wogan on the radio got us through the interminable waiting. He too was sitting in a stationary vehicle, filling in time and talking to the world. Except, he was in a radio van in a car park in Los Angeles preparing his listeners for the Opening Ceremony later that day of the 1984 Olympic Games in the stadium across the road. He was very merry, he had a stream of guests to chat with and everyone was excited.

I have always loved the Olympics. I had worshipped Anne Packer and Mary Rand at Tokyo in 1964. I was enthralled by Coe and Ovett in Moscow in 1980. I loved all the razzamatazz. As the hours ticked by in LA that day, I felt the anticipation growing but I also began to think strange thoughts. Why had I never heard a Brit suggest that we, the UK, should try to host the Olympics? London 1948 was a long time ago. And, since I now regarded Manchester as the centre of the universe, why not Manchester? My eleven-year-old eldest, David, told me, 'Dream on, Dad'. Finally, the AA arrived and we were towed into Thorpeness at about 2am, but my head was still buzzing with Olympic thoughts.

When I got home to Manchester, and the holidays and the great LA Olympics were over, I began gingerly to share my crazy thoughts with friends and a few influential people locally and was struck that no one slammed the door in my face. It was mad, of course, they all laughed, but why not? One friend I told was the admired broadcaster Brian Redhead, who loved big thoughts and he introduced me to his chum, the ex-athlete and journalist, Chris Brasher. 'As a gold medallist in Melbourne in 1956 he knows the ropes,' said Brian. Like many others, Chris chortled but the more he thought about the idea, the more he liked it. He encouraged me to keep going. I talked cagily with the Leader of the City Council, Graham Stringer, who also liked the idea but could not put ratepayers' money in. 'Don't worry,' I replied. 'If this idea takes root, when we have meetings in the Town Hall, I will pay for the coffee and biscuits.' Into the New Year there were chats with more people but I had no idea how to proceed.

The second key date was February 21st 1985 when the pace changed. It would be a busy day. At about 8.10am (the prime spot) on the BBC *Today* programme, John Rodda, doyenne of British sports reporters on the *Guardian*, was revealing his scoop to the nation. He reported that Mrs Thatcher had let her Sports Minister, Neil McFarland, know that, in light of the Los Angeles success, she would like to see Britain make an Olympic Bid. The assumption was London. Later Number 10 hotly denied the leak and it is said that Mr McFarland's career never progressed from that moment. Meanwhile, I went into manic mode. I first phoned Mike Unger, the editor of the *Manchester Evening News*. I asked him if he had heard the Olympic piece on *Today*. 'Yes. Why?' he asked. 'A Manchester Committee is in the process of formation, bidding to host the Olympics,' I lied. 'Really! Tell me more.' 'When do you go to press?' I asked. '11am prompt.' 'You will have the names by then. By the way, you're on it,' and rang off.

I rushed to my office. I talked to the leader, the chief constable, the vice-chancellor, the chairmen of the Development Corporation and the Chamber of Commerce, some friendly businessmen like Sebastian de Ferranti, Sir David Alliance of Tootal and David Plowright of Granada TV. I even reached two of my sporting heroes, Bobby Charlton and Clive Lloyd. In two hours I had a very respectable list. They assumed I was phoning as chairman of this committee. I phoned my list in, lyrical about our virtues. After unsuccessful years of trying to get theatre stories onto page one of the *Evening News*, at last my dream came true, but on a new subject.

MANCHESTER GOES FOR GOLD was the front-page banner headline.

I wondered what to do next. I felt alone, no money, just a shadow team, nothing substantial. I reckoned I had better tell someone in the British Olympic world. I knew no one, not even the name of the organisation I needed to talk to.

With the Queen at Haileybury for its Centenary – November 1962

With sister Diana and brother Andrew in Salisbury, Southern Rhodesia – March 1963

My grandmother Barbara Scott and my uncle Tim Scott

My parents David and Vera Scott

With Richard Burton and Elizabeth Taylor at the Oxford Playhouse - February 1966

Hewison cartoon of Four Degrees Over in Punch - September 1966

With Vanessa Redgrave and Michael Elliott in Manchester - January 1969

With Coronation Street ladies at Royal Exchange Theatre opening - September 1976

My children Tom, Anna and David Scott in Marple Bridge – April 1982

With Bill Beaumont receiving honorary degrees from Manchester University – July 1988

With Princess Anne at Olympic Session in Tokyo – September 1990

With Bobby Charlton at the Barcelona Olympics - July 1992

With John Major and Graham Stringer at the door of No 10 – February 1992

With John Major and Alicia Tomalino at No 10 for a reception - March 1993

With the Mayor of Leningrad, Anatoly Sobchak, the Lord Mayor of Manchester and Vladimir Putin and others at Manchester Town Hall - April 1991

With Prince Charles at St. James's Palace – March 1994

*Alicia's and my wedding in Bermuda with our witnesses
Helen Hindle and Sonia Stewart – November 1995*

My two step-daughters, Raquel and Sara in Montevideo – May 1997

With Mother, Father, Sister, Brother in Milford in Surrey – May 1998

With Louise Ellman, David Henshaw and Mike Storey celebrating Liverpool's victory to be European Capital of Culture – June 2003

In those days the London telephone directory was divided into four volumes, and I looked up in volume three under 'O' for Olympic. I found Olympic Dry Cleaners, Olympic Airways, Olympic Café – nothing on the Games. I thought of B for British and, hey presto, there it was in volume one – British Olympic Association (BOA). I phoned and asked for the man in charge. Dick Palmer, the general secretary, took my call. I explained who I was, why I was phoning, how keen Manchester was to host the Games and that a committee had been formed to promote our ambition. In his gentle Welsh tones, which I came to know well, he was not discouraging. Yes, he had heard John Rodda on the BBC.

He pressed me, 'Now that you have decided you want to have a go – there will have to be a competition, you know – what will you do?' I busked. By now it was noon. 'Well, I am raising money, of course, and we must do lots of research and commission a feasibility study.' 'That's good,' he said. 'Who are you thinking of using?' More busking. 'I think Price Waterhouse would do a good job.' 'No objection to them,' he said, 'but have you considered Arthur Young? You probably know that their Los Angeles office provided the heart of the 1984 Los Angeles Organising Committee.' I had no idea! But I did not admit it. 'I will think about it and I'll keep in touch with you, if I may.' I did know, however, that there was an Arthur Young office in Manchester and their senior partner was called Ken Millichap. I rang him. 'Did you know that your Los Angeles office ran the Los Angeles Olympic Games last year?' I asked. 'No,' he said. 'I didn't. I think you are mistaken. Can I ring you back?' Ten minutes later he was back. 'Do you know, you're absolutely right. I am so sorry. Moreover, we have a young man in the office here, who is working on the Edinburgh Commonwealth Games next year. I've told him to talk to you. He's called Rick Parry.'

Rick was with me by 1pm for a sandwich. We plotted all that afternoon and started a close working relationship. Months later, I persuaded Arthur Young to second him full-time to the committee for some years. Unlike me, he was quiet, brilliant at detail and could stay silent for longer than anyone I have known – disconcerting, but a great quality. We would run the bid from my theatre office, but the size of the team and the research would depend on how much money we could raise. All in all, it was quite a day and a start. Now we could throw our hat in the ring.

First, a description of how the Olympic bidding process worked in those days. It was in two stages. Your first task was to get your city chosen by your National Olympic Committee (NOC) – in our case the British Olympic

Association (BOA). Only NOCs could put forward a city and only one city at a time. The competition was between cities, not countries or governments. Proof of government support, however, as well as a demonstration of popular enthusiasm was critical. Without them, you would be scuppered. Your second task was simply to get forty-five of the eighty-nine members of the International Olympic Committee (IOC) at that time to choose your city over the others in a secret ballot on a specified day.

About nine months before 'decision day' each bidding city had to submit a voluminous, detailed bid document which would be studied by an IOC technical evaluation team. This was a massive exercise. Essentially, the Olympic Games are the World Championships of some twenty-six sports held simultaneously in one city over a three-week period. The bid document had to demonstrate competence and understanding of every detail. A good bid document would not get you the Games, but a bad one would mean failure. The document had to prove you could solve every issue that the Games would throw at you. The technical evaluation team would visit and test you on every detail. The final vote was taken by the full membership. Mystery lingered over how IOC members were chosen. Under Juan Antonio Samaranch, the inscrutable Spanish IOC President, the process was opaque. I never knew why Togo and Uruguay had members and Ghana and Paraguay did not. And why only seven women?

Each city determined its own bidding strategy. City bid representatives were either endlessly in aeroplanes visiting individual IOC members in their countries or the members were visiting each bidding city to 'inspect' it, and, of course, have a good time. This 'gross hospitality' which bedevilled those visits is now forbidden. Each bidding city also had to penetrate the incredibly complex structures of international sport around the world. All the twenty-six summer Olympic sports had their own international federation. Each continent had its own Association of National Olympic Committees. There were consultants and lobbyists selling themselves to the bidding cities as experts with an inside track to votes. It was a circus.

Our task was to join the circus and be nominated by the BOA in July, just five months after that frantic February baptism, as the British candidate city for 1992. The bid committee was formalised. The Duke of Westminster became our president. We hired Manchester's best advertising agency, whose chairman, Mike Dyble, became a key member of the bid team. Sports consultants and other professionals came on board. But we were simply not ready when the BOA had to make their choice. We were green and fell at the first hurdle. Birmingham beat Manchester and London easily and became the British candidate city for 1992. Birmingham had a renowned ex-Minister for Sport, Denis Howell, leading a keen municipal bid. London was jointly led by the Lord Mayor, who knew nothing of sport, and the man who managed Wembley.

Manchester did certain things well, which stood us in good stead later. We were first into the field and before the others got going, I had written a simple appeal letter for £10,000 each from the fifty largest companies in the country and was astonished to raise £180,000 in a fortnight. Our insistence, demanded by Graham Stringer, that it was a private sector initiative was clearly important. With our Arthur Young introduction, we arranged a visit in April to Los Angeles to find out how an Olympic Games was really organised. Four of us went. The Arthur Young LA team were a dazzling group of people and for three days we had a series of meetings about finance, technology, ticketing, sponsorship, security, transport, the village, the facilities (and their after-use), the media and broadcast centres, accreditation, etc. They were proud, after the various troubles of Munich 1972, Montreal 1976 and Moscow 1980, that Los Angeles had turned things around. We were learning but in 1985 we were not ready.

Fifteen months passed but we were not idle. I persuaded the committee not to disband. I was sure that Birmingham would be trounced. Rick and I and others kept talking and learning and we attended the IOC session in Lausanne in October 1986, when Barcelona was chosen to host the 1992 Games. It was an eye-opener. Four of the six candidate cities were led by their heads of government – not, of course, Birmingham, which was overwhelmed, and received only five votes. We came home from Lausanne, chastened, but better informed. We might be able to make a second attempt. We had a small sum left in our funds to keep our hat in the ring.

The BOA decided to sponsor another British bid for 1996. So, we fought again for the British nomination. We began talks with Liverpool, Cheshire and Lancashire Councils about keeping the bid a Manchester bid but one that brought together the whole North West. The councils were very positive, all wanting a slice of the action. The Duke of Westminster became more involved and was a highly credible leader of the private sector. We worked hard in 1987, raising more money, building our team, working on the BOA members, doing detailed research and improving our print and PR. As a result, Manchester beat Birmingham in this new UK nomination battle in February 1988. Denis Howell was very angry.

Now we were in the real fight, not just a British one. Our problem was that we knew almost no one internationally. Our priority was to find out as much as possible about the IOC members. We received a profile of each. In those days they were members for life. Several were over eighty. We scoured the biographical entries for British connections. There were few. One, the elderly Egyptian, was amazingly a 1930s graduate of Manchester University; the Taiwanese was a more recent graduate of Liverpool University; the Nigerian had been a doctor in Glasgow; the Ecuadorian had been Ecuadorian Ambassador to London in the 70s.

We sent copies of each member's biog to the British Ambassador or High Commissioner in the relevant country. 'Please could you tell us if you know any more about this person?' we asked. By and large, they knew less than us. Our Ambassador in Ecuador replied adding a PS that he had asked the Foreign Office to be in touch by telephone. The call came. 'Mr Scott? Candlish here from the FCO, following up the letter from our man in Quito.' 'Oh yes, Mr Candlish. Is it not great news that the IOC member from Ecuador was at the Court of St. James in the 70s?' 'Quite so,' he said. 'But a word of warning. I am afraid that when he left London, he left under a bit of a cloud; actually, quite a big cloud. Unpaid bills. Even fraud was suggested,' he reported. 'Oh no,' I groaned. 'So, if you were thinking of inviting him here, which, of course, you can, you should know that you may not be the only people on the tarmac to greet him on his arrival.' Señor Arroyo was declared innocent, but later was thrown off the IOC at the time of the Salt Lake City corruption scandal!

This kind of research was free but we were going to need money, real money. I talked it over with the Duke who asked how much we needed. I reckoned at least £2 million. I showed him a budget. He was amazing. 'Well, when you started, you managed to raise £10,000 each from a few companies. That must be your method again. Except this time, you should pitch the request at £100,000. I'll start you off with £100,000. And I will write to a few people. Remember you have a better story to tell today. We are properly in the contest now.' He was right and we reached our target of £2m. Furthermore, we sought significant pro bono help – plane tickets from BA, accountancy and legal work, hotel accommodation for our VIP guests, secondments, etc. I had raised money all my life and this was the biggest. People seemed to think the Olympic Rings meant zeros!

Once Manchester was made the UK's official candidate city in February 1988 I realised that we had to get to the prime minister. Mrs Thatcher was not remotely interested in sport. Indeed, she seemed to think that sport was what the great unwashed did on a Saturday afternoon. Her aversion to soccer was total. But I knew we had at least to try to get her onside. Through my brother-in-law, Brian, I got an introduction to Robin Butler, the Cabinet Secretary. Jeffrey Archer helped me meet Bernard Ingham, Mrs Thatcher's redoubtable Press Secretary, and also Willie Whitelaw, her 'best friend' in Cabinet, who slapped me on the back as I left with the words, 'Anyone who can keep it out of London has my support.' They all gave me the same advice. 'Try to interest her husband, Denis. He loves rugby and she listens to him.'

Peter Yarranton, the chairman of the Sports Council, and a friend of Mr Thatcher, offered to set up a lunch for us to meet at the Savoy Grill. Mr Thatcher was like his cartoons: huffing and puffing, downing large Martinis and disapproving of water as my choice of drink. He hated soccer, he hated the BBC, he was rude about foreigners. He was also sharp and asked quite tricky questions. He hardly knew anything of Manchester and was suspicious of the Olympics. When I told him about Athens and Atlanta, our main opponents, he became intrigued and quite competitive. 'No, no, they shouldn't have it – one couldn't do it and the other doesn't deserve it.' He was impressed by how big a part the private sector was playing in our bid. He approved of the Duke's involvement and my meetings with Butler, Ingham and Whitelaw. 'Now then, last question. What's in this for Scott? Why are you so bloody keen?' I thought quickly. 'Glory, sir!' He chortled. 'I like your style. Now bugger off, I want to talk with Peter.' I left fairly pleased, but not at all confident how this conversation would convert into pillow talk with the Iron Lady.

Not long afterwards the Duke of Westminster and I managed to get into Number 10 to see Mrs Thatcher in her upstairs sitting room. Thanks to Robin Butler we had been granted thirty minutes and she got straight down to business. 'How can anyone justify the costs when all you want of these expensive new facilities is just three weeks' use?' We answered that the after-use and the infrastructure were committed. The boost to the most important region outside London could change the whole balance of the country. She looked straight at the Duke. 'I suppose you know what you are doing. What do you want of me?' The one idea she did like was bringing the whole shooting match down to London for a day to celebrate the IOC Centenary at Buckingham Palace in 1996. 'Yes, yes. We could leave the seating from Trooping the Colour in place and have a great parade.' I could tell that all her instincts were entirely for London.

We asked her to accompany the team to Tokyo in September 1990 to demonstrate the government's support. Out of the question. Absurd, even though we pointed out that at least two other prime ministers and one head of state would be there with their teams. Grudgingly, she accepted that a Cabinet minister might come with us. 'I can see that Colin Moynihan won't do!' Her first suggestion was Tom King. 'He's a dear and would do it so well,' she said. I pointed out that the Secretary of State for Defence might be sending an odd message to the IOC. She glared at me. I trembled. 'Well, who then?' she asked. She thought more. 'Geoffrey Howe's an idea. He is deputy prime minister, you know.'

We then got onto the opposition. She could see that Athens was the sentimental choice. I told her that a secret IOC report had come out saying that Greece was planning to raise a special grant of $1.8 billion dollars from the EU; she got agitated and instructed her private secretary, Andrew Turnbull, who was with us, to make a note of this. 'No way! I'll put a stop to that!' she thundered. We got nowhere. We had more than our allotted time and I took unworthy pleasure, when leaving, in walking past Whitelaw, Douglas Hurd and Nicholas Ridley kicking their heels outside the door waiting to go in. In the end, it was Chris Patten who came with us to Tokyo. He was good, but he was not the prime minister.

The British presence in the administration of world sport had declined alarmingly in the recent past. The days of Lord Exeter and Sir Stanley Rous, and Britain saving the Olympic movement in 1948, were well and truly over. Our current two IOC members were obscure – Lord Luke of the Bovril family and Mary Glen-Haig, an Olympic fencer from 1948. They cut no ice in the smoke-filled rooms of the IOC, now dominated by the Latins. Also, the BOA was peopled by other past figures, men like Sir Arthur Gold, who tarred all African sports leaders with the same corruption brush. I had one or two dreadful rows with Sir Arthur. There were a few younger stalwarts like Dick Palmer, John Holt and Craig Reedie. But in 1988 we had no major players at the top table.

The UK had perhaps the best-known sports journalists in the world but that was a two-edged sword. The British view of the administration of world sport was considered hostile by the acolytes of Presidents Juan Antonio Samaranch (IOC), Joao Havelange (FIFA) and Primo Nebiolo (IAAF). The average IOC member loved Samaranch, the average British sports journalist did not. We were haunted throughout by British investigative journalists exposing corruption in sport. In particular, a devastating book called *The*

Lords of the Rings, about IOC corruption, dogged us. The IOC members hated it. The fact that the central message, if not every accusation, turned out to be true did not help us!

In 1988 we attended our first two Olympic Games: the Winter Games in Calgary and the Summer Games in Seoul. Manchester was now a very new and junior member of the Olympic family but our small team was entitled to 'observer' accreditation, which entitled us to go everywhere. We could go into all the stadia and arenas and go 'backstage' as well. Also, we could visit the VIP hotels and the athletes' village. I attended my first Opening Ceremony. I saw my first major ice-hockey match – Canada versus Czechoslovakia – in the stunning Saddleback Arena in Calgary. But our main task was to meet and get to know the members.

As Brits we could not escape the Eddie the Eagle phenomenon. It is hard to credit now how huge it was. I shared a lift with him in the village one day. I asked if he was frightened as he hurtled down the ski jump. 'Not really,' he said. 'I am counting in my head as I ski down to the moment of lift-off but I can't see anything. My goggles mist up.' A young woman, Caroline Searle, was the press officer for the British team in Calgary. It was meant to be her quiet introduction to the Olympic world, ahead of the much greater demands of the Summer Games in Seoul in September. The British Winter Games team was tiny and she was there to learn the ropes. Instead, she found herself organising the biggest press conference of the entire Calgary Games for the world and his wife to meet the Eagle.

The Manchester team had its feet well under the table by the time of the Seoul Olympics. We stayed at the IOC headquarters hotel, and we met the members in the lobbies and the restaurants and at the events. I was trackside in the stadium for the notorious 100m final, when a drug-propelled Ben Johnson flew down the track. He was awarded his gold medal and disqualification on the same day. A fabulous event which I gleefully attended was the men's hockey final at which GB won the gold medal. We also met our bidding opponents – the statuesque blondes who seemed to make up most of the Athens team, the cheerful teams from Toronto and Melbourne, and the slightly folksy lot from Atlanta, whom we all underestimated at the start. Soon, however, we admired the skills of Billy Payne, the chairman, Andrew Young, the ex-US Ambassador to the UN, and Billy's number two, Charlie Battle.

Back in Manchester, we now had a good office functioning, close to my theatre office, so that I could pretend I was working in one when I was actually in the other. The work essentially was researching and preparing the bid document. As far as the visits in and out of Manchester were concerned, we relied on volunteers, and people like Mike Dyble, Jan Heyes, Mike Cuerden, Hilary Brayshaw and Maria Carvath were terrific. Most important, this was when Helen Hindle came into my life as my Olympic PA. I drove her mad but she was the best assistant in the world. In certain countries we had language problems and a Bulgarian from my village of Marple, Anastasia Limb, helped with Eastern Europe and Russia and a volatile Mexican Mancunian, Maria Guadaloupe Rudge, the ex-wife of the Hallé Orchestra's first oboist, helped with South America.

The first time that we travelled as a group after Seoul was to the 1989 IOC session in Puerto Rico. I managed to persuade Graham Stringer that his usual left-wing Labour get-up of jeans and tee-shirt would not be entirely appropriate for an IOC session, even though it was in the Caribbean. We bought him what I believe was his first ever suit, from Marks & Spencer. Like Manchester itself he cleaned up beautifully and is now, as an MP, always smart and well dressed. I claim some responsibility for that.

The Puerto Rico session was the first Olympic meeting that Princess Anne attended since she had been elected an IOC member in place of Lord Luke who had retired. This big meeting also coincided with the news from London that her marriage to Mark Phillips was over. The British press chased her to San Juan. She behaved totally normally. One press incident made me aware of what the Royal Family has to put up with. We came home via New York travelling as usual with BA. The rest of the team had gone home on the direct 747 flight from JFK to Manchester but there were not seats for all of us. Rick and I gallantly said we would wait to the next day. To our amazement we were upgraded onto Concorde at 10am. In the lounge there were copies of the UK tabloids. One front page was a pic of the Princess with her face seemingly buried in a white handkerchief. The headline ran something like 'Princess Anne weeps for her broken marriage.' It sounded unlikely. The photo showed a large shoulder just leaving her face and hanky showing. The shoulder was mine, I realised, and the picture was of the Princess coping with a meringue which had exploded as she bit into it. It went everywhere, in a puff of white. It was not a hanky and was funny at the time. The headline was ridiculous.

Other memorable trips included going with Bobby Charlton to Cairo for the opening of a special Africa and Asia Football Competition. I cannot overestimate the importance of Bobby to the Manchester bid team. Firstly, he was such a lovely man and he always lifted us. Secondly, he was then incredibly famous. Crowds gathered round him, wanting to meet him. The Cairo VIP list included two Sheiks – of Saudi Arabia and Kuwait – (both IOC members) who were extremely grand and impossible to approach. When I sought a meeting I was laughed away, until I got the news through that Bobby Charlton was with me. Walls tumbled. We were virtually carried into the presence. Their Serene Highnesses were boyish in their pleasure at meeting him. Bobby and I were photographed on camels at the pyramids and those pics made several newspapers.

Some of the oldest members, now long dead, were the most interesting. I went to Rome to meet the old Italian tennis player Georgio de Stefani (by then eighty-three) who had opened the new Centre Court at the Foro Italico in Rome in 1935 by playing a set with Mussolini. De Stefani was a freak player because he never played a backhand. He was ambidextrous and played forehands with both left and right. Once he decided he would experiment by facing service with a racquet in each hand. The Lawn Tennis Federation had quickly to introduce a new law of tennis that a player could only use one racquet at a time! He was good enough to get to one Grand Slam final – the French.

One of my favourite members was a Mexican gynaecologist called Eduardo Hay, who single-handedly resolved the delicate matter of the gender-testing of athletes. This was a big issue with some Russian ladies in the 60s and 70s. Expert committees cannot resolve such issues today. He led the successful bid by Mexico City for the 1968 Games. The secret, he said, was to turn your weakness into your strength. 'When we were bidding in 1962, the IOC members, led by Lord Exeter, believed that the athletes would not just suffer from the altitude of Mexico City (7,200 feet above sea level), they would die. For this reason, Mexico could not be considered. I came to London to see Exeter and with evidence proved to him, so long as the distance athletes had time for altitude training, the sprinters and jumpers would not only thrive, they would break world records. Exeter's views were critical then but he listened. I was proved right. Look at David Hemery and Bob Beamon's long-jump record.'

Bidding for the Olympics required travelling the world, round and round several times. I went to Auckland for the Opening Ceremony of the Commonwealth Games in January 1990 because most of the seventeen Commonwealth members of the IOC would be there. I was away for seventy-two hours. I calculated, if I went round the world west to east: Manchester –

Los Angeles – Auckland – Perth – Abu Dhabi – Manchester, keeping my watch at GMT, I would not suffer jetlag. I was wrong. I was ill for a week.

The travelling out and the visits in were extremely costly, as the visits included wives, but planning and constructing the details of our proposals, which made up the meat of the bid document, required massive, expert, expensive research. The bid documents weighed well over 6kg each. We made films and models. We hired teams of consultants with experience and flair. And all the time we were in this extraordinary election battle. You learnt never to believe a word you were told. People were friendly to your face but treacherous behind your back. Graham Stringer remarked that it all reminded him of internal Labour Party elections, where every vote was promised three or four times over.

We ended up as a team in Tokyo in September 1990 for our final presentations and the vote. Apart from a celebratory concert in a major concert hall, we never left the hotel. We had a big team of people there, all with their responsibilities, running our stand, setting up meetings for our Secretary of State (Chris Patten) to meet members, and chatting up those we had cultivated over the past months. Our big set-piece event was a large dinner on the night before the vote with the Princess and Chris Patten and an excellent turnout of IOC members. We encountered Japanese hierarchical inflexibility at its most intense. How many would be attending? We said we could not be sure even with only four days to go. This threw them into turmoil. They had to know exactly how many. We said to plan for forty but it might be less. We could not be certain, because of the IOC disease of last-minute 'no shows'. We said we would pay for forty but we might have to lose a few places. Impossible! It was not the cost, it was the uncertainty, especially with Royalty attending. No manager could take the responsibility of being flexible on the night. With half an hour to go, we took out four places and four chairs and re-laid the table ourselves. By then we knew that thirty-six were coming. The Japanese could not cope at all.

The next day the presentation went well and the vote went badly. We got eleven votes and went out second. At least we beat Belgrade. During the party afterwards news filtered in that Seb Coe had announced in London that as from that evening he was preparing a London bid for 2000, which annoyed a few. The Princess was livid. Atlanta, who had not started as favourites, won. Athens was apoplectic. They considered 1996 as theirs – the Centennial Games to commemorate the first modern Games in Athens in 1896. This was not something a jury wanted to hear. Atlanta's bid was the best I ever saw. Not the best Games, which I thought were ordinary. But the best bid. Atlanta painted itself as a multicultural city to some and a black city to others. And the IOC golfers got to play Augusta! The team had somehow persuaded President Reagan to sit at a bank of telephones in the White House for some hours of the morning before the vote, being put through personally to several key members, and gently soliciting their votes. This was not a performance I could have dreamt of asking Mrs Thatcher to undertake. We had tried but it was not enough.

10

MOSTLY ON AEROPLANES

Two Letters to David at School

Letter one – with Princess Anne in Manchester and Budapest – letter two on the vote trail in Bali, Cairo and Rabat – help from Bobby Charlton and Clive Lloyd

> *A flavour of those crazy days of travelling, schmoozing and bidding are contained in two of many letters I sent my son, David, at his boarding school. I sent him regular bulletins while I was away. They also give a glimpse of trying to do two jobs at once – bidding for the Olympics and running the theatres.*

20th October 1989

Dearest Dee

This last week has brought together all kinds of extraordinary events in the life of a humble Olympic bidder. I hope you will be amused. On Saturday 13th the whole British Olympic Association arrived in Manchester with Princess Anne for their AGM and for an important presentation by our bidding team on the Sunday. Frankly we have not been confident that the BOA was truly behind us. We felt they were just observing us, and several of the senior members were unfriendly. Mary Glen Haig and Sir Arthur Gold, with whom I had my bust-up in Puerto Rico, for instance, are Londoners to their bootstraps. We made a high-tech presentation in a specially adapted Granada TV Studio and we produced an impressive array of consultants, architects, two of the 1984 LA team, police officers, hoteliers, planners, designers etc. We worked off a carefully prepared script and I deliberately took a back seat. It was thorough, there was a robust Q & A session and it went splendidly. The BOA genuinely warmed to the team.

I then had to rush back to my office to put on a DJ because the Princess was attending a 'Harry Secombe and Friends' Sunday night Gala at the Palace in aid of the Army Benevolent Fund. At the end I took her on the stage to meet Harry and friends and finally back to the hotel. It was the kind of event that a few years ago I would have been wetting my knickers over. No more, I tell you. Easy.

Monday was a feverish day in the theatre office until we left at 4pm to go to Liverpool for a bid reception with the Princess and the Duke of Westminster, at the Albert Dock. The Reception was for 350 and dinner afterwards was for forty. HRH was in good form but her voice was in trouble – not a condition she enjoys. She handled it brilliantly, saying not a word but smiling and listening and shaking hands and expressing all kinds of opinions with her eyes and her look. She knew people would speak to her if she said nothing and so it happened – odd but masterly. At the dinner she spoke more fully but she had to have a voice the following day for the Save the Children AGM which she was chairing in London. Philip Carter, Chairman of Everton and of the Merseyside Development Corporation, John Smith, the Chairman of Liverpool FC, the Leader of the Council Keva Coombs and the Editors of the Post and Echo were all tremendously supportive, which for a Manchester initiative was quite something.

Tuesday was another full day in the theatre office, with interruptions from Helen, and at 7pm a car came to pick Rick and me up to drive us to East Midlands Airport where we were being given a late-night lift on an Andover of the Queen's Flight by the Princess, who had been home to Gatcombe and then came back north, via London and the Save the Children AGM, for another Gala in Nottingham. Some schedule, poor woman. Our destination was Budapest for a meeting of the Global Assembly of International Sports Federations (GAISF) – all sports, not just Olympic ones. The Princess was attending as President of the International Equestrian Federation. Somewhere she had managed to change from evening gown into jeans and sweater. The plane was incredibly slow – I am sure I saw cars below overtaking us. It felt like being in a black and white war film, flying across war-torn Europe in a painfully slow bomber chugging through the flak at low altitude. We were met at 3.30am by a very fast, blue-flashing, siren-screaming motorcade which roared us into a deserted central Budapest in very few minutes. The good citizens living by the highway must have been thrilled.

Budapest was a revelation. Having been to Belgrade, Warsaw, Sofia and Moscow recently, I expected another bleak, sad Soviet city. On the contrary, it was utterly beautiful. What I had not realised until we got there was that on the very day of our meeting, the Praesidium of the Peoples Republic of Hungary was meeting to declare independence, renaming itself simply Hungary, and laying down the rules for free elections. The opening of the Conference on the first evening was very moving. The Guest of Honour was the Speaker of the Parliament, who was for a few weeks acting as interim President. He made a speech that would have been impossible just a month before, talking emotionally of freedom and the need for new friends. We were at the epicentre of a global tornado. The earth was moving. Next day the conference was pitifully absurd. The meeting started with seventy-two members; an hour later there were seventy-five. After debate the sports of bandy, sambo and dog-sled racing were added. There was discussion about dope-testing the dogs. I felt like a child gazing from the window of the classroom, longing to be outside.

I almost caused an international incident over a dinner I organised. Unknown to me I had booked the private dining room of the smartest restaurant – Gundel – in Budapest on the same night that Adidas had organised a delegates' dinner. The Princess had agreed for our invitations to go out in her name. Six eminent IOC members (including two Royals – the King of Greece and Prince Albert of Monaco) had all accepted. Bobby Charlton was one of the home team. Adidas were angry and I was told to cancel it. I took my problem to the Princess who said that whatever I *decided she was certainly not going to an Adidas dinner. We went ahead and a good time was had. Marc Hodler, the Czar of the Winter Olympics, is football mad and loved chatting to Bobby. We made real progress with him. The journey back was less exotic than the one out.*

*Your loving
Dad*

December 14th 1989

Dearest Dee
    I have now experienced true happiness. As you know, British Airways give us free seats, and when they can, upgrade us to Business. This time the first leg of the flight was non-stop to Singapore and I begged the office to make sure I was flying Business. Then on to Bali. When I got to the check-in they looked me up on the computer and told me Business was full. I was distraught. My size and Economy for a long-haul flight do not go together. They then said rather apologetically, that if I would agree to it, I could travel First Class instead. I walked through immigration on air, then realised I had nothing to read. I went to WH Smith where I discovered a pile of the latest Patrick O'Brien John Aubrey novel, published that week, which I had been hanging on for. It is my favourite read these days. First Class and a new Patrick O'Brien. Life gets no better. 'Oh bliss. Oh poop poop.' Miles to go, lots of things which could go wrong, but I am feeling fine. So here's to Christmas with lions and elephants and waterfalls.

3 DAYS LATER
Bali was beautiful but disappointing from an Olympic point of view as there were only five Asian members there and we had been promised twelve or thirteen. The meeting was for two days and lasted one and if there had not been eight candidate cities present (four summer and four winter for 1996 and 1998) presenting plans with videos, models, etc., they would have had difficulty filling one day! The Olympic world is a strange, bloody animal. One teeters between admiration and contempt. Admiration for the Games and contempt for the self-important and dodgy hangers-on.

I spent most of my time there with Charlie Battle from Atlanta, who had made the same incorrect calculation as me. He is meant to be a lawyer, husband and father while I am meant to be a theatre manager, husband and father and neither of us, we reckoned, was doing very well at any of our responsibilities. Of course, he should have been my enemy as a key figure in the Atlanta Bidding Team. Like me he is seduced by the Olympic movement. He knows little of life outside the American South. Now his eyes are opened to Europe, Asia and Africa. He has been away from home longer than me. We spend hours together on the fringes of meetings, ingratiating ourselves to all and collapsing into giggles when we consider the absurdity of it, despite the great prize.

The meeting was dull beyond words. The Chinese member Zhenliang He and Francisco Elizalde from the Philippines are hopeless cases for us. The others are more interesting, the two Indians and the man from Taiwan, CK Wu, who is a graduate of Liverpool University. He has two daughters going to universities in the UK. The Indians are a colourful pair, one Raja Bhalindra Singh of Patiala is an elderly ex-Test cricketer who loves his whisky, and the other, Ashwini Kumar, a senior ex-policeman who ran Indian hockey. They remember the Raj fondly and are Anglophiles. They are nice but vain. That's unfair. We candidate cities so flatter and woo them that they would have to be actively hostile to us to counter our ego-boosting ways. Frankly, if we don't get these three votes we have absolutely no hope of winning. So, I stayed up with them and dutifully laughed at their jokes.

The ridiculous meeting apart, I loved Bali. My two other team members left early but I had to wait for a plane to Cairo. A sleepless Garuda flight. Deliberately without a pill, having had three in Bali and saving one for tonight. If the bid makes me addicted to Mogadon I really would be cross! I spent the flight thinking about the elderly Egyptian, Ahmed Touny, who I am to see in Cairo. Manchester University has no record of him but I come armed with a scroll and gift from the Vice Chancellor nevertheless!

2 DAYS LATER
Now I am in a Pakistan International Airways DC10 to Paris. The flight to Paris has begun bizarrely. At the end of a rather energetic take-off there was a considerable jolt and the oxygen masks came tumbling down

on us. Getting them back required yards of sticky tape. It was also the only flight I have been on where the cabin crew cooked on an open flame on the aisle trolley. Worrying but delicious. Late taking off from Cairo, I am worried about the transfer from Charles de Gaulle to Orly.

I spent twenty-seven hours in Cairo dominated by three things – dreadful diarrhoea, an explosive phone call with Mum and a rather good meeting with Touny. The illness was Indonesian, and Mum's fury was because of my absence during a bout of dreadful behaviour by your brother. He had stayed out till all hours and I only made matters worse by suggesting that her worries were pointless. Not clever. I felt dodgy and rather cast down. I had time to nip into the museum to see the Tutankhamun exhibits. Wonderfully empty, badly displayed but breathtaking. Oddly, I loved most the old photos at the tombs. All those long khaki shorts and moustaches.

My two hours with the old gentleman were great. Touny is immensely wise, intelligent and concerned about the way the Olympic Movement is going. He longs for the days of Avery Brundage and Lord Exeter. He pinpointed five huge problems:

1. Gigantism. The Games are too big – too many sports, too many athletes. 2. Professionalism. Paying athletes is a big mistake. Gold Medals for sale. 3. Commercialism. The money swilling around has made the IOC corrupt. 4. Politics. Governments should stay right out – Moscow and LA disasters. 5. Drugs. Doping has been brought about by the other four. Sport used to be an inspiration. Now it is the motivation for greed and selfishness.

Would he be pro Athens? No, he is dead against Greece because of politics. I discovered the truth about his links with Manchester University. He was at the old Co-operative College which was affiliated. This enabled him to run, swim and be a gymnast for the university. He accepted the scroll and gift from the VC with delight and aplomb. Whether he is a vote for us, who knows? His age may stop him being in Tokyo to cast his vote.

3 DAYS LATER
I made the Royal Air Maroc flight from Orly just in time. We have a new team for the Olympic Council of Africa (OCA), which includes the Lord Mayor of Manchester, Yomi Mambu. She is a formidable lady from Sierra Leone, who came to Manchester as a nurse, leaving her husband behind

in Freetown. She is a large lady, rather quiet, who, Graham Stringer tells me, has had a tough life. She is clearly steel underneath. We are dreading the reception we will receive from the OCA President, the famous Jean-Claude Ganga from the Congo. I had a severe dressing-down from him in Seoul about apartheid. His scalding words came from a man who is said to own a string of brothels in Marseilles. The Lord Mayor is looking forward to crossing swords with him! She will make it clear that Mrs Thatcher does not speak for her or her city.

So far Morocco is not to my taste at all. The scene at the airport in Rabat on our arrival was a foretaste of the days ahead. There were people meeting the flights but they were only interested in attending to the VIPs. The Manchester team, I fear, were not VIPs. There were coaches and taxis lined up but when they had all departed about thirty people were simply left behind. The Tanzanian delegate had lost his luggage, spoke no French and was appallingly treated. He was laughed at and jostled. We took him under our wing and grabbed a taxi to go into the Hyatt, a posh hotel where the conference was taking place. We arrived to find that a lot of the booked rooms had been taken over that day by the King and many of us were to be moved to other hotels. It was chaos. But what the King requires, the King gets. Having finally got the team into another hotel, I return to the Hyatt shattered to set up for tomorrow.

This morning the Lord Mayor (she is called that even when she is a woman) and I had a glorious first encounter with Mr Ganga. He was speechless. The idea that the first citizen of Manchester was a majestic African lady from Sierra Leone dumbfounded him. He put his arm in mine and whispered, 'But I like to attack you. Now I cannot.' Yomi played him brilliantly. They kept on bumping into each other and in the end he was showing her off. In fact, she was one of the most admired attendees of the whole conference in her colourful dresses and her chain of office. She enjoyed herself hugely. She will speak well of the bid at home. It will make no difference to the way Ganga votes but we survived a difficult outing. In fact, the event was far more worthwhile than the nonsense in Bali. There were twelve of the sixteen African IOC members present, partly since President Samaranch was gracing the occasion and they love him.

We also included in our team two of our world class sports stars – Bobby Charlton and Clive Lloyd. Bobby is, of course, a hero in football-mad Africa, Clive less famous because there is cricket only in the South.

He was recognised by the Aussie boyfriend of the singer in the bar. 'Hey! Christ! Aren't you bloody Clive Lloyd?' He is a commanding presence – probably the only batsman who has scored a double century (245 in Mumbai) for the celebrations to take the form of the fans burning down a stand in disgust. He and Bobby are real gents. We are so lucky to have them. They never mention money although their fees for appearances are massive.

Our time in Rabat offered evidence of another great divide in Africa – Francophone Africa and English-speaking Africa. It reminds me of a 'bon mot' of your grandfather who said that the only thing the French and the Brits agreed on about their colonial pasts in Africa was that the Belgians were worse. I saw naked racism in Rabat. The Tanzanian delegate never got his luggage and I happened to be in the Conference admin office when he came in on the day before departure to ask politely whether they could send his case on if, and when, it finally showed up. Remember, the staff in that room had the sole duty of looking after the delegates. They flicked his Accreditation Card in his face, asked where he came from, suggested his name was stupid and where was Tanzania? A small postscript: I am sitting with the Lord Mayor on Royal Air Maroc to London. She wants to use her last dirhams on 200 cigarettes. What do we discover? The main Moroccan Airline does not accept Moroccan money.

It has been an incredibly complicated trip. In little more than a week I have flown on British Airways, Singapore Airlines, Garuda Indonesian Airlines, Pakistan International Airlines, Royal Air Maroc, British Airways again and I have no idea what I have achieved. Then the day after tomorrow, when you return from school, off to Harare on Air Zimbabwe. That will be amazing, but I may want a little sleep first.

See you very soon.

Your loving
Dad

11

MANCHESTER AND ABROAD PART TWO

Olympic Flights of Fancy Concluded in Monte Carlo

Second Bid for 2000 – John Major – £55 million for Manchester – Meet Alicia in Greece – Barcelona Games – 'gross hospitality' for IOC Members – team on the road – Queen meets IOC Member in Paris – corruption and British unpopularity – 2nd failure in Monte Carlo – BOA abandons Manchester – still a great legacy

My letters to David rather prove that all our efforts accomplished little. Limping home from Tokyo, we seriously questioned whether we should try again. We had clearly done better than Birmingham, but was it enough? The BOA made up our minds for us when they decided to sponsor another competition to choose a British city for 2000. We could not give up. This time the fight was between Manchester and London. Birmingham had had enough. The leadership of the London bid was led by Seb Coe and the disagreeable Peter Lawson, Chief Executive of the Central Council of Physical Recreation, who a few years later was jailed for fraud. Nevertheless, a serious bid for London, which this was, meant they were immediately the bookies' favourite.

Manchester, meanwhile, was battle-hardened and had done its homework. We had worked assiduously on the people who mattered, namely the electorate of thirty-two BOA members. We were confident we could win. I met a cluster of sports journalists in the gents at the Charing Cross Hotel just before the vote was taken in April 1991 and they asked me for a prediction. I said we would win by more than ten. They guffawed. They were seriously wrong. The voting was Manchester, twenty-seven, London, five. In truth, I think we saved Seb Coe from himself that day because on reflection London, like Manchester, would not have beaten either Sydney or Beijing.

The team which now took Manchester's bid forward was transformed. Rick Parry resigned to start his stellar journey in British Football to be the first CEO of the Premier League and then the boss of Liverpool FC. Howard Bernstein, the Deputy CEO of Manchester City Council and John Glester, the CEO of the Development Corporation, together took on the key planning roles. Under their joint leadership we completely rethought the main Olympic development area and they worked out the chief formulae for pulling the government onboard both at ministerial and Civil Service levels. We knew that Manchester must start building new facilities to be credible. We could not proceed just with plans and models.

The most significant difference between Manchester's two bids for 1996 and 2000, beyond the fact that we now knew so much more about the process, was the change of prime minister. John Major, unlike Mrs Thatcher, loved sport, not only in the elite Olympic form, but also as a grass roots activity. Indeed, it would be hard to name any British prime minister who loved sport more. Chris Patten had brought back to London from Tokyo the key message that if we were serious about wanting the Olympics, the government had to do much more to support the bidding city than Mrs Thatcher had done. He was also privately hopeful that the BOA should stick with Manchester and not change horses to London. He saw the regional benefits and John Major shared this view.

Our first task was to persuade both ministers and senior civil servants that bidding for the Olympics, let alone hosting them, was not a matter for City Councils and tiny sports budgets, but had to be viewed as a national objective. An Olympic bid was much more than a sports issue and responsibility should sit in a major Department of State. Robin Butler, the Cabinet Secretary, and like the prime minister a sports enthusiast, agreed to attend a small dinner at the Athenaeum and promised to bring relevant Permanent Secretaries with him. Five attended, including the key ones, Terry Burns of the Treasury and Terry Heiser of Environment. We were fortunate that we became the responsibility of the Department of the Environment (the DOE) with their new, formidable Secretary of State, Michael Heseltine. He was not a great sports fan but he understood major Northern cities and he became a real supporter. A small unit, led by Jeff Jacobs and Liz Meek, was set up at the DOE and they managed a series of meetings at all levels of government. The fact that everyone in Whitehall now knew that Major, Heseltine and Butler were all personally interested in the project concentrated Civil Service minds. We created an ambitious shopping list and, finally on February 27th 1992, we were summoned to Number 10 to hear our fate.

As the team entered the Cabinet Room to take seats opposite a waiting group including the prime minister and four Cabinet members (Heseltine, Patten, Ken Clarke and David Mellor), two junior ministers and three permanent secretaries, I knew that we had not been summoned to be told just to go away. The atmosphere was warm and supportive. It was my first meeting with John Major, who was impressive, close to. He was taller than I expected. Even with weighty colleagues alongside him he was clearly the leader of the pack and was constantly sending little written messages to colleagues along the table. You could feel his energy. At the end of the meeting, before he took us outside onto the steps of 10 Downing Street to tell a large pack of journalists the momentous news for Manchester, he was shaking hands with everyone with both hands and then putting a hand on a shoulder. He was very tactile. His last words to me as we left the Cabinet Room was a whisper in the ear at the door, 'Keep in with the Chief Secretary (David Mellor) – he's the important guy in this room – for the money.' Standing between Graham Stringer and myself at the door of Number 10 he announced a commitment of £55 million to the city for the initial items on our list. £55 million for Manchester was a big news story.

It meant we could start on three big initiatives: building the new national velodrome, starting the new indoor arena at Victoria Station and assembling and decontaminating the land for the new stadium on old mine workings a mile to the east of the city centre. £2m of the £55m was the government's contribution to the costs of the bid. Our other immediate tasks were working on the new voluminous bid document, organising visits and a strong team to lobby at the Barcelona Games in July 1992. We managed to exceed our target of raising £5m for the bid. By now each IOC member was the 'responsibility' of a bid team member and friendships were being struck up all over the world. A summer Olympic Games is the time when those relationships are consolidated between the IOC members and the bid teams from all the cities. We were at it night and day. Manchester's not-so-secret weapon in Barcelona was John Major. He had a few days at the Games and he met many IOC members at the events, in the hotel and at private meals. He got the message of the value of the prize and the toughness of the battle we were in. He loved it and everyone was pleased to meet him. He promised to be in Monte Carlo for our final presentation in September next year.

Other ministers dropped into Barcelona to help. David Mellor was one, but he got on a plane to Barcelona at least partly to escape the intense press interest in his private life back in London. There had been some devastating phone taps. He had left the Treasury to start a completely new Department of State – National Heritage (DNH). The DNH remit included sport but for David it was unfortunately dubbed 'the Ministry for Fun'. When he got home, he had to resign. It was sad as he had been a good friend to us. I did something with David in Barcelona I have never done before or since. I was out to impress him and invited him to dinner in one of the city's best restaurants off the Ramblas, Los Caracoles. We decided to walk. As we approached the place I saw a huge queue of people waiting to get in. I suddenly realised that I had made no reservation. So, I simply marched him to the entrance, said, 'Of course, I have booked,' and went to the first empty table I could see and we sat down. I was never challenged and we had a good time.

Barcelona was a great Games, the best I ever attended. The highlight events for me were Chris Boardman's cycling gold, Sally Gunnell's hurdles gold and Steve Redgrave's third rowing gold, all of which I saw live. The atmosphere in the streets and squares was electric. It was hot but not unbearably so. People did not seem to sleep. My biggest achievement of the whole three weeks did not advance Manchester's chances one jot. I managed to get free tickets for all the twenty members of our team for the Opening Ceremony. There was a black market on the streets for tickets at $4,000 each. I had asked President Samaranch's nice Chief Assistant, Francoise Zweifel, if she could help me. 'You get two anyway,' she said. 'But I need more, like eighteen more!' I pleaded. 'Well, on the last afternoon I usually have a few left over when all the scroungers and VIPs have had their allocations. In the end I am battling to get rid of the last handful. So, come and see me on the day itself.' The team was told to be patient and miracles might happen. With six hours to go I went back in humble search and found her clutching quite a block of tickets. She was pleased to get rid of them and cheerfully shelled out twenty. I was a team hero for a day. It was not only a great Games, it was also a great Opening Ceremony and we all watched the flaming arrow apparently fly into the bowl to light the giant flame. Later we discovered that it had missed by 150 yards. But the giant flame lit up and the illusion survived.

A real friend and a major Anglophile was Nikos Filaretos, member for Greece, who was responsible for running the International Olympic Academy in Olympia. The Academy hosts a sort of annual summer camp every June held in fairly basic conference huts and halls at the historic site. Every National Olympic Committee is invited to send two young delegates. With staff, lecturers and visitors added there must have been several hundred people attending. Nikos generously and probably improperly invited me to attend as a guest lecturer on the subject of bidding. For me it was momentous for a special reason. Looking after the guest lecturers was a multilingual, beautiful and bright Uruguayan lady called Alicia Tomalino, who had been a delegate before and was now an indispensable member of the Academy summer team. She was a sports psychologist (and an unlikely qualified international weightlifting judge). I realised she could fill a hole that had appeared. Maria Rudge, our Mexican Latin American expert, had suddenly and very sadly died of meningitis. Could I persuade Alicia to replace her? Alicia agreed to do so on an occasional basis up to the vote. In January 1993 we visited seventeen countries in twenty-two days together. In 1995 we were married. See later chapters!

Members' visits to Manchester came thick and fast. A great friend in Cheshire, Sebastian de Ferranti, had an amazing mansion near Macclesfield called Henbury Hall based on a Venetian Palladian rotunda. He was wonderful company and seemed to fill a role as a Favourite Courtier to the Royal Family. Sebastian got me into Buckingham Palace to meet Prince Philip who it transpired had not much enjoyed the Olympic world. I bemoaned the fact that when President Samaranch visited Washington or Moscow he was made a fuss of by presidents and invited to the White House and the Kremlin. As far as London was concerned, I said, he had never even met Mrs Thatcher. 'Well, he should count his bloody blessings,' retorted the Prince cheerfully!

Several members had dined with Sebastian when they visited Manchester. He and Naomi were fabulous hosts and he encouraged me to bring as many IOC members to dinner as I liked. He found them fascinating. One memorable visit was by Philip Von Schoeller, the Austrian, who was the only other member with the Princess Royal from an equestrian background. He was a major target for us. He stayed with the Ferrantis and went hunting with them. We also took him by Sebastian's helicopter to Aintree for the Grand National in April. Except this was 1993 and the Grand National we took him to was the Grand National that never was. The race was aborted after two false starts. It felt like a disaster. I was distraught. Von Schoeller was magnanimous. 'We might have gone to any old Grand National. Instead, you took me to a unique one.' Talking about it was like asking Mrs Abraham Lincoln what she had thought of the play.

On another occasion we hosted the Russian Vitaly Smirnov, whom I had visited in Moscow two years before. As we were driving to Old Trafford for lunch with Bobby Charlton we passed the Cricket Ground. I explained that there was a County Game going on. 'You won't be interested in that, I assure you. It has nothing to do with the Olympics.' I was not getting away with that. 'I wish to see cricket,' he announced. There was no dissuading him. On the mobile I threw myself on the mercy of Jim Cumbes, the Chief Executive of Lancashire. 'Don't worry, Bob, I'll gather together some grandees in the Committee Room for tea and we'll look after him. But I warn you, it's only Sussex and there aren't many in.' He was as good as his word.

He had managed to get together what was for me a glittering gaggle of past and present players, including Mike Atherton, then Captain of England, Clive Lloyd, David Lloyd, Farokh Engineer and, to my delight, the legendary Cyril Washbrook, along with Committee Members. After jolly chats Smirnov announced, 'Bob, I now want to watch cricket.' It was going on in front of three men, two boys and a dog on the other side of the window looking onto what was then a pretty run-down stadium for 15,000. We went out to the hallowed Committee balcony and he watched silently for three or four overs. 'Bob, I have question.' *Oh God*, I thought. *What is he going to ask?* Long pause. Then, very calmly, he asked, 'Why is ball red?' I hadn't a clue, but he clearly was on to something. The white ball for one-day matches had already been introduced! What he made of it all I have no idea, but at least he never asked about the size of the crowd.

There were so many other moments. Brian Chesworth, Alicia and I visited Shanghai for the South East Asia Games – an entirely invented event to promote Beijing – where Samaranch and many IOC members would be present. We had, for twenty-four hours a day, a lady minder assigned to us called Mrs Wu. We discovered she was sleeping in an adjoining room on our corridor, trying to keep an eye on us, Beijing's unholy competitors from England. We had a good time giving her the slip like naughty children. The contrast between Shanghai then and now is mind-blowing. She must have been very relieved when we left.

I shall not forget shopping in the famous 'spy' shop in South Audley Street in Mayfair with Mexican billionaire and IOC member Mario Vazquez Rana. He spent £17,000 on an exploding briefcase and fountain-pen camera and other James Bond Q tricks. He was a leading member of the so-called Latin mafia, a Lord of the Rings, who were running the Olympic movement at that time. He could not make his credit card work and I rather pathetically offered mine. To my horror it was accepted and for a few hours I was seriously in the red. He had come to London in his private Gulfstream, essentially to meet John Major at Number 10, which I had managed to set up. He not only promised his vote (ho! ho!) he gave me a lift on his plane from Luton to Manchester. Very briefly he inspected us.

Every member had his Manchester bid document personally delivered. My father, an experienced Ambassador, went to Ulan Bator effectively for lunch to deliver the bid book to the Mongolian, Shagdarjav Magvan and to Western Samoa to meet up again with Paul Wallwork, an old acquaintance from his days in New Zealand. Brian Chesworth performed the same mission to the Thai member in Bangkok, Nat Indrapana and Mike Dyble similarly to the member in Mauritius, Ram Ruhee. They all came back with good stories. My own best bid book delivery moment was to the two rather solid Swiss members, Marc Hodler and Denis Oswald, at a dinner at the residence in Berne on an evening which went from staid to frisky as Her Excellency knocked back the booze for Britain.

At the end of our South American jaunt Alicia and I flew from Miami to Zurich to see Joao Havelange of FIFA (and, briefly, Sepp Blatter, his general secretary and infamous successor). Havelange adored Alicia and held her hand for the entire interview. We left the meeting, each with extremely expensive FIFA wrist watches and flattering absurdities ringing in our ears about how we only had Beijing to beat, and his money was on us doing it! We flattered them but, boy, did they not toy with us?

I am told that telling stories about the Queen is 'poor form'. However, I think this one is allowed, as it did not come from any private conversation of mine with her and it happened abroad. As a team we were always trying to find ways to impress IOC members in their own countries. One day we heard that the Queen was making a state visit to France in June 1992 and there would be a garden party at the superb British Embassy in Paris. The great and good would be invited and a few would be able to shake the Royal hand. We pleaded that Maurice Herzog, the famous first conqueror of Annapurna and a long-standing IOC Member for France, be invited. Word came back that not only had he attended but also that he and the Queen had been seen to have an animated conversation.

A few weeks later I saw Maurice in Barcelona and remarked that he had been seen with my Queen in Paris. 'Yes, yes. We had a fascinating talk. I was delighted to be introduced.' The Queen told him that she knew a bit about the Olympics as her husband some years ago and her daughter Anne now were involved. 'Ah yes, your daughter, the Princess Royal,' Herzog said. 'I know her a little.' To which the Queen asked, 'Tell me, how do you find her?' Slightly taken aback, he said that she had been an Olympic Competitor, was President of the Equestrian Federation, and was now an IOC member, a splendid and highly qualified colleague. 'But I could see from a twinkle in the Queen's eye,' he went on, 'that she expected me to say more. So, I took my courage in both hands and said *Mais peut-etre elle est un peu dure.*' '*Dure?*' exclaimed the Queen. 'What do you think I have had to put up with for the past forty-two years?'

The members I probably got on best with were two North Americans: the American ex-rower, Anita de Frantz, as honourable and as committed to sport as could be, and the Canadian ex-swimmer Richard Pound, an IOC Vice-President who chaired the committee to cleanse the Augean Stables after the Salt Lake City corruption debacle and was the Founder of the key World Anti-Doping Panel (WADA). The thing I really loved about these two was that they were both serious but loved to share a laugh. Perhaps the most impressive member was Judge Keba Mbaye from Senegal, a member of the International Court of Justice, who assured me that members, including himself, would change their minds endlessly.

President Samaranch was the undisputed king of the jungle. He loved to be loved, but he was wonderfully devious. People spent their lives trying to work out what he was thinking. I suppose, if you have to deal with Havelange of Football, Nebiolo of Athletics and Vazquez Rana of the NOCs, you have to be sharp as a fox. We laid on an almost Royal Visit to Manchester for him with ministers, Dukes, police outriders and helicopters in close attendance. But our biggest success with him was the result of my begging the Princess to entertain him to dinner at Buckingham Palace. She was not enthusiastic, but I assured her that we would, of course, pay for the occasion. 'Oh well, all right!' she said. The extent of the success with Samaranch was that his wife, Bibi, never an enthusiastic Olympic wife, came to London especially for the dinner. Even she, who rarely left home, was not going to miss seeing inside the Palace. I have to say that it was, indeed, very grand in a state dining room.

As far as corruption was concerned the situation today seems to be greatly improved but throughout my few years on the Olympic treadmill it was always on the agenda and the British press and TV led global investigations on an almost monthly basis. Correctly too, but it did not endear Britain even to the innocent member. We always knew certain members were corrupt. Of those who were expelled I can only say that there were few surprises. Whether it was noble or naïve, Manchester never offered a bribe. But we certainly indulged in 'gross hospitality'. Even if we had wanted to arrange a bribe and get away with it, it was pointless. The voting was secret and the evidence was that corrupt members were taking bribes from several cities at once. Slowly but surely, with Marc Hodler, Richard Pound, Jacques Rogge, Thomas Bach leading the way, themselves the clean men of the IOC, have worked hard to rid the IOC of this scourge. But as Ahmed Touny told me in Cairo, it will never go away with so much money swilling around. Unsavoury as it is, I am not certain that lining a few individual pockets has done anything more serious than destroy the IOC's sanctimonious view of itself.

Anyway, we got to Monte Carlo and the September 1993 vote at last. We arrived in Monaco with a lot more hope than we had in Tokyo three years before. We took a prime minister, gold medallists, pop stars, a youth choir, a Guards band, amongst other attractions to boost our case. My good friend Charlie Battle of Atlanta used to say that the last six months were key, the last six weeks vital, the last six days crucial and the last six hours was when the decisions were made. Our final presentation was considered excellent with solid contributions from the prime minister and the Princess. But I could never banish the thought that there were six hours between our leaving the Hall and the start of voting. In that time the only Brits the members would see would be Princess Anne and Dame Mary Glen Haig, who were incapable of working a room. No one admired the Princess more than me, but 'bidder' was not her middle name.

We had also been aware in the last days that the membership was experiencing a massive push for Beijing, with senior players like Havelange, Smirnov and Herzog deploying the argument, probably with the support of Samaranch, that giving the 2000 Games to Beijing would mean that it would be the Olympics that finally brought China back into the comity of nations at the start of a new Millennium – heady stuff. All I knew from my Aussie counterpart was that Sydney was thunderstruck that Beijing had gathered in forty-three votes and so nearly beat Sydney, who squeezed ahead with forty-five. Certainly, in that endless voting calculation we all did, we could never see Beijing getting more than thirty-five votes or so. Members who chose to tell us that they would never vote for Beijing clearly did. In the end Manchester was like the Liberal Democrats in a British General Election – we like you, but not enough to vote for you! We came third, beating Berlin and Istanbul, two impressive scalps, but we had to be satisfied with just thirteen votes. Next day I met over thirty of those thirteen!

That evening we had a party, a big party. It was so good that several of the victorious Aussies joined us. They reckoned our party was better than theirs! Our room was next to the empty room reserved for the Chinese celebrations, which were cancelled. We pinched some of their drink. I had to break away to do live links to the BBC and ITV Evening News. The prime minister was back in London by then and spoke handsomely of our efforts. In my relief that it was all over, I stood on the table, spoke gratefully to a great team and then got down and planted an admiring kiss on the Royal cheek. I knew it was virtually a hanging offence but I did think the world of her. The final denouement was late that night when a group of British press photographers begged me to come to the beach the next morning for one last wistful, defeated pic. I did as I was asked and sat on the sand looking out to sea in contemplative fashion. The picture was in several national papers the next day, all with roughly the same caption: 'Defeated Olympic Bid Chairman surveys the wreckage of his marriage.' Not exactly what I was thinking and it sounded awful.

The team had made visits to all the members of the IOC and sixty-three members visited Manchester. In the end we made two full bids, first for 1996, then later for 2000. By the time we finally left the Olympic bidding fray in September 1993 we knew the extended Olympic world intimately. We had attended meetings in places as varied as Acapulco, Auckland, Bali, Budapest, Cairo, Harare, New York, Puerto Rico, Rabat and Shanghai. Our bidding teams attended the Games of Calgary, Seoul, Albertville and Barcelona. We presented our candidature formally at IOC Sessions in Tokyo in 1990 and Monaco in 1993. The Royal family assisted. One prime minister and other senior ministers became closely involved. Major new sports facilities in Manchester were built. And it all happened because of an idea I had had in a lay-by on the A45 in July 1984.

Mark you, I had to face up to the small, grim matter of the failure of both our bids. Sydney and Beijing were spectacular candidates. It was the turn of the Far East and not Europe after Barcelona. Manchester was not London and lacked glamour. In those Latin-dominated days in world sport, and with a hostile press, Britain was not popular. So, we knew we had to have a second agenda. Graham Stringer and I had shared a belief that the bidding process should always be positive for Manchester: that it must be a race worth entering, even if that meant losing. We would take the Olympic line about 'taking part' rather than 'winning'.

No one in the know really expected us to win either in Tokyo in 1990 or Monte Carlo in 1993. Happily, many have pointed to the Olympic bids as the rocket fuel which first ignited Manchester's revival in the early twenty-first century. It is thanks to the Manchester Velodrome, which became the HQ of British cycling, that Britain has dominated world cycling for five Olympics and pushed Team GB high up the medal table. The new Manchester Arena with 20,000 seats was the biggest in Europe until the O2 at the Dome opened. The stadium we began is now home to one of the world's richest football clubs – Manchester City. Some legacy, even if we lost.

The eight years from 1985 to 1993 were undoubtedly the most exciting and frenetic of my life. For much of the time the most difficult thing I had to do was to work at two entirely different coal faces simultaneously. One day I would be wooing Cameron Mackintosh or Glyndebourne or Topol and the next I would be in Auckland or Budapest or Rabat wooing Olympic nabobs. I spent a long day hosting President Samaranch around Manchester and Cheshire before taking him to Manchester Airport for his departure back to Lausanne. Exactly as his plane was departing, another was landing with the Duke and Duchess of Kent who were coming to the Palace to see Wagner performed by Opera North. Greater Manchester Police rushed me back to the theatre just in time to greet them at the door. I sat next to the Duke for *Die Meistersinger* and I blush to admit I nodded off on his shoulder. He gently nudged me and whispered reassuringly, 'I think it's rather good.'

The chief victims of this crazy time were my wife and children. The marriage had been in trouble from before 1985 but we had soldiered on. I was away a lot and Su went to Australia for six months in 1992/3 which made life more complicated. I knew the parting was inevitable and the children suffered. We separated and I took a flat in the city centre.

After Monte Carlo there was to be no new British Olympic Bid for 2004 or 2008, nor was there a British competition for 2012. London was simply appointed. Even though I know I am putting myself in a small minority, bearing in mind how well 2012 worked out, I still suggest the BOA should have stuck with Manchester. *The Times* ran a leader to that effect in 1993. Our bid for 2000 was an enormous improvement on our bid for 1996. Admittedly, Athens and Beijing were seen as irresistible candidates for 2004 and 2008 and perhaps it was sensible that there was no British candidate for those years. But was it proper that, after the success of the 2002 Manchester Commonwealth Games, there should have been no competition at least to make a choice for a British Candidate City for 2012? Just to hand the baton, as it were, to London with no competition showed the BOA leadership to be cowardly.

I am not saying that Manchester would have beaten Paris or Madrid as London did but if the BOA had stuck with Manchester as their Olympic Candidate City, then I believe that the Games would eventually have come to Manchester and the North West for the same reasons they are going to Brisbane in 2032. The real force in this argument is that Britain as a country would have derived far more benefit from an Olympics in the North West than just more massive spending in London and the South East. Of course, 2012 was terrific. Who will forget the London Games? But its huge cost has simply changed a part of East London. Manchester 2012 or even Manchester 2024 would have been capable of changing Britain. It is not healthy that one city so dominates our public life. Maybe the Northern Powerhouse will change everything. I doubt it. We will see.

Not everyone is interested in the Olympics, I know that. Indeed, lots of people dislike the Games intensely. Princess Margaret was a friend of Sebastian de Ferranti and was a frequent guest at Henbury. I met her there on two occasions and she shall have the last word. Soon after our final defeat I met her again when Sebastian brought her to the ballet, her great love, and she remembered me. 'Oh, yes, we've met. You're that Olympics man. I must congratulate you on a splendid result.' 'Well, that's not really the standard line, Ma'am. We lost.' 'No, no, I insist. Manchester got a great deal of credit and we didn't get the bloody thing.'

12

RUSSIAN ADVENTURES

Wonderful, Woeful St. Petersburg

Love affair with Russia started in teens – Chaliapin and Tolstoy – visits to Moscow and Leningrad – Gorbachev at Bolshoi – Russian IOC Members – Anatoly Sobchak, Mayor of Leningrad and adviser, Vladimir Putin, in Manchester and Leningrad – with Prince Charles in newly renamed St. Petersburg – final work visit to Russia

My love affair with Russia started in my teens. It was not politically motivated. To me, in my post-war innocence, Stalin was merely sinister and Khrushchev a fool, and at that age my interest in Russia was only to do with the romance of the country, the literature and the music. As my voice deepened and my own singing improved, I discovered and adored Russian folk songs and popular music and the Red Army Choir. I was also mad about the liturgical music of the Russian Orthodox Church. I not only loved the voices I loved the sadness and the richness of the music. They put me on the edge of tears and the balalaika backing choked me up. It was the very quiet singing that really got to me rather than the full-blooded roar of a hundred basses. I moved on to the literature and read *War and Peace* quite young. Pierre became my hero. I found Borodino riveting and the Masonic bits baffling.

Another influence was a trio of pictures in my grandmother's house. They were three large watercolours in handsome frames of mid nineteenth-century Russian rural life by Pyotr Petrovich Sokolov. My great-grandmother told me that they had been given to her grandfather, the notable Victorian water engineer, James Easton, by a grateful city for the work he had done in creating fountains in St. Petersburg. Easton, an associate of Bazalgette, had been responsible for the almost impossibly difficult engineering of the fountains in Trafalgar Square and the draining of the Kent marshes. Where two of these pictures are now I have no idea but the best one – of a three-horse troika at the key dramatic moment of overturning at speed in the snow – now sits above the fireplace in my drawing room.

One of my unlikely teenage heroes was the Russian bass Feodor Chaliapin. By this time he was well dead – he died in 1938 – but records remained and his reputation as a formidable, larger-than-life figure lived on. A good friend of my grandmother was the now almost forgotten composer and conductor Lawrance Collingwood, a student of Glazunov in St. Petersburg, who almost single-handedly got Sadlers Wells Opera through the Second World War, touring the company around the country. Gran told me that he had amongst many other things conducted Chaliapin. I was desperate to meet him. She took me to his strange house in a converted disused railway station for tea and I begged to be told about Chaliapin. 'A big man, a difficult man but with a huge voice and an extraordinary stage presence,' said Lawrance Collingwood, who was a very mild man and rather small.

'Like many such artists,' Collingwood said, 'he was not the most accurate singer. Once I remember during a final stage rehearsal for Boris with full orchestra he sang a wrong note in an aria and I stopped him and pointed out his error. He was not best pleased. He marched to the front of the stage and roared at me, "A wrong note! A wrong note! Do you not know, when I am like this, I can kill a man?" I was not impressed and reminded him that it was our job to play and sing what the composer had written. He tried to bully me and I would not have it. Anyway, he was not the best Russian bass I ever conducted. Have you ever heard of the Ukrainian Mark Reizen?' I admitted I had not. He put on his turntable an old 78 and out came this smooth, beautiful, deep voice and that was Mark Reizen. He too sang all over the world but he never created the same stir as Chaliapin. I cannot remember what he sang – it was a song, not an operatic aria, I remember that – but I can hear the voice in my head still. This must have been in 1961 and I am ashamed to say I never met

Collingwood again. Ashamed because he did not die until 1982 and I cannot bear to think of all the conversations I could have had with him.

The final piece in my jigsaw of youthful Russian discovery was a trip to Covent Garden in December 1962. As I have said earlier my favourite master at Haileybury was Basil Edwards who had directed me as King Lear. When it was all over, and had been counted a success, he said that he wanted to give a few of us a present and suggested we go to London to the theatre. I could choose. I said that I had never been to Covent Garden. He got tickets for us to see Boris Christoff in *Boris Godunov*. I did not know quite what to expect and was unprepared for the overwhelming experience. The spectacle, the music, the choruses, the designs, the theatre itself, but above all the performance of Christoff, simply stunned me. I date wanting to be involved in the theatre, particularly then as a singer and actor, from that performance. Some four and a half years later, when I had sensibly given up wanting to be a singer, I wrote off to all the great London institutions looking for work as an 'assistant' this or that. I got an interview with the resident producer at the Royal Opera House, Ande Anderson, who started our conversation with the reasonable question of why I wanted to join an opera house. I answered slightly pompously along the lines of how opera was in my view the only art form that combines everything – music, visual art, dance and drama, and that, when it works, it knocks all the others into a cocked hat. 'Has it ever worked for you like that?' he asked. 'Only once,' I said. 'When was that?' he asked. 'Here, in this very building nearly five years ago, when I saw Boris Christoff in *Boris Godunov*,' I answered. 'Ah, you have done your research, I see. That was my production.' Nothing I could say would persuade him that I did not know who the producer was and that I had not prepared my answer. Anyway, he was very nice and offered me a job, which ultimately I did not take up. I am still not sure why.

Already, by the age of twenty-two, what with Christoff, Tolstoy, Rachmaninoff, the choirs, I was hooked on Russian culture. Then the glorious movie of *Dr Zhivago* was released with its balalaika score, troikas and snow (not to mention Julie Christie) and I was gone. I have never lost my passion for things Russian. Indeed, as my theatre life unfolded my devotion to more geniuses like Chekhov, Prokofiev, Tchaikovsky, Dostoyevsky, Solzhenitsyn deepened. I read about Peter the Great and Catherine the Great. I discovered *Anna Karenina* and the extraordinary story of Tolstoy and his devoted but dreadfully treated wife Sonya. Meanwhile, I had lost my political naivety and read voraciously about Lenin and Trotsky and Stalin. The appalling barbarity was there, but so were the heroism and the magnificence. The experience, however, was always at one remove. It was in the theatre or in the concert hall, on screen or in a book. There was Eisenstein, the Ken Russell films, Anthony Hopkins in the BBC's *War and Peace*, Solzhenitsyn's *One Day in the Life of Ivan Denisovich*, Rachmaninoff's piano concerto in the movie of *Brief Encounter*, *Dr Zhivago*, Prokofiev's *Romeo and Juliet*, *Uncle Vanya* with Albert Finney and Leo McKern at the Royal Exchange. It all fed the fascination. I just wanted to go there, especially to Leningrad.

Finally, I would get to visit. It all began in the late 1980s, when the Royal Opera House had broken their commitment to make Manchester their second home. Russia was one of the countries I decided to visit in search of world class opera and ballet for the Palace. In those days life in Russia was very grim. Although a great thaw would set in with Mikhail Gorbachev, you still had to make very clear plans for a visit to Russia with every flight, train journey and hotel booked and approved in advance. My first trip was in 1985 with a second in 1987. On the first trip I only visited Moscow, the second I went on to Leningrad and flew home from there. I had to have official invitations from both the Bolshoi in Moscow and the Kirov in Leningrad before setting out. Over the course of almost ten years, between 1985 and 1994, I must have made nine journeys to Moscow and Leningrad for very different reasons. During that extraordinary period, the Soviet Union collapsed, Leningrad became St. Petersburg again, the Kirov became the Mariinsky again and the state of the two great cities went from bad to worse. During the same period I hosted several visits to Manchester from the two main Russian cities. What I did not foresee, when I made my first 'arts' visit to Russia, was that sport would also take me there later. Nor did I know then that in 1991 I would meet and get to work with a very famous man indeed.

On my first visit to Moscow I was on my own. Well, sort of. I was met by a black car and I had a Bolshoi host pretty well 24/7. In the faded Hotel National there was a lady at a desk by the lift on each floor checking me in and out. She never spoke nor smiled. The phone made funny clicking sounds. The food was grim and the wine worse. The rouble was a joke, with a pound worth very little at the hotel desk and about seven times more from the shady man who sidled up to me in the street as I left the hotel. Beautiful young ladies approached me in the bar and sought me out. I wandered out of the hotel to sightsee or shop. The sightseeing was sensational, the shopping non-existent. I remember wandering round the legendary department store Gum and passing endless stalls with nothing on them. The only excitement was when a crowd gathered in seconds at one stall, where a consignment of shoes had suddenly arrived. I watched, horrified, as people grabbed whatever they could. Whether they were the right colour or size or design or left or right did not seem to matter.

Sadly, the Bolshoi Theatre itself was closed for repairs, so I was taken to the Light Opera Theatre. The performance was so dreadful I can remember nothing about it, not even the name of the piece I saw. The next morning I was shown round the Bolshoi Ballet School. Now that was fantastic. There cannot be another ballet school with such facilities in the world. It was huge with endless practice rooms, all with sprung floors, and hundreds of almost identical children moving silently and swiftly between lessons. I never saw such perfect behaviour from twelve-year-olds. My first efforts to bring the Bolshoi to Manchester were wholly unsuccessful.

On my second visit to Moscow in 1987 the Bolshoi had reopened and I was given a ticket for a ballet gala. I walked to the theatre to discover extraordinary security in place. I had to show my ticket to get into the square in front of the theatre as well as at the front door of the theatre itself. There was security everywhere. I was in the stalls and everyone was standing, with their backs to the stage, waiting for a celebrity entrance into the Czar's Box – it is still called that! Into the box walked, to a studied silence, General Jaruzelski, the President of Poland, and his glamourous peroxide-blonde wife, followed by Mikhail and Raisa Gorbachev, who were greeted by wild applause. The gala was like all galas with little bits of this and that and it went well. At the end Gorbachev waved to the applauding, cheering audience. He then made a bad mistake. He took Jaruzelski's hand in his and raised it in the air like a boxer. The audience booed violently. I never saw a hand dropped quicker and they all made a speedy exit. This was 1987 and clearly that Russian audience preferred Lech Walesa to the diminutive General in dark glasses. Once again I drew a blank in Moscow despite several meetings.

I went straight from the theatre to the station to catch the overnight sleeper to Leningrad, an experience someone had recommended to me. Although it was April it was bitterly cold and there was a light snow falling. I had a small suitcase which a large, elderly, heavily bearded porter insisted on taking from me and putting on his old-fashioned trolley. He grunted to me to follow him. Picture the scene. I am walking almost the length of the platform, through tiny snowflakes falling in the dim yellowish light, following a large man in a great trench coat, fur hat, boots and a six-inch-wide leather belt holding the coat flaps together. We get to my carriage and he hands me up the steps to a babushka who has a samovar of tea waiting and takes me to my compartment. It was a scene from *Anna Karenina*. The compartment was fairly spartan but I had it to myself and it was warm and clean. The toilet at the end of the carriage was disgusting. The train was slow and I sleep badly on trains. I woke very early and looked out at miles and miles of snow-speckled silver birches rolling by, punctuated by the occasional village waking up with people in smocks and coats and headscarves walking to their work with horses and carts slowly moving about. It looked like a nineteenth-century painting and was beautiful as the sun rose.

In those days the streets of both Moscow and Leningrad were dismal. There was no colour. There was very little lighting. It was a wholly grey world. There were no colourful advertising hoardings. There were no enticing shop windows. The people were colourless too. On both trips it was cold and although the long coats and hats were probably brown or blue or black they all looked grey. There were uniforms everywhere but nothing in scarlet or gold. There seemed to be a lot of police stamping their grey boots on the grey pavement snow, blowing whistles at you if you took one step off the kerb. I had my scheduled meetings with theatre managers and ballet masters and they were friendly. Yes, they wanted to tour to England, but they did not know when or how much it would cost. Now they had met me they would come and visit my theatre soon. 'When?' I asked. They did not know.

Despite the prevailing gloom, I had more success in Leningrad than Moscow. Leningrad was twinned with Manchester and, curiously, Leningrad took the twinning more seriously than Manchester, largely, I think, because twinning trips for Soviet officials out of Russia were highly prized. As a result, on my first visit, I was excellently looked after by the amiable Margarita Mudrak, the head of the House of Friendship, which looked after thirty 'special relationships' with foreign cities. Sadly, the hotel I had been allocated was even more awful than the one in Moscow. It was the infamous and massive Pribaltiskaya Hotel with 5,000 poky rooms on the Gulf of Finland, miles from the city centre. *I will not stay here if I come again*, I decided. My chief target in Leningrad was the Kirov Ballet. I had already discovered that the opera companies in both cities would probably be out of my league financially. I went to see the ballet on two successive nights at the glorious Kirov Theatre. Like the Bolshoi Theatre the Kirov also had a Czar's Box. This is where I sat with seven others. When my next-door neighbour raised her arms to applaud I discovered that BO could pretty well ruin an evening out, even in the most beautiful theatre. *Introducing deodorant to Russia could make you rich*, I thought. In truth, my whole evening was ghastly from start to finish. What I did not fully realise before my visit was that the Kirov had at least five companies and at my first performance I saw what was clearly the fifth company in what was simply the worst ballet I had ever seen: a wretched show with wretched dancers and wretched music. It was the only occasion when I have ever seen two ballerinas circling each other on pointe, chatting to each other. I went to bed deeply depressed. I could not sell that in Manchester. The next night with some foreboding I went again. This time I saw the first company in the first performance of a revival of *Le Corsair*, the same production that had launched Nureyev years before. It was electrifying. Now this was exactly what I was looking for. I finally did get the Kirov Ballet to come to Manchester in 1989 during a Western European tour, not, sadly, the first company, but the second, and they were good, but the music was provided by a scratch British orchestra.

The atmosphere of Leningrad in 1987 and 1989 was like Moscow – grey, cold, poor and deeply unhappy. Yet there was a beauty and coherence about Leningrad that moved me – far more than Moscow. There is, of course, a stunning historic centre to Moscow but away from the Kremlin and Red Square and the river it soon becomes overwhelmingly dreary. Everywhere you looked in Leningrad it was majestic: the river, the canals, the bridges, the Peter and Paul Fortress, the Hermitage, Nevski Prospect, the Smolny, other palaces – you could go on and on. And while I was walking about dazzled by Peter the Great's city, I got very lucky.

The big prize I was always after, but was certain I would miss, was the Kirov Opera. I had more or less dropped the idea on the grounds of cost. Then I was invited to meet Yuri Temirkanov, the music director of the company, and he told me he was in negotiation with a new British management company called the Entertainment Corporation to bring the company to London. 'You must come to Manchester,' I pleaded. 'Fine by me,' he responded. On somebody's advice I had brought with me two bottles of whisky as gifts. He got them both and we became friends! When I got home, I contacted Peter Brightman, the CEO of the Entertainment Corporation, and persuaded him, with guarantees, to bring the company to Manchester for a week after their short season at the Coliseum. It would be their last week in Britain. It was fantastically good fortune – we got the full works – a Russian season of Tchaikovsky's *Queen of Spades* and *Eugene Onegin* as well as Mussorgsky's *Boris Godunov*. The company brought great soloists, including the then unknown but brilliant baritone Sergei Leiferkus, the full chorus and orchestra, with my new chum, Temirkanov, conducting every performance – about 290 people in all.

The Kirov Opera week at the Palace was sensational. I was in the theatre every night. The designs were huge but somehow simple. The chorus was superb and the strings of the orchestra made a noise the like of which I had never heard before, especially the cellos and double basses. We had some interesting problems that week. The company was spread around three mid-range Manchester hotels and the deal was that they got bed and breakfast and a £9 (I think) per diem during their five weeks in the country. Many of them had decided they would live on breakfast alone and save most of their per diems. The poor hotels never knew what hit them. Trays of eggs, sausages, bacon, beans, toast would arrive and instantly disappear. More was called for and then more.

They were also serious shoppers and asked our nice young assistant stage manager – a quiet girl – if she could take a group of them to this famous shop called Boots. 'Of course,' she said. When they got there, she asked what they wanted. 'Condoms,' they said. When they had stripped Boots of every box of condoms in the store, they asked her to take them to other pharmacies for more, many more. She was shocked. Then on the Friday a small deputation of three members of the chorus came to see me to ask politely if I would allow them to miss the last night's performance. 'Why?' I asked. I was not sure I had the authority, but I did not think the audience would miss three people. 'We have hired big lorry and we go to big depot in Luton to collect washing machines, fridges, televisions we order,' – hundreds of them apparently, all to be paid for from their per diems in cash. They had hired a container in Felixstowe and they needed to pay for their 'white goods' and see the container off home. They were going back on Sunday. How could I say no? The only problem for the Palace was that it took weeks to rid the dressing rooms of uniquely grim BO. But they were sensational.

For a year or so Leningrad Opera had to take a back seat as I focused on the first Manchester Olympic bid and our presentation to the IOC in Tokyo in September 1990. However, this other part of my life brought me back to Moscow. As I have explained elsewhere, our search for Olympic votes both in Tokyo in 1990 (for the 1996 Games) and in Monte Carlo in 1993 (for the 2000 Games) took us to every corner of the earth. Russia and Eastern Europe was one of my patches. Anastasia Limb was my wonderful Bulgarian assistant who spoke beautiful Russian and came with me on a complicated journey to Belgrade, Bratislava, Budapest, Warsaw, Sofia and Moscow in August 1990. In each city lived either one or two IOC Members. Moscow was much our most important port of call. The two members there were real IOC heavyweights – Vitaly Smirnov and Marat Gramov – who had both been deeply involved in the 1980 Moscow Olympics. They were not popular in the movement as a whole but they led the Eastern European bloc of about twelve IOC members and no one knew where these votes might end up, assuming Belgrade went out in the first round, which they duly did.

Our first planned event that August night in Moscow was a disaster. The two members and the General Secretary of the Russian Olympic Committee, Nikolai Lents, had all agreed to come to dinner at one of Moscow's most exclusive restaurants, the Stanislavsky, with David Logan, the Minister in the British Embassy (the number two), Anastasia and me. Sir Roderic Braithwaite, the Ambassador, was in London. 'I shall not be surprised if no one shows up,' David said cheerfully. 'Oh, no, surely not,' I protested. 'They have all agreed to come.' He was correct. No one appeared. He rolled his eyes. The three of us ate alone and very well. I quizzed David about Russia. Steeped as I was in all things Russian, I found David extremely sceptical about the glory that is Russia for people like me. 'All the singing and dancing and weeping and loving turns me on,' I said. 'And the defeats of Napoleon and Hitler had been heroic, surely,' I insisted. David gently explained. 'I do not differentiate between Russia and the Soviet Union. The world is divided into those who love this country and those who do not. The Foreign Office has a rule. The Ambassador can be an enthusiast or a sceptic, so long as his deputy is whatever he is not. I am the resident sceptic! My Ambassador is more your type!' During dinner we at least got a message that the meeting at 10am the next morning would still proceed.

Bang on time a big black car arrived at the hotel and Anastasia and I were driven to the newly named Russian Olympic offices. Both grand members were there waiting for us. I was ecstatic. This was what we had come for. We had what can only be described as a robust discussion. At least, Smirnov, who spoke good English, and I did, while Gramov flirted gently with Anastasia in a corner. Smirnov was very aggressive. Remember Mrs Thatcher was still, just, prime minister. 'Why are the British now so unimportant in the world of sports when they used to be number one? Why does your government not support your bid more? Why did Mrs Thatcher try to wreck the Moscow Olympic Games? Why can you not control your lying journalists? Why have you not built the necessary new facilities yet?' I did my best to defend my country, my government and myself and he relaxed. He did this to everyone apparently – attack. 'We will not vote for a US City. Australia is too far away. Athens is a joke. So is Istanbul. We support Belgrade but they will go out in the first round.' This left Manchester as their only choice! I did not believe a word of it. I went home depressed. It was the most direct and open chat I had had with a major player but how could we make up the necessary ground? I knew in my bones that Manchester was simply not glamourous enough. I am confident Manchester never received a single Warsaw Pact vote.

Suddenly and unexpectedly in April 1991 when Manchester's second Olympic bid was rapidly taking over my life, Leningrad raised its head again. The first and newly elected Mayor of Leningrad, Anatoly Sobchak, had been invited by our Foreign Office to make a whistle-stop trip to London. The purpose of his visit was to learn about British inner-city regeneration and all the management issues that needed to be understood and implemented in his city. He insisted that he wanted to spend part of a day in Manchester, his twin city. He would come for lunch. I knew nothing of this until I received a call from a friend Sue Causey, a Russian speaker, who was already working with the Town Hall to develop relations between Manchester and Leningrad. She and I had kept in close touch over securing the visit of the Kirov Companies. This was Thursday 4th April 1991 and she needed help on Monday the 8th when Mayor Sobchak was to be in town. 'Everybody is out,' she explained. 'They have given us no notice and the Lord Mayor is out, the Leader is out, the Town Clerk is out. You have got to come to the Town Hall and host a lunch for the Mayor and pretend you are all the people who cannot be there!' Just three people were coming – Mr and Mrs Sobchak and his Foreign Affairs Adviser. I liked the idea and I enjoyed the lunch. I especially enjoyed the Mayor. By the end of our lunch he was insistent that I should come to Leningrad. 'I need your help,' he said. I was flattered, but I discovered that he said this to everyone and, of course, he was right. Everyone knew that his city was in a serious mess.

The Lord Mayor of Manchester came back to the Town Hall from his lunch appointment and formal photographs were taken with me flanking the Mayors on one side and Leningrad's Foreign Affairs Adviser on the other. He was a short man with blond hair, a puffed-out chest and a Crimplene suit. His name was Vladimir Putin. Sobchak wanted me to come to Leningrad and he said Mr Putin would be my contact. A new chapter in my Russian story had opened. Someone told me that Putin was not the Mayor's adviser at all but his KGB minder. Who knows? They always seemed close. I did not speak Russian and Putin did not speak English, so we communicated through Sue. We wrote to each other and met again several times. Putin proved to be a deeply inefficient bureaucrat, but I noticed that every time he wrote to me his title had become grander. In the mid-1990s when my relationship with Sobchak and Putin and St. Petersburg (as Leningrad had become again) finished, I forgot about him. My astonishment when Putin became President in May 2000 was total. I simply recognised him on the BBC TV News. His meteoric rise seems to me to be one of the most unlikely journeys in history.

As a result of his visit in April, from the 4th to the 11th August 1991 I made a serious visit to Leningrad. I was there as an official guest of Mayor Sobchak and there was competition between various departments of the Town Hall for the doubtful honour of being my host. Sue Causey was the vital interpreter and link. I discovered that Sobchak had created a Renaissance Foundation for the city and he wanted to talk to me about it: a sort of 'Venice in Peril' concept for another city which was going 'under'. My real host that week was another Margarita, Margarita Gromyko, a good deal more formidable than the gentle Margarita Mudrak, the House of Friendship lady. This Margarita was Head of the Inter-City Relations Department of the City Council – the Lensoviet – working to Putin. She was an old-fashioned Soviet bureaucrat and was deeply depressed about the way the city and country were going. She warned us not to believe too much in Sobchak. She told us we could not trust Putin. Prophetically, she said that Gorbachev's days were over, that Yeltsin was contemptible and Sobchak was in her words 'no politician'.

We had no idea that just eleven days later Gorbachev would narrowly survive a coup and his days and the Soviet Union itself would have collapsed by Christmas. On that August visit I met several times with Sobchak; he confirmed his invitation to become an International Trustee of his Renaissance Foundation. I promised to do what I could (very little, I reckoned) to help win influential friends for Leningrad in London. I mentioned Prince Charles who was famously dedicated to the restoration of historic cities and buildings. Sobchak thought that would be fantastic. He told me that his city would soon return to its old name of St. Petersburg and he begged me to get Prince Charles to visit.

The next day at a big press launch in a beautiful palace on the Krestovskii Island, he signed the contract for Leningrad to host the Goodwill Games in 1994. These Games were a poor Ted Turner/CNN concept to bring the sports worlds of the Soviet Union and the USA closer together after the bitter boycotts of the 1980 Moscow and 1984 Los Angeles Olympic Games. Sobchak publicly introduced me as a distinguished guest and major player in the Olympic movement, and also as the personal representative of Prince Charles and Princess Anne. I was deeply embarrassed and appalled that such words might ever be published. Still the week passed memorably. Perhaps the highlight was a private tour around the Hermitage, organised by Margarita Gromyko. Our guide was Vladimir Metveev, the Deputy Director. The tour included a dark and almost dangerous visit to a recently opened-up area beneath the gem-like private theatre – unknown for 150 years – where rooms and passages of Peter the Great's first Winter Palace had just been discovered. A private tour of the Hermitage on a late summer afternoon after the crowds have left is amazing. Just three weeks later, on September 6th, as Gorbachev was fighting for his political life, Leningrad became St. Petersburg again.

When we got home Sue and I set out to try to interest Prince Charles. We began the complicated process of trying to get to Royalty. Happily, the Prince was interested but, inevitably, he and his marvellous Private Secretary, Peter Westmacott, were very cautious about being able to offer much. There was the not inconsiderable family matter of the Romanov assassinations to be overcome. It was agreed that any progress on the Prince's personal involvement should be handled through his International Business in the Community team and slow but steady progress was made. I persuaded Peter to ask the Prince to meet two emissaries from Mayor Sobchak. Sobchak had become something of an international hero for having resisted the coup leaders, keeping the Army out of the city and restoring the name of St. Petersburg. In fact, he was now being talked of seriously as a potential successor to Yeltsin.

Sue and I took Margarita Gromyko and the top St. Petersburg archaeologist Professor Boris Ometov to Highgrove to talk with Prince Charles. An official invitation for the Prince to visit St. Petersburg was handed over and duly noted. He repeated that he would like to come but that the matter was sensitive. During this period I received several letters from Putin, some in Russian, some in fractured English. One nice one was in response to an invitation we sent to Mayor Sobchak to visit the Prince privately in Britain in November 1991:

Dear Mr Scott
    I wish to express my appreciation for your letter where you inform us about the interest of His Majesty Prince of Wales to the problems of St. Petersburg and his desire to contribute to the development of our city.

Unfortunately, the visit of Mr. Sobchak to the United Kingdom is not possible now due to the very difficult situation in the city.

At the same time we would be very glad to meet His Majesty Prince of Wales in our city and ready to assist this visit.

I take this opportunity of wishing you all very best and send my kind regards.

Sincerely yours
PUTIN V.V.
Chairman of the Committee for External Relations
(NB Putin's new title.)

Wheels turn slowly in such delicate matters as a senior member of the Royal Family visiting Russia. In the end the Prince did go to St. Petersburg for four days in May 1994. Once again Peter Westmacott, who later became successively British Ambassador in Paris and Washington, was great. I was a member of the group accompanying the Prince. It was, I suppose, a typical private royal visit. There were welcomes and dinners and speeches and visits to conservation initiatives.

One morning we all made our way to a colossal old warehouse, acres of it, in an industrial zone. It was totally empty except for a very small group of people working with wood and fabric in a tiny distant corner. 'What are they doing?' asked someone. 'Making deckchairs,' was the truthful answer. 'What used to happen here?' asked someone else. 'Oh! This was the biggest factory in the Soviet Union for building bogies for railway wagons,' we were informed. We were all disconsolately wandering about the acres of emptiness and I walked to one large door to the side and opened it. There, almost as far as the eye could see, were more acres of abandoned yard on which were stacked literally thousands of rusting bogies; ones which would never now be attached to a railway engine. Once massive railway bogies for an Empire, now deckchairs. It was pitiful.

At the same time, modest projects were identified, agreements were signed and it was announced that the British Council would be opening an office and library in the city. Putin was in attendance at all times and it is ironic, remembering the part he played in setting up HRH's visit, that it was Putin himself who angrily closed down this cultural exchange effort in 2008. At the time the Prince's visit went well, the ice was broken, and five months after her son's visit, the Queen visited Russia herself. Sue and I felt we had at least made a small contribution to world affairs!

My final working visit to St. Petersburg was in July 1994. I went for three reasons: to attend a Trustees meeting of the Renaissance Foundation, to attend the Goodwill Games and to see Mayor Sobchak. They were all depressing occasions. The Foundation was falling apart with accusations swirling around of financial mismanagement or worse. Certainly, there seemed to be no evidence of any progress. There had been a successful fundraising telethon for the Foundation which had raised millions of roubles. Now people wanted to know what had happened to the money. The answers were thin.

The 1994 Goodwill Games, after the glories of the Barcelona Olympics in 1992, were absurd, with a series of events going on in a deserted stadium which delighted no one. I sat with equally appalled sports journalists from *The Times*, the *Guardian*, the *Telegraph* and the *Mail*, whom I had got to know well during my Olympic years. We watched the most boring athletics event I have ever had to endure, namely the 20km walk, the whole of which took place in the stadium. This meant that the walkers, who looked pretty odd anyway, had to go round and round the track about eighty times in about an hour and a half. The gentleman who came last was so bad that as the winner was crossing the line, he still had six more laps to go, which we solemnly had to sit through. At least in the Olympics the walkers walk nineteen and three-quarters of their kilometres round the streets of the city and only enter the stadium for the last lap.

Finally, my meeting with the Mayor was affectionate but sad. Putin was not with us. I could not imagine the trouble Sobchak was in. On the one hand, he seemed not to be suffering from any stress from his impossible situation – he was resolutely cheerful and optimistic. On the other he seemed almost completely out of touch with reality. He considered the Goodwill Games were a triumph and the progress of the Foundation splendid. He wanted the Olympics in St. Petersburg and wanted me to help him get them. We kept in touch for a few months but I wondered how long he would be in office. The answer was little more than a year.

On my last day I had a meeting in a flat on the fourth floor of a crumbling block with Manchester's representative in St. Petersburg, Catherine Philips. Almost my last thoughts on St. Petersburg and Russia come straight from my diary of that visit.

The entrance to Catherine's block of flats is horrendous, smelling of urine, with a rubbish skip full of rotting waste with cats digging into it, smelling in the heatwave, right across from her front door. Her flat is very pretty but the common areas disgusting. I decide to take the trolleybus from her flat back to the hotel. I stand in a queue behind a woman who has the most terrible elephantiasis of one arm with a claw of a hand on the end of it. In front of her is a man with clearly dreadful jaundice who is almost completely yellow. Everybody seems to be pale and ill, enjoying the last few days of sunshine before the autumn and then the winter viciously descend in September.

St. Petersburg is utterly confusing. It is so beautiful, so magnificent. Russians, one to one, are lovely. But it is rotting. You feel a little like an aid worker must feel in the Congo. What do you do? It is so vast, so crumbling. I love it here but I thank God when the plane for home takes off. Poor Russia.

I never saw Sobchak or Putin again. In 1995 St. Petersburg descended into major internal power struggles and in 1996 Mayor Sobchak was deposed as Mayor and he fled to Paris. In the same year, Deputy Mayor of St. Petersburg Putin (yet another promotion) moved to Moscow to work for Boris Yeltsin before succeeding him. On the 20th February 2000 suddenly, and some say suspiciously, Anatoly Sobchak, aged sixty-two, died on a visit to Kaliningrad. Some say Putin was loyal to the end, others say he was no friend at all. It was clear, however, that they had once been close.

I have been back once to St. Petersburg again, as a tourist with Alicia in 2017. We met none of the people I used to know. I had gone on and on about the city and she wanted to see it for herself. It is very different now. There is lots of colour, the shops seem full, the hotel was excellent. The Kirov Theatre is the Mariinsky Theatre again and we saw a good production of *The Flying Dutchman*. The number of uniforms on the streets in the 1990s used to make it a very safe city to walk in. You see few uniforms now. It feels threatening. You watch where you go. Sad for such a sensational city.

13

ROUNDABOUT ROUTE TO GREENWICH

Apollo, the Commonwealth Games, Bermuda and a New Life

Marriage over, no job, a knighthood, awards – strange time – portfolio life – Alicia moves to England – Apollo Leisure – London Lyceum fiasco – Commonwealth Games and wedding in Bermuda – leave Manchester for Greenwich for Millennium planning

By the end of 1993 I had lived and worked in Manchester for twenty-five years. I had been involved in building, restoring, running theatres and turning a bingo hall back into a theatre. Raymond Slater and I had had both fun and success but now the theatres had new owners, Apollo Leisure, and I was only involved part-time. The Olympic bids had been a demanding mistress, but that affair was over. I was still married to Su but we had separated, never to speak again, and I had begun living with Alicia. My children were angry with me and that is miserable when you want to be a good father. It all brought a sense of failure even though I was blissful with my new partner. Overall, I suppose the balance of success and failure in love and work was fairly even, but I was muddled. I had 'won a few and lost a few'. I was determined to be positive. It was clearly high time to have another victory or two. But who and what was I now?

It was a strange period. I had income from various sources but it was barely adequate. Divorce, I discovered, was expensive. I had become the chairman of Manchester's commercial radio station, Piccadilly Radio, which was interesting. I had various small consultancies. I received fees for after-dinner speeches. The city agreed to pay me an Olympic clearing-up fee. I was receiving my reduced fee from Apollo. I had also become quite well known. I received a knighthood 'for services to the community and sport in Manchester'. Yet I could not throw off the bleak feeling that I had only been awarded it for another worthy British failure. Indeed, Olympic effort or failure – call it what you will – combined with my theatre work had brought me a clutch of honours – Honorary Degrees and Fellowships, Mancunian of the Year (twice), the French *Ordre des Arts et des Lettres* (in the same list, I might say, as Arnold Schwarzenegger), 'Man of the Year' awards from the English Tourist Board and the Institute of Public Relations – but mostly I felt failure. I also knew that my life, either with a move to London or remaining in Manchester, had to be resolved. I had never formally applied for a job but I thought I might have to start looking soon. I was nearly fifty and the truth was that I did not know what I wanted or was competent to do.

When the theatres had been sold in 1991 to Apollo, I could frankly have been out on my ear the next day. Partly because I had been so identified with the revival of the theatres and partly because Paul Gregg, the Apollo Chairman, could see that I might be able to help his expanding empire, he asked me to join Apollo on an annual consultancy fee with a car. This was generous at the time because I needed an income to allow me to continue my Olympic adventures and he knew that I would be away a lot. I was frank with him that my new consultancy role would have to be 'occasional' – I could help him in Manchester, assisting his new manager, and on any special project that might arise as an 'ambassador'. At this time Apollo was busy around the country buying up grand old theatres which had been run into the ground and I helped with the setting up of new management of some of them. Apollo also had cinema interests and I got involved with those. One day I would be in Glasgow, in Liverpool or in Torquay. It helped Paul with some of the main London producers for them to think that I was still involved with the Manchester theatres, the most important commercial theatres outside London. I got on well with his theatre division director, Sam Shrouder, and his property man, Steve Lavelle. However, for much of the last three years I had often been absent from my own theatre office and that was going to get worse.

Friends and colleagues in the theatre world were rather disapproving that I could maintain a relationship with Apollo after they bought the two theatres. They wondered how someone with a background in the Royal Exchange Theatre, who had brought both the Palace and Opera House from commercial into charitable ownership, who was a member of several Arts Council committees and panels, in short, someone who seemed to have the 'subsidised arts' gene in his DNA, could stoop so low as to join the ultra-commercial and somewhat predatory world of Apollo Leisure. They suggested I had 'sold out'.

Inevitably, I did not see it as they did. My chief motivation for several years had been the Olympic bid and I had been determined not to draw a penny from our bid funds as a salary. I needed income and Paul Gregg provided it. The theatres had to be sold because Raymond Slater was in trouble, not because I had failed. No one else was offering me help. I think Paul Gregg rather enjoyed my Olympic aspirations and he was happy to enable them. Now with all thoughts of another Olympic bid dead and buried I felt it was my duty to start working a bit harder for him. Apollo had been good to me. I felt honour-bound to repay the debt.

Perhaps my best work for Paul was in helping him secure a great London theatre against fierce opposition. The fabulous Lyceum Theatre, Sir Henry Irving's famous building just off the Strand, had had a chequered history and since the war no one had been able to obtain sufficiently long-term tenancy to justify proper investment. The theatre was in a poor state. For years it had been a Mecca Ballroom, living on six-month licences. It was also official post-war London County Council policy that the theatre would be demolished to make way for a giant roundabout at the north end of Waterloo Bridge. The Lyceum was in limbo. The LCC would not sell a long lease or a freehold but demolition was forbidden when the government, after great pressure, invoked the Theatres Act 1968.

At last things began to move. The property developer George Walker, the brother of the boxer Billy Walker, secured title to the building but he never had sufficient funds or planning clout to develop it in the way he wanted. The Theatres Trust, a quasi-government agency, had helped stop the theatre being demolished and expected it to fall into its own hands as a result of these prevarications. Under their noses in 1994, Apollo, goaded on by me, stepped in and did a deal with George Walker direct. We relied on the maxim that possession was nine parts of the law.

Like the other vultures circling we had decided the Lyceum was an incredibly valuable performance space because there were too few large 2,000-seat theatres in London for the big musicals which were now, after years of famine, multiplying at a great rate. The shows had a life expectancy way beyond that of *My Fair Lady*, *West Side Story*, *Hello Dolly!* and *Oliver!* – twenty years, possibly, rather than three. Just think of *Superstar*, *Evita*, *Cats*, *Les Misérables*, *Phantom of the Opera* and *Mamma Mia*. And to prove the correctness of our thinking, Disney's *The Lion King* has now played over twenty years at the Lyceum. The potential audience had grown massively as the middle class expanded and had more spending power. The London theatre establishment were furious with Apollo, but Paul Gregg had acted wholly properly and boldly.

What happened next was ridiculous and, ironically, involved the subsidised arts world, namely the Royal Opera House and the Arts Council. In my view they behaved contemptuously towards a so-called greedy commercial operator. It still enrages me. The talk of the London arts world was how the Royal Companies would deal with the necessary two-year closure period of the Royal Opera House for massive alteration and restoration. It was unthinkable to sack the orchestra, chorus, dancers and technical staff for those two years. Touring was considered prohibitively expensive, so Apollo put in an offer to help. The Royal Companies could have first use of the Lyceum.

The Lyceum is about a hundred yards from the Royal Opera House. Of course, the new Lyceum stage, while huge, would be smaller than that of the Royal Opera House. However, with some financial help from the Arts Council we could improve and increase our facilities beyond our own existing plans and the ROH would be able to show a repertoire of their more modest opera and ballet productions – Mozart and Puccini rather than Wagner. It would suit everyone. The Royal Companies could be kept going with some compromise. They could run the Lyceum themselves for an appropriate rent and then reopen Covent Garden with a big bang and major new-minted productions, which was what everyone wanted. Their audience would not be inconvenienced even if some of them turned up at the wrong theatre a few yards up the road. Apollo in turn would get a better equipped theatre and a proper rent. A good deal for everyone.

There was one problem. The decision had to be taken quickly because we were about to start building works and we were in the last stages of negotiation with Andrew Lloyd Webber for his revival of *Jesus Christ Superstar* to reopen the theatre. There followed a great deal of technical discussion, which went well. The chairman of the Royal Opera House liked the idea, the Arts Council were OK with it but were understandably nervous about contributing too much public money to a commercial building. We assured them that they would be saving a fortune. The net result would be the cheapest solution. The Royal Opera and Ballet directors were also happy. But one or two others, who had impossibly grandiose dreams for a temporary Opera House somewhere on the banks of the Thames for two years, had other ideas. Their thinking was fantasy.

The ROH board and management dithered; deadlines came and went and Andrew LW wanted to secure his date and start selling tickets. Finally, this really good idea for the ROH was aborted. What was so infuriating was that an enormous amount of work and high-level meetings had gone into planning an acceptable solution, only to come to nothing. And as we predicted, the closure period famously ended up being a mess and costing taxpayers millions. An enraging coda was that months later, after our building works were well under way and thousands of advance tickets for *Superstar* had been sold, I had a call from Virginia Bottomley, the relevant minister, asking us to reopen the Lyceum/ROH question as everyone now agreed it was the best solution. She got short shrift. It is long ago now but the saga was little short of scandalous. I have certainly had a bumpy ride with Covent Garden over the years.

All the way through this confused and unsatisfactory theatre period there was one unexpected and enjoyable sports diversion. A new opportunity had opened up. Manchester and the BOA had put away Olympic thoughts after the denouement of our second failure. However, the chance of securing, from left field, as it were, the Commonwealth Games of 2002 was forced on Manchester by the Commonwealth Games Council for England (CGCE). Only weeks after our return from Monte Carlo, the CGCE decided that they wanted to choose an English city to make a bid for the 2002 Games at the General Assembly in Bermuda in 1995. They wanted applications from cities by December 1st 1993. Strangely, there had never been an English Commonwealth Games and 2002 would be the Queen's Golden Jubilee Year. This was a big idea, not one to be cast aside.

The bid team were naturally tired and most had departed the field, but those who remained could not bear the thought of another city suddenly muscling in on our patch and taking a real prize, even though it was a lot smaller than the Olympics. Once again, Graham Stringer, Howard Bernstein, John Glester and I put our heads together and agreed that we had to throw our hat in the ring. Graham agreed that we had exhausted our ability to raise private money and that this would have to be a city bid. The costs, both of the bid and the underwriting of the Games, would be a fraction of their Olympic equivalent, but the Commonwealth Games remain the second biggest multi-sports event in the world. Birmingham and Sheffield also made bids for the English nomination. Manchester won easily. London could not even put a bid together. We were chosen by the CGCE to be the English bidding city in February 1994 and our opponents were likely to be Adelaide and Cape Town.

Although this was now essentially a municipal bid, Graham wanted a reduced international bid team to remain in business and be seen to be leading the process. Automatically, I suppose, I became chairman of this bid too. There were many Commonwealth Members on the IOC and we knew that we had a head start against any competing Commonwealth city from our Olympic experience. We knew who to talk to, how to do the work and of course we now knew so many people. We made various trips out to some old and some new targets but now our destinations were not Lima, Moscow, Cairo and Bali but the Isle of Man, Belfast, Jersey and Gibraltar, all of whom had a vote.

Our biggest expedition in search of votes was to the rather modest Commonwealth Games in Victoria, Canada in July 1994. I went back to Buckingham Palace, to see Prince Edward this time, and was able to brief him on our pitch for the 2002 Games now that he was preparing to take over the duties of Patron from the Queen. We saw more of him in Victoria. Our sizeable team was so successful that the other competing cities announced during those Games that they were withdrawing their candidacies from the process, offering the excuse that England was the proper country to host the Golden Jubilee Games. We left Victoria certain that Manchester would be unopposed in Bermuda in November. There was talk about which sports we might choose. The Commonwealth Games have always favoured a programme of sports between individuals rather than teams. Sports between individuals are easier to organise, involve fewer athletes and are, therefore, cheaper. Team sports, however, were currently being fiercely discussed with several voices raised in different parts of the Commonwealth about the desirability of including cycling, soccer, cricket, hockey and rugby sevens.

With the new Manchester Velodrome now finished, cycling was a certainty. With soccer and cricket there were difficulties with the international governing bodies (FIFA and the ICC), which already had full schedules, as well as the problem of costs. Hockey was agreed and rugby sevens made it on to our programme and was a popular choice. Rugby has its roots in the Commonwealth and has proved so successful that it is now included in the Olympics. The whole bidding process was part-time and low-key but there was a lot to prepare and we were very conscious of costs because we knew there would be no blank cheques. Once again Paul Gregg was generous in giving me the time to lead the team. We had a problem with shooting, which is both difficult and expensive to stage and brings in virtually no spectator or TV income. The Dunblane massacre was a recent, raw memory. Many countries were happy to see shooting fall off the list of sports, but one or two others were outraged, especially New Zealand, who said they would vote against England if we persisted, pointing out that a unanimous vote was needed for an unopposed candidate city. Against my advice, as the New Zealand threat was an empty one, Manchester gave way.

In November 1995, British Airways flew a Manchester team to Bermuda for the Commonwealth Games Federation general assembly and vote. Alicia and I were now an 'item' and she had moved from a Uruguayan Passport to an Italian one courtesy of the delightful Italian consul in Manchester, who helped, on the legitimate grounds that all Alicia's four grandparents were of Italian stock. November 3rd 1995 was an auspicious day for the two of us. Manchester was safely confirmed as the 2002 host city in the morning; in the afternoon, secretly, with our dear friends Helen Hindle and Sonia Stewart in attendance as bridesmaids and witnesses, we were married at the main Registry Office in Hamilton.

There was a big party for all the delegates that night at the close of the assembly and we told the splendid Mike Fennell, the Jamaican Chairman of the Commonwealth Games Federation (CGF), what Alicia and I had been up to that afternoon. Immediately he turned the event from being a Commonwealth Games celebration into a big wedding reception with several hundred guests. And what a great success the Manchester Commonwealth Games were. I had nothing to do with the organisation, but I was tremendously proud at the Opening Ceremony in 2002 and that the two unsuccessful Olympic bids and the successful 2002 bid had made the Commonwealth Games possible. Even the frequently ungracious Seb Coe has admitted that Manchester did the groundwork for London getting the 2012 Olympics by improving Britain's credibility in the multi-sports world.

I had already mutually agreed with Graham Stringer that Bermuda would be my Manchester swansong. I did not want to be the chairman of the Organising Committee for the next seven years and I don't think others wanted me either. I had learnt by now that a little of me in one role goes a long way. To put it mildly, I can be over-zealous. By 1995 I had spent twenty-seven years in Manchester directing one special project after another and frankly I could not think of another that would be suitable or exciting. For another thing, Alicia, even though she had made close friends, did not feel comfortable in Manchester with my old ghosts haunting the streets. She was not mad about the weather either. We needed a clean break. Maybe I should have fought to stay where I had belonged so long, but I too had itchy feet. Also, Graham was giving up the leadership of the city to become an MP and it just felt as if an era was coming to a close. The city gave me an amazing dinner/send-off in the Town Hall with 200 guests, once the Commonwealth Games prize had been landed. There were very generous speeches and they gave us a handsome canteen of elegant antique cutlery. And by happy chance a new future was already taking shape.

My internal struggles about 'what next' were sorted out by the first of two life-changing phone calls. The second would come six years later. This one was from the Senior Partner at Price Waterhouse in Manchester, whom I knew slightly. He had a Partner in London who had been given the job of looking for someone to help the London Borough of Greenwich. The Millennium was approaching and they had decided they needed to get the best out of it. Greenwich had not really been thinking about the Millennium at all until, sometime in 1994, the Royal Observatory received a call from a large Swiss watch company, asking how much it would cost to book the Observatory for New Year's Eve 1999 and New Year's Day 2000. To which the response had been, 'Why would you want to do that?'

Someone in authority finally got the message and in 1995 the Borough was certainly beginning to think Millennium thoughts. What Greenwich Council apparently told the man from Price Waterhouse in London was that the person they were looking for was someone who could do for Greenwich the sort of things I had been doing in Manchester. The partner in London asked his chum in Manchester to find out if I could think of anyone like me! As he knew me, he phoned to say that he had an odd commission. Did I know anyone like me? And explained why. I went silent for a time as if I was thinking. Pause. 'What about me?' I innocently asked. They could not exactly dismiss me out of hand as a possible solution if I was supposedly the model.

In quick time a meeting was arranged for me to meet Len Duvall and

Bob Harris, the Leader and Deputy Leader of Greenwich. We got on fine and an offer was made. They were prepared to pay quite well. I insisted that this could not be an exclusive contract, which would mean I could keep my Apollo retainer going for a bit longer! A decent income at last suddenly looked possible. I agreed to move to Greenwich and set up, with the full involvement of the local politicians, an 'independent' trust company in a public/private sector partnership which would prepare Greenwich for the Millennium.

The government (still Conservative then) had just announced that it would be setting up plans for Millennium celebrations. So, we had to be ready for whatever they announced. Substantial grants would be made available from the sensational success of the Lottery. The only condition Len Duvall and Bob Harris gave me was that Sir Brian Jenkins, a resident of Blackheath, an ex-Lord Mayor of London as well as Chairman of the Woolwich Building Society, should be chairman and I would be chief executive. We met and I was delighted. Together we would pick our fellow non-executive directors. I was very fortunate to be given Andrew Parry (the second important Parry, after Rick, in my life) from the Council's development team as my assistant and we remained colleagues and friends for years: a very good man. We had an attractive office in West Greenwich. The arrangements seemed perfect to me.

My work in Greenwich started in June 1995 and Greenwich has been my home ever since. Rather like Manchester in 1968 I thought I might be in Greenwich for just a few years. So far I have been living in the Borough for twenty-seven years – as long as Manchester. My slightly unconvincing excuse to myself for leaving Manchester for London was that Greenwich wasn't exactly London. It was a very particular place with a fabulous history and a worldwide Millennium resonance – the Royal Observatory being the exact spot on the earth from where time and space are measured. I also discovered from my first conversations with my new political friends/masters that the five miles which separate Greenwich from Westminster had some similarity with the 180 miles that separate Manchester from London. There was a similar tension not unlike that between a wilful child and a domineering parent.

In 1995 the Borough of Greenwich was not even on the Tube map. It was not just in the unfashionable East of London but in the dodgy 'Sarf East'. The heart had been ripped out of Woolwich. Both the Royal Naval College in Greenwich and the Royal Arsenal in Woolwich were closed areas as 'secret' Defence establishments. From Greenwich to Woolwich, the south side of the river was largely empty and squalid with the shining exception of the Thames

Barrier. There were acres of dereliction on the Greenwich Peninsula roughly halfway between the two parts of the Borough and one of the most polluted sites in the country. Road and rail links were early Victorian. There were just 200 bedrooms in a handful of hotels in the entire Borough. It desperately needed a lift and the Borough Leaders thought the Millennium might be a launch-pad into the future.

The prize, though none of us had an inkling in 1995, was to be the Dome. All we knew was that the government was going to devote a big lump of money from the Lottery to celebrate the dawning of 2000. Fighting for that money was to be the main initial work of the Greenwich Millennium Trust, the name of the body which Sir Brian and I, with the Borough, created. We brought together a splendid, supportive board including Lady (Sue) Hollick, David Quarmby, Trevor Philips, Sir David Hardy and our two outstanding Council leaders Len Duvall and Bob Harris. Our first task, as we saw it, was to persuade London itself that Greenwich should be where the Millennium should be celebrated for the entire country. However, we first needed to know exactly what the government was planning. We had picked up that they were contemplating a national competition and we needed to know the rules of engagement. By now I had good instincts for bidding, which presumably was why I was engaged. Getting into the heads of the competition devisers and judges had always been a first priority. But who were they and what were they after?

In 1995 Britain was experiencing Lottery fever. The government had introduced the new National Lottery at the end of the previous year, which was proving a huge success. Its profits were to go to five good 'causes', 20% to each of: the arts, sport, heritage, charities and a new body, the Millennium Commission, run by seven Commissioners, appointed by the government. The two senior politicians in the group of seven were Michael Heseltine and Virginia Bottomley. By 1996 it was clear that the Lottery would have billions to distribute. Amongst many early decisions that the Commissioners took was to run two competitions to determine firstly 'where' and secondly 'what' those Millennium celebrations should be. 'What' also implied 'organised by whom'. They would support major projects all over the country to mark the Millennium year. But determining the main celebrations came first.

What happened was a wonderful British muddle. The first task was to identify on what piece of land exactly the celebrations should be held, the second was to choose an operator of the celebrations, who would conceive what it would be and then run it. The problem of 'where' was relatively straightforward. There were fifty-seven candidates for the location and we lobbied hard for what we said was the blindingly obvious choice of Greenwich. Not London, but Greenwich. We were keen not to make the choice difficult for the government. We must not offend the regions by fighting merely in the name of the capital city. It was a possible trap I was particularly alert to. We offered not the Royal Observatory but the derelict and contaminated tip of the Greenwich Peninsula through which the '0°' Meridian Line passes. Our offer was not just the Greenwich Meridian and GMT but also an opportunity for the regeneration of horrendously polluted land, originally the site of Europe's largest gasworks. We even tried to persuade everyone that Greenwich could be to the Millennium what Bethlehem was to Christmas, somewhere for the whole world to mark. Our USP was the magic word Greenwich.

Meanwhile the much more complicated competition for 'who' and 'what' was being decided alongside our simpler competition for 'where'. As the day of announcement approached it was clear there were not going to be clear decisions. Although history barely records it, the winner of the 'who and what' competition was a small but brilliant design house called Imagination, owned and run by a man called Gary Withers. His concept was a huge circular new exhibition hall/tent which would continue life after 2000 as the new flagship hall of the National Exhibition Centre in Birmingham. He, therefore, was putting 'where' and 'what' together. For the Millennium Year only, he proposed that there would be a new Great Exhibition recalling the Great Exhibition of 1851 and the Festival of Britain in 1951 and that it would be in Birmingham.

In short, the small Imagination team was trying to win both competitions. Gary constructed a large, expensive and brilliant model to demonstrate his concept. We heard that the commissioners loved it. But when he was asked to work out if he could put his hall/tent, later christened the Dome, on the Greenwich site, we knew we would probably win our part of the competitive process. In crude terms, it now looked as if the 'what' and the 'where' questions had been decided – a huge tent in Greenwich with an exhibition inside it.

The big, big question of 'who' was still up in the air. Imagination could not run it. The obvious potential operators like Disney, Warner Brothers, Madame Tussauds and other major theme park operators did not want to touch it with a bargepole. The big film and theatre production companies on both sides of the Atlantic said 'no, thanks'. They all considered the Commission's attendance projections of twelve million paying customers in the year to be wildly optimistic and that it would take years to bed down such a massive brand-new attraction. I remember meeting the manager of the Motor Show, which had moved from Olympia in West London to the NEC in Birmingham. He told me that the first two years of the transferred show had been chaos and they only began to feel on top of problems in year three. The exhibition to go in the Dome, with all guns blazing, had to be completely ready on January 1st 2000, and cope with 33,000 visitors a day from day one.

The next difficulty was that there was a General Election fast approaching with the almost certain prospect of a change of government. The Millennium Commission's competitions had been a Tory initiative championed largely by Michael Heseltine and Labour was not prepared simply to rubber-stamp the decision, if they took office. Tony Blair, of course, won his massive majority in May 1997 and New Labour immediately set up a review of Greenwich and the Dome. To our joy, six weeks later they did confirm it. Indeed, they went further. Mr Blair and Peter Mandelson, who took charge of the Dome, despite some protests from New Labour ranks, wanted it to be even bigger and better than the Tory proposals and the new government would have its sticky fingers all over it. Indeed, if a substantial commercial company did not want to run it, then they would do it themselves. Ministers would become impresarios. The rest is history – well, part of the next chapter is – and I had a bird's-eye view.

14

GREENWICH

The Dome and Way Beyond

The Dome – cock-ups – Jennie Page – new life in Greenwich – consultant and chairman – Picturehouse Cinemas, Greenwich Theatre, Greenwich Waterfront Partnership, South London Business, the Oval, Bexley Heritage, Trinity Laban Conservatoire

The Millennium Dome in its development and first year was a strange, unhappy story. I was pleased that I had played my part in making sure that Greenwich was centre stage for the Millennium celebrations. In a way, I had done my job. But the plans for the main attraction in the Dome, the Millennium Experience, as it was to be called, always bothered me dreadfully. From my theatre experience I knew clearly that there was a huge difference between building and running a theatre on the one hand and putting on a show on the other. The second is much more creative and much more dangerous than the first. Quite different skills are needed for each. I had done both but on a much, much smaller scale and never at the same time. Even getting the Royal Exchange Theatre built and going were two distinct operations run by separate teams.

As soon as Tony Blair gave the Dome his full-hearted backing in June 1997, the Greenwich Millennium Trust gave a rousing cheer and the Millennium

Commission went into frenetic mode. It was thought by some that the events and design company, Imagination, had supposedly won the competition to create both the building and the show for the Millennium Year, but Imagination all but disappeared from view. They worked on the stand sponsored by BT but that was all. The design of the Dome is credited to the Richard Rogers Partnership working with the engineers Buro Happold. The word Dome, whoever invented it for their enormous erection, was pretentious. It was more just a bloody great tent.

The Government and the Commissioners took charge and created a delivery vehicle called the New Millennium Experience Company. Jennie Page was mysteriously elevated from being chief executive of the Commission (1995–1997) to being chief executive of the Millennium Experience Company (1997–2000), without any kind of competitive process. She was paid handsomely but she was way out of her depth. She had never overseen the construction of a big building and she had never been the producer of a show, let alone perhaps the biggest one ever attempted in this country. Of course, she appointed teams of experienced people to assist her – Stephen Bayley the design guru came and went after six months, Cameron Mackintosh toyed with it and said 'no thanks' – but Jennie was the boss and was required to do both tasks together. Inevitably, I suppose, she did not want to admit her fundamental lack of experience. It was all too exciting. More seriously, neither did her political masters. Tony Blair trumpeted it as 'a building which would be the envy of the world' and it was he who appointed Peter Mandelson to be Minister for the Millennium and become the Dome's political boss. Mandelson's fall from grace and his departure from government at the end of 1998 was a bleak precursor to the fate of the Dome in 2000.

For over two years Jennie had run the Commission well, as you would expect from a senior, imaginative and tough civil servant, who had previously been director of English Heritage. But an impresario she was not. And that is what she was required to be. Looking back now it does all look insane. On January 1st 2000 at 10am the greatest exhibition/show on earth was set to open. But there was the small matter of putting on a completely different extravaganza for the Queen, the prime minister, the Cabinet and one of the biggest A-lists in London history the night before. Included in the audience of thousands were the editors of every important newspaper and TV channel in the land, most of whom finally arrived after the show had started, thanks to terrible transport and security cock-ups. Then, within hours of this massive gala, they were meant to move seamlessly to the long-running and quite different exhibition/show. Even PT Barnum would have said, 'You're crazy!' I have had some bad notices in my life but the stories next day were scorching.

I am not simply being wise after the event. When Jennie was first appointed, I saw quite a lot of her – I think she saw me as a local friend – and I helped her bring onto the Millennium Experience Company the two best businessmen on our own Trust – Sir Brian Jenkins and David Quarmby. Indeed, I thought she might ask me to join and was slightly put out when she didn't. Now, of course, I am deeply grateful that I was left out! I saw her a lot, gave her advice and warned her about problems ahead, both from my Greenwich and theatre experience, at breakfast meetings, which she took increasingly badly.

When, weeks after the opening, she was sacked, she understandably blamed ministers. She was correct that they thought they (and she) could walk on water. 'They' included the prime minister, ministers and Robert Ayling, the chairman recruited from British Airways to run the Millennium Experience Company. Peter Mandelson had been absurdly over-involved. Yet Jennie did have friends who tried to warn her. 'Concentrate on the Millennium Eve Party OR the Show. No one can do both eight hours apart.' 'Tell the Cabinet and the Royals to celebrate somewhere else or have the one-night thrash at the Dome and delay the Millennium Show proper until the weather gets better? Easter, maybe.' Once, I remember her showing me in her office in December an array of different plastic champagne flutes for the picnic hampers on the night. 'Which one do you like?' *If that is what she is thinking about, she has her priorities wrong*, I thought. Sadly, she came to regard people like me as enemies.

Funnily enough I think the Arts world generally has to take some of the blame. We spend our lives in the subsidised sector – art galleries, museums, opera houses, theatres, concert halls – complaining that we are kept on permanently short commons and if only we could have more money, then what glories we could achieve. Well, here was an occasion when money was no object. You could have what you wanted. So, given unlimited funds, even Peter Mandelson reckoned he could be a successful impresario – guaranteed. Sadly, it does not work like that. Ask Steven Spielberg. Ask Cameron Mackintosh. In the case of the theatre, the ratio of financial return is roughly eight failures for every one success. With the right money you can get the venue right, but you can never guarantee the show will succeed. And some experience is useful. There is no such thing as a formula. And, however striking the theatre is, the play's the thing. The show is what people buy tickets for, not the building. You do not buy tickets for Her Majesty's, you buy them for *Phantom*.

The Festival of Britain in 1951, against all odds and with no money, got it triumphantly right. Working from a garret sometimes works. The Dome in 2000 with all the money in the world did not. I was at the infamous Gala Opening on Millennium Eve. Because we came in from the south side and not the north, thus getting there in good time, we were given double portions of the goodies on offer because so many had not arrived. The VIP latecomers, who came in from the north, went hungry as well as suffering other appalling problems. It was a fiasco and managed by itself to condemn the reputation of the Dome for the whole of 2000. It will be hard to forget the quartet of the Queen, the Duke, Tony and Cherie Blair awkwardly holding hands and trying to look cheerful singing 'Auld Lang Syne' with the rest of us. It could have been even worse. If it had been typical January weather that night, there might have been no show with no audience at all! In fact, the weather on Millennium Eve was fine, if cold. Nevertheless, it was sad and wrong to see Jennie by herself take the can for so many people's gross mistakes and get the sack.

Mercifully, the O2 Arena, which finally opened in 2007, now sits as Britain's largest indoor arena in a sea of shops and restaurants in the middle of the Dome. It is a real success. Of the 2000 disaster there is no trace. I was at a meeting in Greenwich in late 2001 when Lord (Charlie) Falconer, who had been appointed to rescue what he could from the ashes of the year, told us that a preliminary deal for a long lease had been struck with Philip Anschutz, the legendary Los Angeles billionaire who, amongst many other huge projects, had conceived and now owned Staples Center in Los Angeles. London badly needed a new first-class indoor arena (both Birmingham and Manchester had better ones) and the best man in the world for the job was prepared to deliver it, albeit on exceedingly favourable terms to himself. It was instantly clear, even if the government took a financial caning in the final negotiations, this was the best solution. It was great news for Greenwich, which would now boast another major London attraction, but it took six years to come to fruition. It opened finally in June 2007.

For most people the Dome is now the O2 and the O2 is the Dome. Millennial memories have faded. Millions of people have visited the great arena and it is now said to be the highest earning place of entertainment in the world. The Tube station, the bus station, the ferry stop and the cable car are all excellent transport connections but the road links will always be unsatisfactory. There have been some big problems when public transport very occasionally fails but the O2 has prospered. And, although it has not gone as fast as we all hoped, the build-out of the rest of the Peninsula proceeds well. Ravensbourne College, Greenwich Village, hotels, schools, pubs, shops, offices, flats and houses – indeed, all the construction that makes a prosperous part of London – are going up at an increasing speed after a slow start. The big question will be, and there will not be an answer for some years yet – 'Will the designers and planners have created a thriving district?' You cannot build a community around just an arena. There are either too many people crowding in at one time or it is deserted. The O2 Arena, rather like Staples Center in LA, is only one of several attractions on the Peninsula and hopefully it will not take too long to establish a significant new 'quartier' of London.

My happiest memories of the years around the turn of the century are domestic and local. Alicia brought two stepdaughters into my life, the older one Raquel who is now a doctor in Valencia with a boy and a girl, the younger one Sara with two daughters and who still lives in Montevideo. Today they feel like my own girls and I am close to them. Well before 2000, Alicia and I had fallen in love with Greenwich and Blackheath and we were sure we had found where we wanted to put down our roots. We had discovered for ourselves what everybody already knows, namely that London consists of a collection of villages and these were lovely ones. We lost good friends in West and North London whom we had known before we came south, but that is the way London works. We have a big group of friends in our 'villages' in SE3 and SE10. Nick and Alison Raynsford have been particularly real and generous friends. And there are many others to whom we are devoted.

We were now determined to plan lives beyond the Millennium but we knew, at our ages, it might not be easy. The Borough was very happy with the way the Trust had secured the Millennium celebrations. They asked the Trust to stay in existence up to and beyond the year 2000 to maintain the drive that comes from the public and private sectors working together. There were great opportunities ahead. The Old Royal Naval College was to be opened up and brought into new use and management. There were new development schemes proposed along the waterfront between Greenwich and Woolwich. New rail services were under construction. New relationships were being forged with Canary Wharf across the Thames. Tourism was a major area for growth. The development potential around the Dome and in the whole of the Peninsula was enormous and exciting. There was the perennial and growing problem of car parking and traffic management. There was also the vexed question of new river crossings in East London. The Borough wanted the Trust to be involved in all these issues. In particular, they wanted to give the public the chance to contribute to the debates.

Fortunately, Greenwich is a place which likes to meet. I became involved in groups and projects that involved endless meetings in the Borough, which turned out to be not only fruitful but were also successful in raising Greenwich's twenty-first-century profile. Quite soon I became a member or chairman of various forums and partnerships and business associations concerned with all these wider waterfront and Borough issues.

In twenty-five years the transformation has been dramatic. The Jubilee Line and the Docklands Light Railway, soon to be joined by the Elizabeth Line (Crossrail), along with boat services and massively improved bus capacity, have utterly changed the transport connections. The glorious Old Royal Naval College, once out of bounds, is now the home of Greenwich University and Trinity Laban Conservatoire of Music and Dance. Along with the extended and improved National Maritime Museum and the Royal Park, Maritime Greenwich was designated a UNESCO World Heritage Site in 1997. The Woolwich Arsenal, with its magnificent buildings, has been transformed, and Woolwich, the town, improves every year as the new transport systems arrive. To cap it all, the Borough has been given 'Royal' status.

When I was first married in the early 70s my wife had a flat in Chalk Farm near the Zoo and if you go there now there is little difference after almost fifty years. This is not how Greenwich is, with its wholesale changes and its extraordinary views of Canary Wharf just across the river. The event that made us feel that we had properly said goodbye to Manchester was that we were lucky enough to find and buy a house beside Greenwich Park ahead of the explosion in property prices. Alicia took out British citizenship and started work in local schools as a psychologist and counsellor. We had really settled in. Greenwich was home.

My Apollo years were also over. I was now pursuing with my Greenwich work a portfolio career with several paid and 'pro bono' roles. Life became more complicated in 2001 when a new but part-time job came my way back in the North West, but that story comes in the next chapter. Meanwhile, life south of the River Thames was busy and growing. Rather reluctantly, I took on the chair of the famous little Greenwich Theatre from my old friend Eddie Kulukundis. The Arts Council had withdrawn their grant on the spurious grounds that they now had to favour the regions over London. Spurious because the sum was tiny in terms of assisting the regions but significant for Greenwich Theatre, which is a local rather than a London theatre. As a result, it became merely a receiving house and good small-scale touring shows were scarce. We attempted some in-house production, including a dramatisation of Dava Sobel's novel *Longitude*, but we consistently lost money. Debts were mounting and we were saved by a major VAT decision won by a theatre in Hampshire which meant that the taxman had to repay quite substantial sums to several arts organisations, including ours. Saved by the taxman – unusual! With our debts paid off and following the appointment of a good new director, after seven years I thought I had done my bit and retired. It was also small beer, frankly, after my rich theatre life in Manchester.

I accepted two commercial appointments, both of which were fascinating. Thames river transport was talked about a good deal. Here was an empty highway in a city whose roads were clogged. Two go-ahead brothers, Peter and Richard Lay, who knew about boats, were keen to exploit the potential of the Millennium by introducing a new service from Westminster via the Tower on to Greenwich and the Dome. 2000 itself was a good beginning but there was no sustainable afterlife. The service, called White Horse Fast Ferries, fell between two stools. It was neither a competitive transport service – too slow – nor was it a tourist experience – too fast. I liked the Lays and admired them but good ideas are fairly easy. Implementation is the problem.

A more satisfactory appointment for me was the chairmanship of the restored Greenwich Cinema as part of the Picturehouse chain. A local chair was wanted to help negotiations with the Council, who owned the building. I admired the chief executive of the group, Lyn Goleby, and her small senior team. I visited several of their other sites and they ran their operations beautifully. Each Picturehouse, whether in Brixton, Brighton or York, felt like a true community asset. In fact, Lyn and I got on so well that she asked me later if I would become chairman of the group. She had two major shareholders who had never really got on. They agreed that an independent chairman was needed. This meant more meetings around the country, an acceptable fee and a small allocation of shares.

The notable achievement of my Picturehouse period was that we pioneered the concept of the live relay of opera, ballets and plays to cinemas. The key word was 'live'. Video recordings of past productions do not have the same audience pulling power at all. We were the first in the country to do it and our opening contract was with the Met in New York. The first relay was of the live Saturday matinee of *Eugene Onegin*, 2pm NY time, 7pm London time. Perfect. Lyn had also done a deal with a German cinema group to come in on the experiment simultaneously. The only problem was that in the British cinemas we contrived to show the sur-titled translation in German and the German cinemas got English. Consternation! Even worse was that we could not change the transmission until the interval. But it was only an early blip.

Sadly, for me at least, the group became so successful that the big boys got interested and the group was finally sold to Cine World. Picturehouse so far successfully lives on inside Cine World with the same policies and image as before. Of course, the Cine World acquisition meant that they no longer needed me. I have always enjoyed working with women and Lyn was one of the best I have known. They seem to me more flexible and freer thinkers. But I stepped down in good heart and with a welcome cheque for my shares in my pocket.

Another enjoyable consultancy was at the Oval with Surrey County Cricket Club. I adore cricket. County grounds all over the country were building new stands and improving their spectator experience. One of their motivations was to become good and big enough to challenge the big six – Lords, the Oval, Trent Bridge, Old Trafford, Headingley and Edgbaston – for the right to stage Test Matches. These six have all had to look to their laurels. Now Southampton, Cardiff and Durham have joined the elite. With the growth of the one-day game, an excellent England team and Sky TV money, cricket is looking much healthier financially. For me Test Matches are best but white ball cricket is a great earner.

Surrey's great problem and opportunity was the Vauxhall end of the ground. At that time it boasted the very outdated North Stands and probably the oldest temporary stand in the country, made up of old reconditioned containers piled on top of each other. For a wholesale development Surrey needed two things – the permission of the Duchy of Cornwall, who were the land-owners, and also considerable new money. The Prince of Wales, well known for his architectural obsessions, took a lot of persuading that our plans, which everyone now agrees have produced a beautiful, modern, green stand, were acceptable. The problem was that word 'modern' again. In 2001 the chief executive, Paul Sheldon, who became a friend, asked me to help with raising money.

We came up with all the usual fundraising wheezes but two stand out. Paul's great idea was to put together a one-day match between famous players from Asia and players from the Rest of the World in 2003. Paul did all the hard work. A free Sunday was fixed. With the help of Kapil Dev he assembled the first cricket XI where Indians and Pakistanis played together on the same side. Sachin Tendulkar agreed to captain Asia, which helped to drive the whole project, and he and Kapil Dev chose a sensational team from India, Pakistan and Sri Lanka. Paul asked Alec Stewart with his perfect Surrey and England credentials to recruit and captain the Rest of the World side with an equally stellar team. Unlike most charity matches (and this must rank as one of the most glamourous in history) the ground sold out. The result did not matter, the event was everything. Asian fans flock to the Oval, so we were pretty sure we were onto a winner.

My contribution was ensuring that the players who would be assembling the day before were properly looked after. I organised dinner on the Saturday night in the Painted Hall in Greenwich and arrival from Westminster Pier to Greenwich Pier in the smartest boat on the river. Our chief host was the then president of Surrey CC, John Major, and there were VIP guests as well as cricketers. We found sponsors for the whole evening. Both the party and the match the next day went a treat. The surplus, despite some substantial international travel and hotel expenses, was over £300,000, which went straight into the fund.

The second memorable effort also involved John Major who, throughout the campaign, was superb. One of the unexpected benefits from the charity match was that we made some seriously rich friends from the Indian community, several of whom came to the dinner in Greenwich and to the game. Chief among them was Gulam Noon, later Lord Noon, who has sadly died. He was always known as Noon. This fundraising idea was essentially his. All Paul and I had to do was produce Sir John at a private lunch in the Bombay Brasserie in Gloucester Road. Paul and I would be there but the guest list would be Noon's. There were ten guests, all of them big fans of cricket and Sir John, and mostly Noon's suppliers.

Nothing relevant to the cause was mentioned during lunch. Lots of talk about cricket but nothing about Surrey's needs. Right at the end, when it seemed that we were about to rise from the table and Paul and I were getting slightly desperate, Noon, almost as an afterthought, stood up and said that these chaps – Sir John, Paul and me – had had this idea of creating a large room in the new Vauxhall End stand which could be used as a giant dining room for Test matches and as a conference facility on quiet days and in the winter.

It was planned that the room would have portraits of great Indian cricketers down the years all around and would be called forever the India Room. He thought a proper sum to support this should be £500,000. And he intended to raise it now. He would contribute £100,000 and he had proxies in his hands for another £100,000. He was, therefore, looking to his friends here at lunch to make up the rest. 'How about £50,000 from you, £75,000 from you, I'll let you off with just £25,000.' How could Noon's suppliers and advisers say no? It all came neatly to half a million pounds in about ten minutes and the India Room finance was delivered. Brilliant.

A privilege for me was the occasional visit during important Test matches to the hallowed Committee Room. And in the famous Ashes year of 2005 when the new Vauxhall End stand had just opened, I had the incredibly good fortune of watching from the best seats in the house the whole of Kevin Pietersen's famous innings of 158 (his maiden Test century), which secured victory in perhaps the greatest Ashes series of all time. I hope I contributed a little bit to the Oval but for me it was not like work.

The next-door Borough to Greenwich going East is Bexley, a Tory Borough, which had in 2000 a go-ahead chief executive called Chris Duffield who left in 2003 to become chief executive of the City of London. He was having problems with two historic buildings in the Borough – Danson House and Hall Place and Gardens, both Grade One listed buildings. He wondered if I could help. Danson House, an exquisite Georgian Palladian mansion dating from 1768, had been dreadfully neglected for years and was officially described by English Heritage as one of the most important buildings in London at risk. Hall Place, another splendid building, part Elizabethan and part Stuart, had been taken over by the Army in the war and then became a school. It too had not been well kept. English Heritage was prepared to pay for major restoration to Danson House but wanted a body other than the Borough to run it when it was completed. Chris Duffield's idea was to create a trust to take over both buildings in an arms-length partnership with the Borough. He insisted to his Borough masters that the trust should be private-sector led. He asked me to be the first part-time chairman. I agreed.

For seven years, things went well. With Chris Duffield we assembled a good group of people to be trustees. English Heritage were true to their word and put £4.5 million into the restoration of Danson House between 2000 and 2005. It was exquisite. We even had the bonus of a Royal opening by the Queen in the spring of 2005. Hall Place had various problems and work progressed slowly until a Lottery application for £2m was successful and the building was dramatically improved. The trust had the benefit of two successive, excellent chief executives – Martin Purslow and Elizabeth Wedmore. They were both superb – Martin was a tireless and imaginative go-getter who invented brilliant events and found true period furniture for Danson House. Elizabeth was quite different, a consummate financial controller who managed the Lottery bid and the restoration of Hall Place brilliantly. They are both gone and the trust is a shadow of its former self. After seven fractious years it was clear that I was not to the taste of some Bexley politicians and officers. We rowed about car parks and promised grants. In 2008 we parted company on frosty terms. At least by then the most important work on restoring the two beautiful buildings had been completed. The difference between the good governance policy of Greenwich Council and the hostility of Bexley Council was marked. I have always preferred to work with Labour Councils rather than Tory ones. Give me Manchester or Greenwich anytime. Not Bexley.

The most demanding responsibility which came my way in this portfolio period of my life was to take on the chairmanship of the board of governors of Trinity Laban, Britain's only Conservatoire of Music and Dance. This new institution, essentially a small specialist university with now its own degree-awarding powers, was formed by the amalgamation of Trinity College of Music (founded in 1872) and the Laban Dance Centre (founded in 1958). They had different reasons for seeking to merge. Trinity was the smallest of the four London conservatoires and needed to grow while Laban needed to move to university status but could not do it alone. The simultaneous arrival of the two institutions in Greenwich and Deptford, a mile apart, led to early conversations.

Two people were crucial to the merger: Gavin Henderson, the principal of Trinity, who had been responsible for moving Trinity to its new home in Greenwich from Marylebone, and Marion North, one of the leading figures in British contemporary dance and who had run Laban in different places for years. They were both charismatic figures in their worlds and were each now responsible for a sensational building: Marion for the new award-winning Laban Dance Centre in Deptford, designed by Herzog de Meuron and which won the Stirling Prize for Architecture in 2003; Gavin for King Charles Court in the Old Royal Naval College, part of the great Christopher Wren baroque masterpiece. The two schools together boast a world-class estate. When Marion retired in 2003, Gavin became the first principal of the merged institution.

Mergers are tricky and reducing two governing bodies to one was a problem. It seemed impossible to achieve without giving offence to someone. A new chair was needed who had been on neither body. The lot fell on me. Settling one new board of governors was my first duty, mastering a set of financial problems was my second. With some blood on the carpet, we got through. Trinity Laban took over the Concert Halls in Blackheath, which has become a successful performance and rehearsal venue – a fine addition to the estate. By the time my eight-year term of office (2004–2012) was over we were fairly healthy, even though chairing a Higher Education institution can never be described as straightforward. Derek Aviss from Trinity and Anthony Bowne from Laban became joint principals when Gavin resigned, until Anthony became the sole principal.

I do wonder how long universities can remain the responsibility of wholly unpaid boards of governors. The Vice-Chancellor, or whatever he or she is called, is the accounting officer and is exceptionally well paid, but unpaid boards work very hard and are constantly being reminded that the buck stops with them. Having said that, I must say that Trinity Laban is a wonderful institution, full of brilliant teachers and students, and Degree Days were inspiring experiences, especially in those buildings which are the setting for all that skill and hard work. It is thrilling to walk through the seventeenth-century grounds of the Old Royal Naval College and hear the sounds of expert music making. The formal student performances at Blackheath and in the theatre at Laban and frequently in the ravishing Greenwich Chapel are always scintillating.

The Greenwich Millennium Trust, the Borough Partnerships, South London Business, Greenwich Theatre, White Horse Ferries, Picturehouse, Bexley Heritage Trust, The Oval, Trinity Laban – these formed the South London part of my portfolio existence. I won a few and lost a few, but on balance I think I am ahead. They do not, however, by any means tell the whole story of my first ten or twelve years of the twenty-first century. My second life-changing phone call came in 2001.

15

LIVERPOOL

European Capital of Culture 2008

Liverpool – Chief Executive of Liverpool Bid to be European Capital of Culture in 2008 – weekly visits – compare Liverpool in crisis and Manchester booming – heart attack – Liverpool wins – bumpy build-up to great year – International Ambassador – Cities on the Edge – Granada Foundation

This phone call came six years after the first and would take me back to the North West on a part-time basis, to Liverpool rather than Manchester this time. It led directly to my final bid, which happily was wholly successful. For the best part of seven years I was in Liverpool for at least two days a week and in 2008 Liverpool had a ball.

You would have thought, since I had lived a large part of my life in Manchester thirty-eight miles down the road, that Liverpool would have been very familiar to me. On the contrary, I had been there many times but I hardly knew it at all and I certainly could not speak the language. I have never worked out exactly where the Manchester accent changes to Scouse but there must be a point on the East Lancs Road where it happens. It is a really curious thing about North West England that these two adjacent great cities, which almost invented the modern world in the early nineteenth century, Manchester and Liverpool, should know so little of each other. The first inter-city railway in the world was the Manchester–Liverpool Railway, which opened in September 1830. The connections were powerful. But they were separated. And, of course, they were fiercely competitive.

Their conurbations almost touch but they remain foreign to each other. This ignorance goes beyond rivalry between fans of football clubs. I am writing of ignorance, some disapproval but not hatred. I was told that things were changing, that the councils, the universities, the Arts bodies, the big firms, the NHS in the two cities were working together. I'll believe it when I see it. People down south think that the cities are connected by the Manchester Ship Canal. They are not. The canal does go roughly from one to the other but it was built to keep them apart, to give Manchester a free passage to the Irish Sea. It was built by Manchester men to bring the sea to their own city, thus avoiding Liverpool and what they considered their ruinous harbour duties. As a result, from its opening in 1894, Manchester for some years had the third busiest port in the country.

Liverpool is older than Manchester with many fine eighteenth-century buildings. Manchester has virtually none. The old cliche of the 'Liverpool gentleman' and the 'Manchester man' may explain something from a long time ago but it is not helpful now. Manchester knows what is going on in the rest of the country, and somehow looks out. Liverpool is complete unto itself, and looks in. Liverpool is generally more handsome than Manchester and the weather in Liverpool is better. But since the war Manchester has certainly had the better of things and if the Northern Powerhouse is really to happen it will be Manchester that will be the capital. As a privileged outsider in both cities, I can truly say that I loved them both and was very happy in both. The spirit is different but the warmth I felt in both cities is equally powerful. Without dreaming of taking sides, I am proud to have worked in both cities. Indeed, if I have one real claim to fame, it is that in 1981 and 1993 I was Mancunian of the Year and in 2003 I was Scouser of the Year. A unique double, I believe!

My bidding career in Liverpool was in two quite distinct phases and they properly qualify as two bids, but one led directly from the other. The first bid was in a consortium competition to be determined by Liverpool City Council. The second bid was to win a national battle between several British cities in a special contest to be decided by a jury, set up by government. The phone call was from a firm of architects who were assembling a team of consultants to bid to manage a major review into the future of Liverpool city centre, which had been struggling for years. There were seven high-powered design and planning consortia in the competition and the prize was a fee of over £1 million. The big London office of the American architects SOM (Skidmore, Owings and Merrill) had assembled a high-class team of professionals. They then decided that they needed an X factor, someone, if you like, to speak for the cultural quarter, who would not be on the other teams. They chose me for my work in Greenwich and Manchester. I accepted immediately.

My job was specifically to think out of the box. I gave the team the idea of positioning the plans and ideas within a timeline from 2001–2007 or 2008. I chose 2007 and 2008 as alternative end dates deliberately. 2007 was the 800th anniversary year of the foundation of the city. King John had given the town Borough status in 1207. So, 2007 would be an anniversary for Liverpool anyway and the city would be in festive mood. 2008, however, was the year when the European Commission had ruled that one British city would be chosen to be European Capital of Culture – the first since Glasgow in 1990. Implicit in our bid was that Liverpool should make a European Capital of Culture bid for 2008 and if, by any chance that bid was successful, then that year would be the climax of our timeline.

The Government was just starting to think how to organise the process. No one, of course, could guarantee that Liverpool would be successful – far from it. But 2008 would be a national celebration and my thinking behind the idea of a timeline was that it would be essential for everyone to have worked really hard in the upcoming five or six years to change the whole look and feeling of the city. Our consortium (with me explaining the timeline) made our presentation to the Liverpool Committee and we won. And that very day, in fact before our victory was announced, the City Leader Councillor Mike Storey (later Lord) and the chief executive, David Henshaw (later Sir), who were the key figures on the interviewing panel, took me aside together at lunch and asked if I would be interested to put my ideas into practice and put together a bid for Liverpool to be European Capital of Culture in 2008. It was a good day.

Exactly as I had done in Greenwich, I suggested we would need to set up a bid trust company and, again, it could not be an exclusive contract. I would not be able to move to Liverpool, but I would come up every week. They agreed but said that I must accept the choice of Peter Toyne, the Vice-Chancellor of Liverpool John Moores University, to be the chairman. I was delighted and the deal to engage me was done. My one concern was how Liverpool and the local media would react to someone so identified with Manchester parachuting into the city. They seemed to take the line that they had somehow stolen me away.

My first impressions of Liverpool on my early visits were mixed, to say the least. There were Grade One buildings, handsome streets, elegant parks, the magnificent waterfront. And, of course, the wonderful history. Everyone knew that. But plum in the heart of the city centre you could take the most dismal walks imaginable. It was as if in certain places the Luftwaffe had only just left. There were crumbling, deserted streetscapes, waste land, neglect, somehow conveying a lack of pride. It reminded me of Woolwich a few years ago: stunning buildings and stunning dereliction side by side. Admittedly I would only be visiting Liverpool. Home was now definitely Greenwich. But, if I had moved there, I would have inevitably chosen to stay in some attractive neighbourhood away from the city centre. As it was, I commuted for two or three days a week for almost eight years and always stayed right in the city centre. I got to know it very well. Virgin Rail must have carried me well over 150,000 miles in total between Euston and Lime Street. I stayed in one of two ordinary hotels in Liverpool, both of which have now been knocked down. In the evenings I would walk a great deal, turning up both jewels and boarded-up buildings and broken glass on almost every route I took.

Things had been critical for Liverpool for years but now midnight was approaching. You could tell the difference between Manchester and Liverpool's economic situations simply by arriving at Euston station and looking at the packed train for Manchester standing at one platform next to another where the much emptier train for Liverpool was also ready to depart. The problem for a great port is that when it loses its function – and you saw very few ships on the Mersey in 2001 – it ceases to be a destination. Practically all the maritime trade today is in the considerable number of container ships in and out of Seaforth Docks five miles north of Liverpool. Some days the only ship you saw was the ferry. Like most coastal towns there are very few ways in and out. Manchester has a 360 degrees hinterland, Liverpool's is roughly 180 degrees. The great boat trains for Liverpool have gone for ever. There were no passenger ships at all. Cruise ships are arriving now but not in 2001. Commercial firms were closing their Liverpool branches. Crewe to Liverpool was in danger of becoming a mere branch line.

I also detected what I thought was serious local nonsense. I disliked the word Merseyside. No one would suggest Greater London should be called Thameside. The name with history and romance is Liverpool. Inventing the word Merseyside just to keep the people of the Wirral, St. Helens, Knowsley and Sefton happy was ridiculous. People from those Boroughs say they are from Liverpool if they are asked where they come from while lazing on a Spanish beach. Secondly, charging a toll to use the two tunnels across the Mersey (essentially from one part of Liverpool to another) is a killer both for business and evening life in the city. Paying a toll to go to work is bad enough. Paying extra to travel to a football match, show or a concert is appalling. You only pay a toll to cross the Thames once, fifteen miles east of Westminster at Dartford, nowhere else. Our 2008 bid did a lot to promote the name of Liverpool and reduce the use of the word Merseyside but we could do nothing about the toll.

At the same time what you could never deny was the majesty of Liverpool. The city has a claim to possess the two finest 'public' buildings in England from the nineteenth and twentieth centuries: St. George's Hall and the Anglican Cathedral. The more I visited them, the more I admired them. What's more, they were both designed by architects who won their commissions in public competitions when they were twenty-five and twenty-two years old respectively – Harvey Elmes for St. George's in 1839 and Giles Gilbert Scott for the Cathedral in 1901. Imagine my Lords Foster and Rogers in the so-called bold and youth-obsessed age of the early twenty-first century losing to a twenty-two-year-old in an open architectural competition! What a splendid, brave city Liverpool must have been in those days to take such risks.

It is both a bold city and a magnificent city. The setting, for a start, is handsome – on a gentle hill rising up from the magnificent waterfront. The Three Graces, the Albert Dock, Lime Street Station, the Walker Art Gallery, the Town Hall, the Picton Library, the Philharmonic, Hope Street connecting the Cathedrals, the wealth of statues, the parks, the Georgian squares all tell a story of wealth, taste and confidence. The challenge in 2001 was to preserve the best and change or get rid of the worst. Most important of all, Liverpool had to start building again. At that time it was a city sky-line without cranes. A successful European Capital of Culture bid could be the jet fuel the city needed to launch itself into the future. Of course, there were all kinds of political initiatives already under way – some had been going for a long time – but they inevitably lacked the public interest, enthusiasm and money that this competitive bid could harness. Happily, it was an initiative shared by all political parties. Indeed, the whole city would finally back the bid. It was a prize even the fans of Liverpool and Everton Football Clubs could share.

Entering the competition was a gamble – the bid could fail. Indeed, it probably would. Greatly to their credit the politicians and the officers never went missing. They backed the small team all the way. Mike Storey and David Henshaw were totally supportive throughout. A few Liverpool grandees stood back, watching, until we won but that was no surprise. Ultimately twelve British cities made bids and these were whittled down to six in a shortlisting process. We made that shortlist, which was a relief. Britain's final choice would be announced in June 2003. The government appointed a jury of twelve people. Unusually for Britain, it was made up of six men and six women, under the powerful chairmanship of Sir Jeremy Isaacs. They were an impressive group of people who were clearly going to make up their own minds and not be influenced by ministers or anyone else. Liverpool was never confident of victory and we were never the bookies' favourite but we planned a good campaign.

Early on, I had the good fortune to receive out of the blue a phone call from a senior civil servant, by then retired to North Wales, who had been responsible for advising the Arts Minister back in 1986 about the choice of the first British European City of Culture in 1990. It is a dreadful confession, but I cannot remember his name. There had been over twenty cities which had put their names forward and he and a colleague had travelled the land meeting representatives in each interested city. After several weeks they came back to their minister in London and told him that they had little difficulty in making a recommendation. 'Glasgow,' they said. 'Oh hell, why could you not have given me a Conservative City to offer Mrs T?' asked the minister. 'No,' they insisted. 'Glasgow must have it.' 'But why?' the minister again asked. 'Because they want it the most,' they replied. Hunger and enthusiasm had won the day.

I never forgot that phone call and we worked very hard not only to stir up the enthusiasm of the citizens with endless public meetings and media coverage but also to find ways to build up and parade public support. We also had to get the whole cultural community singing from the same hymn sheet. This was tougher than you might think. Several leading players, who shall be nameless, were not enthusiastic. They saw the exercise as shameless, even cynical, Council opportunism in a city where arts grants were falling. Finally, the sceptics were won over, partly because the Leader and the chief executive saw to it that grants should suddenly start to rise and partly because the doubters could see that there was no mileage in open opposition. Who knows, we might just win and then they would surely feel the benefits.

Liverpool

We got up to all kinds of stunts. Every Council vehicle, including rubbish bin lorries and fire engines, carried stickers. Every shop and lamp post took our posters. Even the police horses had badges on their saddles. No visitor to Liverpool could miss the fact that the city was bidding. Our logo was everywhere and our catch phrase was 'Liverpool – the World in One City'. One particular way of enthusing ordinary people was to hold a series of city-wide projects to discover what it was that Liverpudlians loved most about their city. One such scheme involved us making a list of what we calculated were the top ten qualities of Liverpool life – Liverpool football, Liverpool music, Liverpool humour, Liverpool buildings, Liverpool writing, etc. – which we asked people to list in their order of importance. We wanted to know what they were proudest of. We printed the 'competition' in the newspapers, we promoted it on local TV, we distributed forms to be filled in in schools, libraries, work places and churches. We got back many thousands of completed forms. The impressive result was that 57% of all people responding – easily in first place – put 'our buildings' as Liverpool's proudest possession. Not football, not the Beatles. It completely killed the notion that fine buildings only interest the 'posh'. We also sent round to 2008 groups and individuals large plastic jars for sweets and asked people to put their concept of 'Liverpool culture in a bottle' – objects, pictures, poems, etc. Again, the response was amazing. Some were so original that Tate Liverpool mounted an exhibition called 'Bottled Liverpool'.

There was a small team in the office but our tentacles spread far and wide into the community. Clare McColgan, Carol Rogers and Lorraine Ashworth were my chief assistants and they were fantastic. Peter Toyne was a marvellously energetic chairman. David Henshaw drove all the departments of the City Council to be properly involved. The government decided that there should be a complicated official questionnaire to complete, issued by the Department of Culture, Media and Sport (DCMS). This we transformed into a colourful bid document. Peter Gingold from the Philharmonic and I wrote it. We emphasised the city's great cultural traditions – the Philharmonic, the Playhouse and Everyman, the Walker, the Liverpool Tate, the Bluecoats, the Biennial. We promoted our unique history of popular culture from the Beatles to football to writing. But we focussed the bid on our confidence in the creativity of our young people and our hunger and determination to win this great prize for them.

We made the point very clearly that we saw the prize as a scholarship rather than a cup. We specifically did not say we deserved the prize for past achievements. We said we wanted the prize in five or six years' time, after years of planning and improvements on the timeline, for all the benefits our young people could gain from it. We were even more interested in grass-roots activities than major events, which, of course, we also took very seriously. Above all we insisted that we concentrate our strategy on getting into the heads of our electorate of twelve good men and women. We did a lot of research into who they were and what would concern them. They were the ones who mattered. We wanted to be the first choice of five or six of them and be entirely acceptable to the rest.

Then, on November 1st 2002, about seven months before Decision Day, I had a heart attack. I was lucky. I was whisked from my hotel to the Royal Infirmary and, later in the morning, to the famous Broadgreen Cardiac Unit to have three stents inserted in my clogged veins. This was only a few weeks after the Liverpool FC Manager, Gérard Houllier, had had a much more serious and publicised attack and who had been taken to the same place from Anfield. The marvellous staff at Broadgreen were impressed by the small flood of enquiries and flowers that came in for me from the Lord Mayor, the Leader, the Town Clerk, the Lord Lieutenant, etc. and they decided I must be a kind of cultural version of Houllier. Alicia came up and stayed at the hostel attached to the unit and I had a few weeks off. David Henshaw and Mike Storey were especially helpful and considerate and saw to it that we did not lose impetus but they wanted me back as soon as I felt OK. I returned after Christmas fully fit again, by when the main task was to prepare the city for the visit of the jury. The bid book had been important but the visit was the key event we had to deliver well. We approached it like a military operation. Every minute was planned.

The jury was to spend a day in each of the six bidding cities. Some were daytrips, others involved staying overnight. They arrived in Liverpool on a Thursday evening after a day in Birmingham. I argued that if they spent the night with us they could start their inspection early on the Friday morning and get back to their homes not too late in the evening. It seemed to me critically important that they should spend the evening before their day with us in Liverpool rather than the Midlands. Fortunately, I had my way. What it meant was that we could look after them cheerfully on the Thursday night and on the chance that they wanted entertainment we could give them a shopping list of things they could do. It worked perfectly – some went to the Phil, some to the theatre, some to dinner, some on a pub crawl. Without fully realising it, they were gently hosted by people who never revealed themselves as planted hosts.

For instance, at every pub there was a carefully placed and briefed character or two who astonished their 'victims' with their knowledge of and enthusiasm for the city's cultural life.

The next day, the big day, we resolutely spared them meetings with men in suits in Council offices. We thought very carefully about what would interest the women members. They went to a school and got down on the floor with the children, we walked through carefully chosen streets and bumped into carefully chosen and briefed citizens like newspaper sellers and shopkeepers, we visited Sefton Park and talked about Green Liverpool, we took a short river trip on the Mersey Ferry.

The highlight set piece was at the gorgeous Picton Library when small troupes of schoolchildren, nurses, police officers, fire officers, actors, teachers, local Mayors, footballers, shop assistants, etc. were paraded before them in a slick ceremony MC'd brilliantly by Carol Rogers. The event began in an empty Reading Room with only the mystified jury members present in the front row of rows of empty seats looking at an empty stage. Carol came on stage, welcomed the jury and then introduced the groups one by one onto the stage from the back. Each group leader made a very short, quickfire two-minute presentation and then each group went to sit in the seats behind the jury. Within forty minutes the room was packed with serried ranks of enthusiastic supporters, many of them in uniforms, all of whom by one means or another had pledged their support and involvement. It was a risky piece of theatre which could have looked a mess because it had had minimal rehearsal. It went superbly. Determined to give nothing away Jeremy Isaacs told the crowd of enthusiasts, 'Well, we are indeed surrounded but we do not surrender.'

Finally, as their various trains left Lime Street to take them home, they all had copies of that day's *Liverpool Echo* in their hands with pages of photographs of themselves reviewing the bid over the evening and day they were with us. It was rather against the rules but we knew that people love looking at pictures of themselves. The *Liverpool Post* and the *Liverpool Echo* played blinders right through the process.

The jury's decision was broadcast live by Tessa Jowell, the Culture Secretary, at 8.30am on BBC Breakfast Television on June 21st 2003, reputedly to their largest audience of the year. The programme flicked from city to city where crowds had assembled in public places in Birmingham, Cardiff, Bristol, Oxford, Newcastle and Liverpool. Our 'studio' was the main bar at the Empire Theatre. We learnt later that the London newsrooms had had to choose where to send their journalists for the result and many of them had chosen Newcastle, the bookies' favourite. One or two key broadcasters were apparently gently advised by an insider that it might be an idea to go to Liverpool. All I can say is that I was not in the know.

When Tessa Jowell made the announcement, Liverpool erupted. In offices, schools, factories and hospitals there was a good deal of hugging and cheering. There was something about the competitive side of it all that excited the average Scouser. A bus driver stopped his bus, got out of his cab and ran across the road to shake my hand! Beating the others, i.e. winning, was a great motivation. It is worth remembering that the city was not used to winning this kind of prize, a prize which delighted everyone. Liverpool was more used to being reviled by the rest of Britain. And it is worth remembering that even when Liverpool FC wins a Cup, half the city goes into mourning! No, this was a remarkable moment. You could swear you felt the earth move.

Tessa Jowell and Jeremy Isaacs immediately got on a train to Liverpool to join the city in its celebration. It was the closest Tessa had ever come to being treated like royalty, she said. Cherie Blair, a passionate Scouser, wrote me a sweet letter and the prime minister congratulated us. The Newcastle *Journal* had a front page with a one-word headline two inches high which simply said BETRAYED. Absurd! By whom? I know why they lost – at least, I think I do. Newcastle played to the wrong audience. They convinced the papers that they deserved to win and would win, which is not what an independent jury likes to be told. It was up to them to decide, no one else. We knew we were fighting for our lives before a particular jury of twelve. We were not fighting in the Court of Public Opinion.

We had decided to make no plans in advance for a party that night, but we certainly had one – at very short notice – in the Town Hall. An amusing thing happened earlier that day which then played well at the party. Sometime in the morning I got a call on my mobile from a man saying that he had been hired to fly a light plane that afternoon round and round above the centre of Newcastle with a message on a streamer attached to the plane, which read '2008 – WE DID IT'. He said that he had now been told to stand down as the plane was no longer wanted. He was just phoning me to ask if we might like it, flying over Liverpool. I had to explain that much as I might like it, we had badly overrun the budget and we had not a penny left. 'Oh, don't worry about the cost,' he said, 'it's all paid for.' So, I told him we would be delighted to see him and his plane flying over Liverpool at Newcastle's expense. At the party I received many plaudits. None was more heartfelt than the ones expressed for the confidence I had shown in booking the plane and its triumphant message. The one regret I felt that night was for my brother Andrew. He was running Education at the Sage Centre in Gateshead and his wife was a GP in Newcastle. They wanted and expected Newcastle to win. Sorry, bro!

Promoting and winning a bid is a complete project in itself. It has a beginning, a middle and an end, quite distinct from the process of organising and carrying out the event itself. The bid, however, sets the tone and lays down the strategy for the year. In the same way organising an Olympic or Commonwealth Games is quite different from bidding for them. A few members of the bidding team may stick with the project right through to the end, but very few. The problem with this, of course, is that an Organising Committee does not always care to carry out all the undertakings of a Bidding Committee. Sometimes they may not even know what those promises were because they have never bothered to read the bid document. They would like to behave as if they are writing on a completely clean page but it can create endless problems. Fortunately for Liverpool, I believe, Clare McColgan and I went right through both processes (albeit in new roles) and we more or less kept the bid philosophy intact. After 2008 she became the city's cultural supremo having been one of two artistic directors for the year itself. Briefly I took over the chairmanship of the committee, but Liverpool 2008 needed a resident chairman and full-time directors and staff, and I could not do that. So, I became Liverpool's international ambassador. I was part-time and non-resident but at least I went right through the messy build-up to the year. At the end of 2008 I gave up my almost weekly Liverpool visits.

The great problem in those build-up years after the bid victory was that the Culture Company and the city went through an appalling number of senior personnel changes. From the outside, indeed from the inside, it looked and felt like chaos. Artistic directors and general managers came and went, and even more publicly, the Leader and Town Clerk of the City Council fell out so spectacularly that they both resigned from their exalted positions. Nevertheless, one got a peerage and the other a knighthood, so there may have been chaos but no disgrace. Two people must be excluded from the mayhem. Indeed, at different moments they kept the show going – Sir Drummond Bone, the Vice Chancellor of Liverpool University, who was the chairman for much of the time and Phil Redmond, the eminent Liverpudlian TV and academic guru who ended up as managing director of Liverpool 2008. He did an amazing job.

The road from 2003 to 2008 was extremely bumpy and the media understandably gave Liverpool a hard time. I was no longer at the centre of things and it would be invidious to go through all the resignations and sackings. I had been involved in some of the senior appointments several of which had ended in flames but I was now assisting rather than leading. Indeed, many of the blazing rows came as great shocks to me and I never saw them coming. Ultimately, after much pain, it all turned out all right on the night. The first weekend in January, which could have gone badly wrong, was a triumph. It was very cold but dry. There were three days of major events and the coverage was sensational. An excellent relationship had been forged with the BBC, so, for instance, the Opening Ceremony, starring Ringo Starr and many local celebrities, was beamed all over the world. The next day the new 11,000 seat Kings Dock Arena opened officially with a stunning concert anchored by the Phil. From those January days on there was highlight after highlight. Tate Liverpool put on a superb Klimt exhibition. Local boy Simon Rattle conducted both his own Berlin Philharmonic and the Royal Liverpool Philharmonic Orchestras on consecutive nights. There was a spectacular Liverpool Biennial. Paul McCartney sold out Anfield for a sentimental concert. John Tavener's *Requiem* ravished the Metropolitan Cathedral.

Major annual national and international events were specially held in Liverpool in 2008. The Open Golf was held at Royal Birkdale. The Turner Prize came from the Liverpool Tate and the MTV Music Awards and the BBC Sports Personality of the Year were both staged in the new Arena. Most memorably perhaps, La Princesse, a 50ft high, thirty-seven-tonne giant mechanical spider, specially created by the French company La Machine, prowled the streets and the waterfront for a summer weekend to the delight of some half a million visitors. Everywhere it went it was accompanied by tens of thousands. At one point it climbed up the side of an office block and down the other side. Its departure from the city centre was brilliantly conceived as it disappeared for ever down the Mersey Tunnel – paying no toll I trust. Many of the kids in the crowd openly wept as they waved goodbye to their amazing visitor.

Another memorable night was the first showing in the big cinema at FACT of a documentary film of the making of *LOVE*, the sensational show which is still playing twice nightly in Las Vegas. It was put together by Cirque du Soleil as a spectacle with a completely re-engineered soundtrack of Beatles songs produced by George Martin and his son Giles, all closely overseen by Paul McCartney. The film premiere brought together Paul and Ringo with Yoko and Olivia, the widows of John and George, with George Martin and his son. The film and the reception were great but the live show is spectacular. Alicia and I had an amazing night at the show eleven years later in Las Vegas when we were ostensibly visiting the Grand Canyon but dropped in on the Strip en route. Ah! The sound of the Beatles, again! I can never get over that they were my contemporaries. Especially now that I am fourteen years past being sixty-four.

The special project which took up some of my time was one that I managed with Franco Bianchini, an Italian-born academic from Leicester, called Cities on the Edge. It was our most important specific European project, bringing together five cities which Franco and I chose and which had the distinct flavour of Liverpool about them – Marseille, Naples, Bremen, Gdansk and Istanbul. The passport for entry to this select group was that they had to be ports, they had to be belligerent and at odds with their capitals, they had to be creative, funny, football mad, music loving, sinful, dangerous – on the edge in every sense. Managing them was like herding cats and, inevitably, we did not achieve all we aimed for. There were a lot of meetings and visits but not enough results. There were some excellent moments. There was a brilliant production of Donizetti's virtually unknown *Emilia di Liverpool*, written in Naples and with some of the musicians brought together by the European Opera Centre, based in Liverpool. The opera, which is set in the leafy groves of Liverpool (well, according to Donizetti it must be a beautiful place if it is so famous!), was staged at the newly reopened and exquisite Concert Hall inside the great St. George's Hall main building. It was amazingly well reviewed.

We arranged a major international Serious Crime conference with the Merseyside Police. The cities got involved. It was extremely well received and at the end of it we had a riveting presentation by Roberto Saviano, the author of *Gomorrah*, the story of the Neapolitan Camorra, Italy's other mafia. A book entitled *ReBerth* was produced, which was an anthology of short stories from writers in all five cities. Top-class photographers from the cities travelled to the other cities to produce a special exhibition and book. A Marseille film director made a film exploring the nature of being a football fan in Liverpool, Marseille and Istanbul called *Football: The Edge of Passion*. Incidentally, Istanbul was included because, in those heady days, Turkey was officially bidding to join the Union. It was fascinating. The whole project was a brave attempt to get different and very interesting European cities to talk to each other. Sadly, there was no follow-up or legacy, but it was good while it lasted.

In Liverpool itself every month there was at least one huge event, but what gripped the city most was the almost unbelievable number of small events involving thousands of people which took place in every corner of the city, including the most deprived areas. The statistics tell their own story. 10,000 artists took part. 67,000 children performed. 1,000 official Volunteer Guides helped the visitors. There were 3,500 Creative Community events involving 160,000 participants and 15 million people attended at least one event at some time during the year. It was calculated that there was an £800 million economic benefit to the City Region and £200 million global media value. These are just some of the figures which were tracked in a sophisticated research and evaluation programme called Impact08 expertly managed by Beatrice Garcia.

The most interesting result from such energy and enthusiasm was that almost every positive development which happened in Liverpool in the first ten years of the new century was laid at the door of the European Capital of Culture initiative. The new Arena, the new Convention Centre, the new Museum of Liverpool on the waterfront, the new Liverpool 1 Shopping Centre, the restored Everyman Theatre, the Lime Street Station improvements, new hotels, new flats, new roads were all somehow explained as part of the great year. Crazy! The legacy was part truth and part myth. Some of the developments were happening anyway, others took time to come to fruition. Certainly, the cranes returned to Liverpool.

Everything seemed to go back to that early morning in June 2003 when we surprised the country and won the prize. After seven years my time in Liverpool came to an end in 2008 rather as my time in Manchester came to an end in 1995. Essentially, I had completed two working periods of my life and the projects were finished.

Just one activity still keeps me coming to the North West – the Granada Foundation. This work takes in Manchester and Liverpool but includes Lancashire, Cheshire and Cumbria – the region that used to be called Granadaland, when the country was divided up into distinct ITV areas. Granada was one of the great success stories of the early days of commercial television. The original owners were the Bernstein brothers, Sidney and Cecil. They did so well and made so much money that they decided to set up a Foundation, called the Granada Foundation, with an allocation of shares in 1965. Its remit was to support the Arts and Sciences in the Granadaland region. Ironically, it is the Foundation that keeps the name Granada alive today. Granada TV has long ago bitten the dust. Now, some fifty-seven years since it began, the

Liverpool

Granada Foundation has distributed over £6 million in grants and still has £4 million in reserve to keep the work going. There have been just two chairmen – Sir William Mather and me – dividing the years roughly equally. We have an excellent Advisory Council which meets three times a year and gives away about £150,000 a year in grants – not big but very welcome, I know. I greatly enjoy the work and it keeps me in touch with what goes on in the region. It is the only activity in my life – I joined as a member in 1976 – which spans continuously my years from the Royal Exchange Theatre to now.

16

EUROPE

Almost a Eurocrat

President of European Commission Jury for European Capitals of Culture – much travel for no pay – highlight when Marseille wins for France – UK involvement now finished – a Remainer – resists concept of one European Culture

The concept of European Cities of Culture was born in 1984 when the famous Greek Culture Minister, the film star Melina Mercouri, came up with the idea in a conversation with her French counterpart Jack Lang. The Member States of Europe was about to rise to twelve and the talk was about a United Europe. She is said to have persuaded him that one way to bring Europe more together would be to appoint one European city a year to host a major arts festival on a rotating basis. No surprise, therefore, once the idea was accepted, that the first city chosen should be Athens in 1985. Each chosen city thereafter would be called the European City of Culture for that year. By a process that is now murky the next four were quickly chosen: Florence – 1986, Amsterdam – 1987, Berlin – 1988, Paris – 1989. In truth, the idea was only quietly taken up in the early days as the first five cities all considered themselves important cities of culture already and they did not need to do anything special to prove it.

Surprisingly, it was not until it was Britain's turn to nominate a city for 1990 that the concept really took off. This was because the British government of the day in 1987 decided to set up a competitive process to make its choice and did not just plump automatically for London. To demonstrate how unprepared the bureaucrats in Brussels were for the UK government announcement that it had chosen Glasgow, one EU document listed the European City of Culture 1990 as Glasgow, England.

The impact of Glasgow 1990 is still felt. It was Glasgow which provided the key motivation for all those who came after – a bold legacy. Every nominated city throughout Europe now aims to use the title to change the city for the better: its cultural institutions, its international image, its reputation, its tourism potential, how it sees itself. Glasgow was the first city chosen by a competitive process and some sort of competition has been the rule ever since. Generally, capital cities have not done well in those competitions, largely I suspect through hubris. The Council of Ministers determines which country shall be chosen each year while the European Commission is the body which administers the process.

As EU membership has grown, the Capital of Culture programme has become more complicated. Growth from twelve to twenty-eight Member countries in thirty-seven years is bound to create problems. For the first fifteen years there was just one City of Culture each year. The year 2000 was a particularly unusual year when no less than ten Cities of Culture were chosen, some not even from EU States. There have been some awful, political choices too. The confirmation of Liverpool 2008 in 2003 gave us experience of the mess. When you think what a poor reputation the UK has had as a Member State of the European Union, it is interesting that between 1985 and 2000, Glasgow in 1990 was considered by most to have been the best ECOC of those years and between 2000 and today, Liverpool in 2008 is considered one of the best, if not the best.

It was, therefore, unsurprising that in 2007 it was generally agreed that a new process was formally required both to choose the cities and also to monitor them during their preparations. However, by then the nominated countries had already chosen their cities up to and including 2012. So, it was agreed that, while the monitoring process could begin immediately, the start of a new process of city selection would have to wait until 2008 when it was time to choose the cities from France and Slovakia for 2013. The Commission's grant to each selected city was increased to 1.5 million euros and was named the Melina Mercouri Prize. The scheme was also renamed European Capital of Culture, not City of Culture.

In 2007, when preparations for Liverpool's year were well advanced, I was approached by the Commission in Brussels to see if I would agree to be one of their nominations to the so-called panel of experts or jury to take forward the new process. The appointment would be for four years and we would start by monitoring the cities which had already been chosen for 2009–2012. We would not start the process of selecting cities until later but then we would look at applicant cities from six countries for 2013, 2014 and 2015. Our jury would be only seven in number for the monitoring period but when we started the process of selection we would be joined by six nominees from each of the countries, making a selection panel of thirteen. Members' pay would be notional but I would get to know parts of Europe I did not know at all. We would be the guinea pigs for the new process and would have to make up new rules as we went along.

I cheerfully said yes, I would be pleased to join. From my first talks with the Commission it was clear that they were deeply under-resourced and the ECOC office was just a tiny cubby hole in the Education Directorate. It was rather neglected, even though the ECOC Programme had a high EU profile outside Brussels. In October 2007, innocent and virtually unbriefed, I attended my first meeting in Brussels. We were given a warning that there were lots of problems to solve. We met as seven new boys and girls with almost no prior information. We exchanged our 'how do you do's', quite keen to get to work. It transpired some more than others. To this day I do not know how my colleagues were chosen.

The first thing we had to do was choose our Chair. Silence. We, by the way, were three ladies from Greece, Poland and Ireland and four men from Austria, Spain, Finland and the UK. It was explained to us that the basic duties of the Chair were both to chair the meetings and write reports in English. In fact, all our work was to be conducted in English. Quick as a flash, the lady who became my best friend in the group, Mary McCarthy from Ireland, and the only other native English speaker, and who had been very much involved in Cork ECOC 2005, proposed me. Approved unanimously. Very soon I realised I had let myself in for much more than I had bargained for. It is strange that Britain's parting gift to the EU is that most meetings will continue to be held wholly in English. When I first started going to Brussels some years ago there were just twelve Member States and each meeting room had a bank of simultaneous translation booths at the back for everyone to get the speeches in their own languages. This was abandoned for most ordinary meetings, and we were deemed ordinary, and English has become the almost universal language of the EU, which was not to the taste of the French especially.

It would be tiresome in the extreme for me to go through every meeting where we questioned cities on their excellent or inadequate preparation as monitors or made the final, sometimes controversial, choice as selectors. I will, therefore, only recount those moments which stick out either on the grounds of crisis or curiosity or tension. Unearthing my notes from those years has astonished me by how much I undertook.

Monitoring already selected ECOCs was quite difficult especially in the new Member States of the EU. The two which caused us the most difficulty were Vilnius, the capital of Lithuania, ECOC – 2009 and Pecs, a small but proud Hungarian city in the south of the country, ECOC – 2010. I had had nothing to do with the selection of either but as the chairman of the jury I was asked by the stretched Commission staff to visit both cities to see what was happening on the ground, whether the negative rumours we were getting were correct and what, if anything, we could do to help. I went alone because they could not afford to send more of us.

Vilnius 2009 had become a much-kicked political football with changes of government, both local and national, the sacking of several members of the cultural staff and the slashing of promised grants. I was hoping to make it a quiet visit to spy out the land, talk to key players and report to my colleagues. Without any warning I was in the middle of an angry slanging match where I was cast as referee. The first meeting was with the artistic team and there were clearly tensions. Then I was thrust into a packed press conference with political opponents on each side of me, disagreeing violently. All I could do was preach peace and reconciliation and remind them of their pledges during the selection process, about which I knew little. I was forceful in condemning the politicisation of the 'year'. I take no credit for it but they managed to offer a much-reduced year. Whether it was successful or left a genuine legacy, I do not know. I rather doubt it. Good people lost their jobs and the politicians took over.

Pecs 2010 had a different set of problems. Again, they had had big personnel problems but it was not their fault. The previous Mayor who was the chief supporter of the bid in the early days was still lying in a coma after a car crash two years before and his successor had died of cancer in October 2008.

Three Deputy Mayors were holding the fort, their cultural programme had been decimated and there was no sign on the streets, with nine months to go, of their approaching year. I spent time in Budapest with a senior civil servant who insisted that Pecs 2010 was a priority of the Hungarian government and would be funded and go ahead. After several false starts there was now an artistic team of three. They did OK but again their year bore little relationship to the written bid promises.

When it became known that I was prepared to visit ECOCs in preparation, I was swamped with invitations. I took this responsibility seriously because I had experienced for myself in Liverpool the turmoil that can engulf a city in its build-up to its year. In two years or so I briefly visited and reported on the plans of six other cities which were all very different. My expenses were paid by the cities but, pleading poverty again, the EU offered no fee, just thanks! Satisfying the jury in our 'monitoring' role was seen as a big deal because the granting of the 1.5m euros Melina Mercouri Prize hung on our recommendation. In truth, I wonder whether we would have ever been able to deny the city their cash prize even if we had thought their plans were hopeless. I fancy the national government in each case would have demanded what they saw as their due. The monitoring meetings were always held in Brussels, a city I came cordially to loathe. I know you can eat well there but our per diems were so inadequate that we usually found ourselves in wretched hotels, just snacking. I occasionally glimpsed the gracious old town but we had to spend our time in the Europolis district, where the buildings scrape the sky and from which the workers get out quicker at 5pm sharp than I have ever seen. They looked as if they hated Europolis too.

Away from Brussels, I had a fascinating time. I visited Essen for the Ruhr 2010 campaign, which I found amazing. I did not know Germany at all well and found I liked Germans much more than I expected to. I loved Istanbul (2010) (that famous European city!) and I also loved their team led by the renowned Nuri Colacoglu. Again, I loved the Turks I met. I went to the slightly dull Turku (2011) in Finland, Maribor (2012), the second city of Slovenia, Tallinn (2011), the beautiful capital of Estonia (beautiful if you give the old Soviet bits a miss) and the gorgeous Guimaraes (2012), the ancient capital of Portugal. Northern Portugal is magical. Anyway I have happy memories of them all. I was treated extremely well because they both wanted help and no black marks at their monitoring meetings. I forged real but brief friendships in several of them. As a jury we met them each twice in Brussels; the second meeting was the key one because it was then that they got the green light and their money. And, of course, the smaller the city, the more the money meant to them.

The selection role, once it started, was even more demanding than the monitoring. What made a good bid? Were we looking for a specific programme for the year, which I warned my colleagues would probably change dramatically? It certainly would if Liverpool was anything to go by! Were we looking for enthusiasm, proof of good management both artistic and financial? What about political commitment, knowing that the leadership might change? Did they have an overall concept which we found European? As a jury we each had different priorities and concerns. The successful city would have to touch lots of bases. We all thought that being 'hungry' was vital. It should not be a parade of buildings or a catalogue of past glories. Aiming to involve and enthuse the young was key. What special European partnerships could they explore? We were giving the prize to a group of people and we needed to trust them.

By now I realised how my past bidding experience had been totally turned on its head. From being the grovelling supplicant, I had become the wooed but inscrutable judge. I remembered my Olympic experiences vividly. To describe the blow-by-blow experience of all the visits to France, Slovakia, Latvia, Sweden, Belgium and the Czech Republic (two cities had to be chosen for each of the years 2013, 2014 and 2015) would be too much but they all had memorable moments. Top of the pile was certainly the battle to be the French city in 2013. It reminded me of the Liverpool bidding saga – big competing cities in a major first-world country, all very anxious to win. France offered eight cities and they all made presentations to us in Paris. When I received my box of bid books from the eight, I weighed the box and it was more than twenty kilos. We shortlisted four great French cities – Bordeaux, Lyon, Marseille and Toulouse. Two of us must visit all four because they had all made huge efforts and spent good money. Mary McCarthy and I would represent our colleagues, along with two of the French delegates, and report back. It was clear that the whole jury should have visited, but no, it would have been too expensive.

The four of us spent a full day in each city and were treated like royalty. The scene in Bordeaux for instance was incredible. We visited many famous sites, attended several presentations and then in the early evening were invited to walk from our hotel to the Town Hall through the city centre for a grand civic dinner to catch the feeling of the city at night. What we had not realised was that what seemed a large percentage of the population would turn out to escort us to the arms of Alain Juppé waiting at the great door. This was a man who had been prime minister of France and was also Mayor of Bordeaux. The photos from above are of us engulfed in a sea of people. Another extraordinary moment was in Toulouse. The meeting with the local business community was arranged in a specially built small 'theatre' in a corner of the biggest aircraft hangar in the world – the A380 Airbus hangar – where three of them were standing side by side in different stages of construction. Astonishing.

Lyon was almost disappointing with a new, seemingly uninvolved Mayor. Nevertheless, Lyon was very beautiful and we had a wonderful lunch on a marvellous boat on the river. We went up the Saone and down the Rhone – or was it the other way round? We were all dazzled by Marseille. Their bid was near perfect. They were also the hungriest, they wanted it the most. The charismatic Mayor Jean-Claude Gaudin, who was also the Vice-President of the French Senate, enveloped us. Bernard Latarget, the artistic director, led a superb team of businessmen, artists, academics, children, acrobats – you name them, they were there. We even visited the central prison to see a performance by inmates. The jury's decision would rest on the presentations before the vote and announcement in Paris.

I had met the French Minister for Culture in advance and I warned her that the final day and announcement would be monumental. She was sceptical but at least they put us in a wonderful set of rooms in the Louvre for the four presentations. The plan then was for us to have a report from the four who had visited the cities and then have a general discussion about the four presentations we had received. This would be followed by lunch, after which we would continue our debate, finishing up with the vote. There were thirteen of us, seven European experts and six French representatives from the Arts world. 'After our first talk, shall we have a preliminary vote before lunch to see if we can narrow the list of four to three?' I asked. This was considered a good idea. In less than five minutes we had the papers back. By a reasonably complicated system I thought I had invented, the ballots came back, in effect saying – Marseille 12, Bordeaux 1, Toulouse 0, Lyon 0. 'Good God!' I spluttered. 'What do we do now?' 'We have a long, slow, delicious lunch,' suggested our French members. We did. No more discussion was needed.

The press conference at 4pm in another part of the Louvre was also extraordinary – about twenty-five camera crews and countless journalists and photographers, falling over each other. The smart money was on Juppé versus Gaudin, Bordeaux versus Marseille. The minister could not believe her eyes.

She assumed that as Paris was not involved, a man and a dog might turn up. Good training for her! She learnt that French Culture does not start and finish in Paris. It was a great occasion in a magical setting. I coped with announcing the result in French, but not with the questions.

We attempted to treat Slovakia (2013), Sweden and Latvia (2014), Belgium and the Czech Republic (2015) similarly. Inevitably they were all lower key. We managed to persuade the Secretariat to up the budget a little and pay for a group of six of us this time to travel around each country to see the shortlisted candidate cities. The weight of all the bid books that arrived at my house in Greenwich was overwhelming. I had a suspicion that not all my fellow jury members read everything they were sent. Perhaps they just weighed them. After our travels around the countries we met as a full panel of thirteen in the capital city of each to receive presentations but this time with six Slovakians, six Swedes, etc., making up the thirteen. We would have full, quite heated discussions and then vote. In Slovakia for 2013 we had an uncomfortable problem. The national Slovakian panel members had clearly been instructed how to vote and we were fortunate that one decided to disobey orders. We saw the usual antipathy to the capital city, Bratislava, whose delegates seemed to think they just had to turn up to be chosen. The second city, the capital of Eastern Slovakia, Kosice, finally won. It was a good decision.

Latvia and Sweden were the nominated countries for 2014 and we chose two very different cities on either side of the Baltic and for very different reasons. Even though it breached our experience of not awarding the prize to capital cities, we were virtually obliged to choose Riga, the capital of Latvia, which with a third of the total population is easily the largest city in the country. Its competitors were tiny and not capable of being capital of anything. After the horrors of the War and the Soviet years we were impressed by how all strands of society in Riga were working together. The young, attractive Mayor was of Russian descent. I loved Latvia and its passion for music, especially singing. Umea, the Swedish winner, was up against more famous cities in Sweden but won because it was a well-constructed bid with a good team led by a committed Mayor. It is an attractive city of over 100,000 people with a high-class university and serious cultural ambitions. Umea is near the Arctic Circle and works with the Sami people, which went down well with the jury. Of the Swedish candidate cities Umea clearly was the hungriest.

The competition for 2015 in the Czech Republic came down to a straightforward choice between the eventual winner, Pilsen, famous for its beer and with a strong economy, and Ostrava, a recovering city with an industrial history. Of all the decisions we made this is the only one I never completely trusted. We may have got it wrong. It was a very close-run thing. I just hope Ostrava gets the prize when it is the Czech Republic's turn again. My European Panel members were very cross about Belgium, the other country nominated for 2015. We were offered only one candidate city – Mons. It was a return to the bad old days. This was entirely a political decision. Candidates from the north, Flanders, were disqualified by their own Cultural Ministry. They wanted a city from Wallonia and they wanted Mons. We went through the farce of a presentation. Some of the panel members wanted to reject Mons on principle but the national sovereignty argument prevailed. It was ironic that EU discipline does not stretch to Belgium of all places. With its well-known problems of choosing a national government we wondered how long the country of Belgium would survive.

My time of being president of the jury was up. Spain and Poland were preparing their bids for 2016. I was now a free citizen again, no longer obliged to visit Brussels. Unexpectedly in my new retirement I received an approach from a Polish candidate city – Wroclaw – to advise them. I decided to accept – a gamekeeper turned poacher. It had been called Breslau when the city was inside German borders. I liked the city, the team and the Mayor but I did not like some of their bid. Two members of the team came to my house in Greenwich for three days and we rewrote the bid book. To my delight, Wroclaw won. A little over two years later I was approached again, this time by the Black Sea city of Varna in Bulgaria for 2019. I went there several times and I always stayed in one of the best trendy hotels I have ever stayed in anywhere. I enjoyed my association with the team, especially the superb secretary, Stanislava. I did my best, but Varna was beaten by Plovdiv. Varna was a mess politically with a change of Mayor during the bid process. Ah well. Win a few, lose a few.

For me the chief question now is how long the competition will continue. When the number of Member States soared to twenty-eight, as I have said, there were several smaller cities from the old Eastern bloc who were chosen and struggled to cope for one reason or another. And, of course, there is the problem of Luxembourg. By the end of this century, if federal equality is maintained, it is probable at the present rate of rotation that every village in Luxembourg will have been a European Capital of Culture. Malta, Cyprus, the Baltic States and the new applicant countries are very small too. I suppose, as long as the prize of 1.5 million euros is offered and national interest is maintained, the competition is safe, but there will be some pretty minor European Capitals of Culture ahead.

By the end of my time in some glamorous and some remote corners of Europe, my health had become seriously dodgy. I was completely over my 2002 heart attack but I was in real pain and found walking and standing for any period of time very difficult. I seemed to spend my life looking for a chair! And, of course, I was juggling jobs all through this time and that was rough. A meeting with an orthopaedic whizz in Valencia, Spain, where my stepdaughter is a doctor, confirmed what I had always suspected. Nobody in Britain seemed to agree but I knew he was right. I had two problems, not one. And he took X-rays to prove it. Both hips needed replacing and I had scoliosis of the spine. To cut a tedious story short I had both hips replaced and in a quite separate operation I had a steel rod inserted into my lower lumber region. Both operations were complete successes. I got to know Guys and St. Thomas' Hospitals intimately and, like most people who have serious experience of the NHS, I thought it was brilliant. I discovered I hate sleeping in hospitals but that's me, not them. I went from an occasional wheelchair to walking three miles a day in under a year. It is eleven years since the fun of the knife and now I am just aging normally. I do not like that much either. Memorial services for friends are becoming too regular.

I was not sad that my time with the European Commission came to an end. After what I have said about Brussels, I was always a Remainer who was astonished when the Brexiteers won a majority in the 2016 Referendum. But as I have already indicated it was hard for me to love Brussels or the way it functioned. The quality of civil servants I met was way below that of their British counterparts. I also reject a central belief of many Europeans in the whole concept of a single European culture. It is a nonsense. French culture, German culture, Spanish culture, Swedish culture, etc. are real and profound. Why try to pretend that there is one culture for a United States of Europe? One of the experiences which I disliked the most, and was not always able to escape, was having to attend conferences hijacked by so-called cultural experts all fighting for their own absurd version of a single European cultural strategy. I always ended up just wanting to stand up, shout 'Bollocks' and leave the room. Interestingly, a lot of the 'experts' with academic titles doing the talking seemed to be German.

European cultures are far too ancient, diverse and precious to be stuffed into one pot. Of course, there is endless common ground but the great thing about my years traipsing around Europe was how much variety there was to see and savour. I loved visiting so many places as a worker, not merely as a tourist. I am not a beach bum nor a sun worshipper. I greatly prefer mountains and forests and rivers and waterfalls. But what I really love are fabulous buildings where fascinating people work and live. How blessed I am that I was allowed to indulge this passion for several years in the best continent in the world for matchless, glorious CITIES!

17

SOMERSET TO GREENWICH

Reflections on a Life Mostly Lived

Reflections – world in crisis – is our blessed generation to blame? – Uncle Tim – bidding – marriage – travel – Alicia – win a few, lose a few!

It is one of the conceits of achieving a reasonable age that you think that the world has changed more in your own lifetime than in any other. I am seventy-eight at the time of writing and if I go back that number of years from my birth in 1944 to 1866 I find my conceit is entirely misplaced. The seventy-eight years before my birth were even more remarkable than the seventy-eight years of my lifetime. In 1866 the American Civil War had been over just one year. The relationship between the United States, Great Britain with its Empire and the great European States began to change fundamentally and inventions of the years up to my birth included electricity, the car, the aeroplane, the machine gun, radio, the telephone, penicillin, television, the computer, splitting the atom, etc. My generation followed and they continued to invent – Atom bombs, DNA testing, space travel, the internet, bar codes, biofuel, 3D printing, etc. Most of the key players, however, of this generation were essentially brilliant 'developers' of earlier inventions. Meanwhile, population, power, plastic, pollution multiplied. Undoubtedly, the chief outcome of the sum of both periods – just 156 years in all, a nano-second in history – is the massive leap we have taken towards the destruction of our planet.

My closest friends were born in the 1940s. I have always regarded us as a blessed generation. Our country's position in the world has further diminished during our lifetimes but we escaped the horrors of our parents' and grandparents' times. Today we see our children and grandchildren are having a harder time than we did. We had so many advantages. We have completely missed out on war. For most of us, education was free. Most of us left home when we wanted to and have usually not suffered either the fears or the realities of unemployment. The guilt of Empire was lifted from us even though more and more people kindly agreed to speak our language. We grew up in the 60s and if ever there was a time for the young, it was then. We have lived under Conservative and Labour Governments and have benefitted from the positive policies of both lots. The Welfare State was invented for us, inflation usually came at the right economic time for us, and society, for all its imperfections, is certainly more liberal. I insist on being optimistic.

The rhythm of our lives has been a good one and life for most of us has been on an upwards trajectory. We were brought up in a time of real austerity: no bad thing because the quality and colour of life kept gradually improving with better education, trips abroad, cheap housing that grew in value and amazing advances in gadgets and comfort. We were even able to visit the great wonders of the world before they became overrun by millions of tourists. We look with envy at very few previous generations, or other countries for that matter.

With all this good fortune, however, and with some fifty-six years of so-called career now behind me, I still find it hard to say what I do. This is perhaps why I have recently been removed from the Birthdays List in *The Times* after over twenty years of gracing the 22nd January editions. Presumably they do not know what I do anymore either. A neat, single word of description, a word like actor, footballer, author, minister, general, does not fit.

I have been successively a happy child, a boisterous schoolboy, a show-off student, an actor, a theatre manager, a theatre builder, an Olympic and big projects bidder, a businessman, a consultant, a sort of Eurocrat – all sorts of things. My life has been mainly in the arts and sport but always playing different roles in different places. Maybe I will settle down one day. It has been exciting on good days and frivolous on the less good. I have never completely thrown off the sense of being a bit fraudulent. To leave Oxford without a degree is shameful, not lessened by later being awarded honorary academic honours.

Like so many others, I have thought I had a decent story to tell – either amusing or interesting, I hoped – but I was intimidated by the blank sheet of paper in front of me and I am the most despicably 'distractable' person in the world, especially by my mortal enemies and dear companions, the television and books. At least I made various starts by beginning an occasional diary which lasted a few days at a time. The trouble was that I was confused between wanting to set down honest memories and pondering pathetically the possibility of publication.

I have kept records and during my Olympic wanderings wrote long letters to my son David at airports around the world recounting strange encounters and conversations. All this I could mine later, I thought. I read *The Assassin's Cloak*, an anthology of great diarists which rang clear bells of guilt, self-loathing, vanity as well as describing the same conflictive search for both honesty and storytelling. These gave me a sort of hope and I began to feel stirrings of self-motivation.

My Uncle Tim was a model. I loved him dearly and towards the end of his life we were close. We had a real bond. He had a wonderful skill for friendship and laughter, taking me up on virtually everything I said. There was his endless worrying about Pasang, his long-term, much younger Nepalese lover and finally his spouse, our shared relationship with his mother, my grandmother, his rich bank of friends, his joy of being gay, his real talent for watercolours, they all just made me sad that I had discovered him so late in life. I was into my fifties before I really got to know him. We have scores of his pictures on our walls, all framed. He could not believe that pages from sketchbooks, some eighty years old, were now on display on the walls of a home. In fact, he wept. He kept diaries, which are now in the British Library, and we talked about his mother, weakness, death, friends and lovers and we laughed a great deal.

Hence the efforts at a diary, hence this memoir. But back to my question of what I do. I am greedy, certainly. I eat too much, talk too much and read too fast. I do not listen to others properly and my voracious reading empties my mind of my own uncomfortable thoughts by filling it with the thoughts of others. I devour books and forget them almost immediately. I am lazy, I am not good on my own, I seek approval. At the same time, I know I am effective. I have both the good and bad qualities which go with leadership. I can amuse people. I can make things happen. I can command a room. I remember Tim telling me that the fact that I had no fear at all in addressing a room full of people was more enviable than I could imagine. He dreaded speaking in public beyond everything. The truth, however, is that I consider my virtues are mere good luck while my weaknesses are avoidable faults. On the one hand I hardly drink, I don't smoke, I don't gamble, I have never taken drugs. But how can I take credit for that? On the other, my lack of the virtues which I admire – brains, courage, modesty, patience – seem to be grievous shortcomings.

So where does all this leave me? Have I made a difference? Will I in any tiny detail be able to say that I will leave the world a better place than I found it? I just hope that Manchester, Greenwich and Liverpool benefitted a bit from having me around. Of one thing I am certain. The best thing that ever happened to me in my life was meeting Alicia. I do truly and unconditionally love her. I know I don't deserve her. My parents loved her and my mother always warned her not to spoil me. Alicia, thank God, did not listen. We have a wonderful life together. And I have inherited two stepdaughters whom I adore.

My first marriage started fine. Following my common course, we were an unusual pair. I was twenty-seven, she was forty-one. I had a cottage in Derbyshire, Su had a flat in North London. We both had jobs in Manchester which we liked, she at Granada and then at the BBC in documentaries, I with my theatre company. Quite early on she became pregnant. I cannot even remember if it was deliberate or a mistake. We both instinctively wanted the baby, so we married. I don't remember proposing, it just seemed the right thing to do. David was born but there were going to be no more births. Su wanted to have a family so we entered into the adoption process happily. Tom and Anna arrived via the Oldham Adoption Society. Tom was six weeks and Anna nine months old. Their difficult starts in life were not really made known to us. They were three outgoing and nice-looking children and I loved them. For some years we were a happy family of five. In his teens, Tom began to go off the rails and has had a difficult life. Anna could be tricky but turned out fine. David and I got on well and still do.

Things seemed acceptable if not special. I never questioned my lot. We had a few years of happy family holidays with our dear friends, the Shorrocks, in Cornwall in May and in Suffolk in August. These sadly finished when the two wives fell out. After a while, I admit, there were other ladies. Of course, this was wrong, but it wasn't vengeful. All was quite calm and I was sure they would not cause the break-up of the marriage. Guilt and bad conscience, yes.

Gradually, the relationship deteriorated. I suppose the age gap did not help. She used to complain that she spent her life having to talk with people about me and my doings. I began to realise that it would all end at some point, but I had no clue when. Su was spending time in Australia and we were facing in ever more opposite directions, but to me, separation was unthinkable as long as the children were still at school. Nevertheless, the break-up of our marriage seemed inevitable. Only the timing was uncertain. Our lives had become a constant series of bitter rows punctuated by equally harsh silences.

Then I met Alicia in Greece on my Olympic travels, which was like a thunderbolt. I knew almost immediately that I had found someone who made sense of the possibility of changing everything. But with her living in Montevideo and me in Manchester, that was not going to be straightforward. She too was married but she and her husband were living separate lives. It is interesting how many people who have lived through a divorce say that their marriages were over long before the final separation. This was true for both Alicia and for me.

You never lose the scars. Su never forgave me. It was a tough time for everyone, especially the children, but everything was finally, if acrimoniously, sorted out. The house was sold. Universities and colleges were found. After the separation, Su moved to Cambridge, got a PhD, made more visits back to Australia and wrote a book. All in all, her life went rather well from 1994 until her unexpected death in 2008. For me, money was tight but Greenwich beckoned. Meanwhile Alicia began her much calmer and more civilised divorce. Now, twenty-seven years later, my second marriage has already lasted quite a lot longer than my first.

From the age of two I have travelled. The early years in Manchester from 1968 was the first period of my life when I was solidly based in one place and travel was limited to holidays in England. In the late 80s the Olympic bug brought travel opportunities back with a vengeance and from then I have longed to be in a plane visiting somewhere completely new. Whenever I hear a plane overhead I always look up, try to identify it and wonder where it is coming from or going to. Alicia shares this passion of going 'abroad' and since we both retired we have made at least three foreign trips each year, not including almost annual visits to see her family in Uruguay. I have worked out I have spent at least one night in 105 countries so far. Only ninety more to go. COVID in 20/21 has been a terrible downer on this fun. So far, I repeat. There are still lots more destinations I long to discover. Uzbekistan, Namibia and Bolivia are three particular ambitions. If I ever write again, I might recount some of the memorable and often bizarre experiences we have had away from home.

For me, being alive is being involved. Involved doing things, meeting people, going places. I have no religious faith. I have always loved the Christian story and it seems to me a good blueprint for living. Of course, I think about dying. My main conclusion is that the death of others can be very tough for the living. For the dead, it is simply a fact, which comes to us all. I have always liked the saying, 'This is it, this is not a rehearsal'. And as every actor or sportsman will tell you, you win a few and you lose a few. Crucially you must make the most of today. OK, I have written this, and that means I have been looking back, not forward. But I still aim to get up enthusiastically tomorrow and maybe, just maybe, something surprising and enjoyable will happen.